Writing Communications
in Business
and Industry

Third Edition

Writing Communications in Business and Industry

Nelda R. Lawrence

Professor Emerita

University of Houston

Elizabeth Tebeaux

Coordinator of Technical Writing

Texas A & M University

Prentice-Hall, Inc.

Englewood Cliffs, New Jersey   07632

Library of Congress Cataloging in Publication Data

Lawrence, Nelda R
   Writing communications in business and industry.

    1. Commercial correspondence. I. Tebeaux,
Elizabeth, joint author. II. Title.
HF5726.L34 1981   651.7′5   80-25642
ISBN 0-13-970467-1

Editorial/production supervision and
   interior design by Natalie Krivanek
Cover design by Zimmerman/Foystor
Manufacturing buyer: Edward O'Dougherty

Printed in the United States of America

10 9 8 7 6 5 4 3 2 1

Prentice-Hall International, Inc., *London*
Prentice-Hall of Australia Pty. Limited, *Sydney*
Prentice-Hall of Canada, Ltd., *Toronto*
Prentice-Hall of India Private Limited, *New Delhi*
Prentice-Hall of Japan, Inc., *Tokyo*
Prentice-Hall of Southeast Asia Pte. Ltd., *Singapore*
Whitehall Books Limited, *Wellington, New Zealand*

Contents

Preface

This workbook text is primarily for college students who must develop the ability to compose written communications as part of their career responsibilities. It also provides instruction and practice for improving the written messages of persons already employed in business and industry.

For this in-depth revision, the material on good writing style had been updated, enriched, and organized for easier study. The book has been completely restructured to accomplish five specific new purposes:

1. To display and analyze abundant examples of both good and poor writing.
2. To provide a full coverage of graphics as aids to written communication, with clear examples and numerous practical exercises.
3. To give realistic examples of resumes, application letters and business letters, together with specific analyses and plans for these letters.
4. To show students the characteristics of technical writing as it is used in typical on-the-job documents and to demonstrate these qualities in examples.
5. To clarify the function of word processing centers and their current and potential effects upon company writers.

Students will find the problems and exercises realistic and interesting because most of them originated in documents from actual companies. Too, these practice materials have been tested in college classrooms and modified to reflect the needs and suggestions of both teachers and students. The graphics section is unique.

For examples of actual written communications in this third edition, we are especially grateful to Richard Lee Hearn, Micronet, Inc., Washington, D.C.; Elmer E. Folk, Exxon Company, U.S.A., Houston, Texas; Professor Charles R. Dunbaugh, University of Houston, Houston, Texas; Linda Pierce, Shell Oil Company, Houston, Texas; Dr. Andrew J. Thacker, University of Houston; Harold A. Lott, Volume Builders, Inc., Houston, Texas; Kay Evans, Exxon Company, U.S.A., Houston, Texas; Wesley Knebel, Connecticut Mutual Life Insurance Company, Houston, Texas; and Professor Fred D. Lewallen, University of Houston.

Special thanks are given to Elizabeth Seufer, University of Houston, for generous participation in accumulating and screening source materials.

For their practical assistance in reviewing and evaluating the manuscript, we appreciate the help of Jene Tebeaux, Southwestern Bell Telephone Company, Houston, Texas; Kenneth E. Lawrence, Southern Pacific Transportation Company, Houston, Texas.

For special assistance in Word Processing techniques and in-house procedures, we wish to thank Mrs. Bernell Lovett, Ms. Gladys Abbott, and Mrs. Glendell Rose of the Exxon Company, U.S.A.

We sincerely thank Sadie Vesey, Center for Counseling, Union Baptist Association, Houston, Texas, and Jan Want, Texas A&M University, College Station, Texas, for their assistance in preparing the materials in this book.

We are also indebted to the following students who allowed us to use their fine work as examples: Carol Seamans, Barbara Shimaitis, Marianne Greenfield, Donna Quinn, Jack Davis, Stephen Williamson, Charlotte Holmquist, Janet M. Barnes, Kenneth Walker, Keith Devenney, Stephen Dorcheus, Gary Bohuslav, Gregory Case, Dan Brock, David Mosher, Estrella Hawthorne, Joy Durrant, Paula Logan, Clint Fagala, and Dan Sherrod.

Writing Communications
in Business
and Industry

1

Producing and Processing Written Communication

YOUR ROLE AS A WRITER

In business and industry, in government, in professions, in organized groups of every kind, people must exchange thoughts. The flow of adequate and timely information to and from the persons who make up an enterprise keeps it alive and growing. As one of those persons, you have recognized the value of language as a means of expressing your thoughts. In fact, without skills to communicate ideas clearly and effectively, your professional knowledge will be of little use to you as you strive to work within an organization.

When a company describes the various positions in its organizations, each description assumes that the person filling the position has the reading and writing ability to succeed in that job. You should never forget that your success in any organization depends as much or more on your communication expertise as on your technical knowledge.

ANALYZING THE COMMUNICATION CONTEXT

After you make a decision, you must communicate with someone to put it into effect. If you act on another person's instructions, you must then report the result of the action. That is, you routinely transfer your thoughts from your mind into the mind of someone who needs the information. To preserve a record and furnish the essential reminders to people in all businesses, you most often write the messages.

However, before you write, you must do some groundwork to prepare your message. What you say in your message will be determined by how you answer the following questions:

1

1. Who is the person to whom the message is addressed?

2. What is the level of this person's educational/technical expertise?

3. What is this reader's attitude toward the subject?

4. What other readers may see the message?

5. What is their educational/technical level?

6. What is their attitude toward the subject?

7. Why are you writing the document? What situation has made your writing this document necessary?

8. What should the reader know after reading the document?

9. What should the reader's attitude be after reading the document?

10. What is the context (situation) in which the document will be received?

11. How long will the information be useful or available to be read by readers you are not aware of?

Too often messages are ineffective or misunderstood, because the writer has not anticipated who the reader(s) will be and what knowledge and attitude they have toward the topic. For example, what you say in a report that will be read and used by a reader interested in a subject will differ from what you would say about the same subject to a reader who is hostile or apathetic towards the subject. In addition, many times writers fail to realize that reports, accessible in files, may be read over a long period by a number of readers unknown to the writers. For that reason, you should be careful about what you say and how you say it.

To better help you keep these important questions in mind as you plan your message, we suggest that you complete the Document Analysis Work Sheet before you begin either to plan or to write any report or letter. Once you complete the analysis, keep it constantly before you as you begin to organize your report or letter.

Unless you consider each question, your communication will probably not be effective; that is, it will probably not achieve the goal you intend. Writers who develop documents by thinking only of their own needs and views about the subject often forget the purpose of the message in terms of the reader. The message wanders aimlessly, is usually too long, and leaves the reader confused and angry.

Because audience analysis and message purpose are so important to the success of any document, you will see the communication situation stressed throughout this book. The underlying point is very specific: *every aspect of style, organization, content, and visual aids should be designed to fit the document's audience and purpose.*

```
                    DOCUMENT ANALYSIS WORK SHEET

                   ( to be completed for every document )


    Topic:                                    Kind of Document:

    AUDIENCE:

    Primary Reader--person to whom the document is addressed:

        educational/technical level:
        position--job title and responsibilities:
        attitude toward the document subject:

    Secondary Reader--others who may read the document and use it:

        educational/technical level:
        position and responsibilities:
        attitude toward the document subject:

    PURPOSE:

        What should the primary reader know after reading the document?
        What should the primary reader be able to do after reading the document?
        What should the reader's attitude be after reading the document?

    DOCUMENT CONTEXT:

        What is the context in which the document will be received? Describe.



        How long will the information be applicable or useful?
```

FUNCTION OF WORD PROCESSING—
ITS EFFECT ON THE WRITER

You may be assuming at this point that a typical communication situation operates something like the diagram below:

Organizational Purpose		Organizational Purpose
WRITER		**READER(S)**
Ideas ——————→ Language ←—————— Ideas		
encoded	decoded	

That is, a writer translates thoughts into language. The reader then decodes the message. Hopefully, the idea the reader finds in the message is the same as the one the writer intended.

However, this simple communication diagram does not parallel the communication situation found in a growing number of companies today. Producing information and handling incoming and in-house communication are done by a highly developed system known as word processing. Basically, you need to know what word processing is, how it affects communication development and transmittal within an organization, and how it affects you as a writer.

Word Processing is the system that combines people, efficient procedures, and sophisticated equipment to originate, process, store, and distribute communications. Today Word Processing Centers within companies handle all or most documents originated within the company. What this means is that all communications—letters, memos, reports, and manuals—are handled in centralized units whose sole function is to process and distribute information.

However, to help you fully visualize the effect that Word Processing is having on company communications, you need to review the process you, as a student, follow in developing your written assignments:

1. You write the assignment in longhand.

2. You type, revise, and retype until you finally produce an acceptable copy.

3. You proofread this copy and perhaps make last-minute changes. You retype some pages or make "handwritten" corrections or insertions because you do not have enough time to retype every portion that needs corrections.

4. You perhaps make a photocopy of the paper (in case your instructor loses the original).

5. You submit the paper to your instructor.

A once typical office situation more than likely followed a similar, time-consuming procedure:

1. A boss dictates a report to a secretary, or he writes the report in longhand.

2. The secretary then types the report.

3. The boss checks and/or revises the report.

4. The secretary retypes every page which contains errors.

5. The boss rechecks the retyped copy.

6. The secretary photocopies the report for filing and distribution.

7. The report is distributed by mail or courier.

Word Processing, designed to streamline all communications, has changed this office situation. Equipment designed for originating, storing, editing, disseminating, and filing information has made the entire process of producing communications faster and more efficient. In fact, Word Processing Centers (or Systems) are frequently integrated with a company's computer system. Therefore, the distinction between data processing and word processing is rapidly diminishing. The phenomenal advances in the development of computer hardware and software have made possible the equally phenomenal advancement of Word Processing equipment. The types and variations of Word Processing equipment available to offices is entirely too complex to begin to describe here. However, a description of how a document might be processed in a Word Processing Center should give you some idea of how Word Processing has changed the communication situation for the writer within an organization. Consider the following situation:

An employee originates a document by dictating it into a recorder. A typist in the Word Processing Center transcribes the document, recording the document on a magnetic disc, tape, or card. The originator then receives a "hard" (typed) copy of the document to revise or edit as necessary. However, at this point, the WPC (Word Processing Center) does not have to retype pages on which corrections or revisions are necessary. The stored document is recalled from storage and displayed, a page at a time, on the cathode ray screen of a text editor. By using a keyboard, the operator can key in all corrections, literally moving words, sentences, and even paragraphs on the electronically displayed document. Once the changes are complete, a printer, attached to the text editor, prints one or more perfect copies for distribution. The now corrected and revised "original" can be preserved on a storage medium such as microfiche, magnetic disc, or magnetic card. From these, error-free additional "hard" copies of the document can be made within a few minutes at any time.

Furthermore, documents stored on magnetic discs or microfiche take significantly less space than traditional filing cabinets. Many times a document can be distributed without mailing it. The stored information can be transferred to another storage system by phone transmission. A document, for example, can be transferred from disc to disc at an approximate rate of nine hundred characters per minute. The receiving storage terminal, connected to a typewriter or printer, can produce error-free hard copies at the rate of 50 characters per second or more. Even by a telephone remote copier hook-up, a letter-size original message can be transmitted and delivered from coast to coast in the U.S. in two minutes.

Much of the effectiveness of Word Processing depends on effective, efficient origination of documents. In both the office of today and the office of the future, documents are originated by machine dictation. The need for efficiency in communications has virtually decreed the death of longhand origination. Longhand is slow, as the average speed is ten words per minute. Longhand is difficult for the typist to read. Machine dictation, in contrast, can be six times the speed of longhand and twice the speed of shorthand dictation, which requires an additional person, a stenographer, whenever a document is originated.

Therefore, you should be aware that a good skill for you to begin learning is proper dictation using an outline only. That is, you want to be able to originate as many documents as possible by dictating from an outline rather than laboriously writing the entire document in longhand before you dictate it into a recorder. If you try to write every document before you begin dictating, you will at least double the time necessary to originate every one.

To help you further prepare for the reality of the modern office and the effect that Word Processing will have on you as a communicator, you will find the topic outline or "plan" approach for every kind of report and letter presented in this text. You will always want to make a topic outline—as detailed as necessary—before you begin to write. None of the suggested plans is inflexible; each one is only a guide to the type of report or letter discussed. However, the suggested outlines or plans should show you how a report or letter could be developed.

Developing your assignments should, then, follow three steps:

1. Complete the Document Analysis Work Sheet.

2. Plan your message by developing an outline.

3. Write the message from the outline.

This procedure will help you learn to plan and write every document in a reader-centered, organized way. The more you practice writing, the better your reports and letters will become.

If you have access to a recorder, try to "speak" your assignments from your topic outline to practice dictation. Once you have dictated (try a short letter first), listen, as objectively as possible to how you sound. Have you clearly dictated a document so that it could be accurately transcribed? Below is a list of dictation aids which will help you practice dictation.

DICTATION AIDS

Organize Before You Dictate

Know the purpose of the document.

List the points you want to make.

Make an outline, as detailed as necessary.

Consider the recipient. How do you want him/her to respond?

Analyze the proposed message with organization, purpose, and recipient in mind.

Give Complete Instructions Before You Dictate the Message

Identify yourself.

Identify the type of communication (letter, memo, form, etc.)

Specify the stationery type (letterhead, memo blank, etc.)

Specify the number of copies.

Specify who will receive copies (in addition to the distribution list).

Specify the spacing, the form, etc.

Give Complete Instructions As You Dictate

Give complete inside address.

Note all punctuation, particularly commas.

Note where paragraphs end. Say "period, paragraph."

Indicate special procedures (underline, center, quote, all caps, etc.)

Spell unusual words or words that sound alike.

Spell all names clearly.

Speak Clearly

Do not place the microphone too close to your mouth.

Do not begin before the machine is ready to record.

Use normal speaking tone.

Enunciate the ends of words: do not lower your voice.

Avoid speaking either too rapidly or too slowly.

Speak Effectively

Embody your points in natural language patterns. Do not try to sound formal.

Avoid sentences that are long.

Speak the way you talk in ordinary conversation; this will keep your message from sounding stilted.

While writers in smaller and medium-sized firms may need only typewriters, copiers, telephones, and other such conventional equipment, their composed messages are as vital as those in the larger businesses. The reason is that the message must still be composed of words in the language of the ultimate reader, regardless of company size or sophistication of transmittal devices.

When you consider the thousands of written documents produced by the average major firm every day, and when you consider how important most of these are to the decisions made by management within these firms, you can understand why companies are willing to spend extraordinary amounts of money to make communication processing more efficient. If the written messages efficiently accomplish their purposes, the money is well spent. But if the report is wordy and poorly organized, if the memo confuses the reader, if the letter is misleading or arrogant, the company has wasted time, lost confidence, and damaged its image.

You are now concerned with how to make your messages accomplish the purposes for which you write them and at the same time retain that priceless asset of goodwill so basic to any profitable enterprise. Of the customary kinds of written messages, you will likely have three to begin with—in-house memorandums, reports to management, and routine letters. As your career responsibilities change, you may add such documents as formal reports, computer software, policy manuals, technical evaluations, and so forth.

However, no matter what you have to write, you will need to show the same qualities of good expression to communicate. Your study of the most representative kinds of documents will help you, therefore, to acquire the good qualities for all your on-the-job writing.

WORK PROJECT 1

Pretest of Communication Ability

Write a personal letter to your instructor, answering the listed questions about yourself. Express your thoughts concisely and completely with your best grammar, spelling, and word choices. Construct paragraphs and arrange your ideas in the order you consider logical to present this information, and sign the letter with your regular signature. Use the best format you know for a personal letter on a business subject. Place the letter on a white, unruled sheet 8½ × 11. Either type your letter or write in ink. The date of the next class meeting should appear in the heading.

For correct name, spelling, and data about your instructor, consult your college catalog or the faculty directory. See the letter of application in Chapter III for the necessary letter parts and the placement of the letter on the page.

1. How many college English courses have you had? Where were these courses taken, and what was the general content of each one (i.e., grammar and composition, Eighteenth Century poets)? Briefly appraise your ability in the use of oral and written English.

2. What other courses have you had that will help you communicate on the job? Remember courses in your major field and those helping you know yourself better.

3. What oral communication experience have you had on the job by telephone, face-to-face with individuals, and with groups?

4. Has your working experience required you to write reports? memos? letters? proposals? What writing duties do you have on your present job?

5. Can you type well enough to turn out a document with the format and appearance needed to please an up-to-date reader?

6. How are you classified in school and what is your major field of study (i.e., engineering, electronic technology, industrial supervision, and so forth)?

7. In the career you are planning, what possible use do you foresee for the ability to communicate through writing?

8. What is your plan for acquiring the skill needed to communicate successfully?

2

Business and Technical Style

USING THE RIGHT WORDS

Words are the smallest units of language that people use to speak and write what they think. Probably every thought you have can be clearly expressed in words. In attempting to express your thoughts to another person, you must select words the person understands and use them with their common meanings.

When you write the message, your words on paper must make the idea crystal clear in the mind of the reader on the first reading. You would not wish to impose on the reader's time and patience by requiring a second reading at a word-by-word pace. Here are some ways to select words that make your writing clear.

Specific Words

Sometimes you will find it difficult to select the exact words to express what you have in mind. You will search for a word with just that fine shade of meaning you want the reader to understand. You try to make the mental picture so clear that the reader will "see" your idea.

Determine what you want the reader to think and choose words so specific as to give a keen, vivid impression. By carefully selecting those nouns and verbs that name definite things and specific actions, you focus the picture at once. Otherwise, you scatter the reader's thoughts and delay understanding by using abstract and general words. Here is an example:

> A recommendation letter for a young man was written by a friend who had previously employed him. The letter contained three sentences of general words, including, "John *is* a *fine boy* and *would make* a *good employee*." The prospective employer saw John as a hazy adolescent figure with mediocre traits—not a company asset. By changing the vague words shown in italics, you can insert strong, specific words that create a vivid picture.

"John works accurately with quantitative data and understands how to *use such statistics* in *informative reports.*" John now appears to be a capable person with the specific expertise the would-be employer is seeking.

In the following examples of vague writing, the italicized words are too general and abstract to make a clear picture.

General	Specific
1. We are in receipt of the *information* relative to the *matter* involving our *commitments* in connection with the *previously mentioned documents.*	1. Thank you for sending us the dates and amounts to insert on agreement forms 62A and 62B.
2. *Relatively fewer* jobs in the technical field relate to more than a *general knowledge* of computer languages.	2. Only those jobs that use repeated scientific data require skill in a mathematical computer language such as Fortran IV.
3. We will be *more than happy* to answer *any* questions you may have in *the future.*	3. We will be happy to answer your questions about other shrubs and trees suitable to your climate.

Simple Words

As a rule, the familiar words which business people use to talk of business actions will convey your ideas the best. To express your thoughts quickly and directly, use more short, powerful words instead of words with many syllables. The reader's eye span will thus be able to grasp more of your message at a glance, moving through the written lines in easy stages. Good writers try to see that their messages contain more than fifty percent words of one or two syllables, if possible. You do not need to apply such a rigid rule to be a good writer, but any reader will appreciate your saying what you have to say in simple, plain language. The writers of the items in the left column here did not value the time of their readers.

Original Version	Simple Version
1. to effect an alternative procedure	1. to make a change or to change
2. to finalize the proceedings	2. to end (close) the action
3. in view of the aforementioned	3. therefore
4. in the majority of cases	4. usually
5. relative to the subject of	5. about
6. This corporation considers it obligatory to conscientiously endeavor to exercise the most diligent and strenuous expenditure of energy directed toward the accomplishment of those objectives consistent with our philosophy.	6. We try harder.
7. to instigate an investigation of the residential premises	7. to begin searching the houses
8. In the event irregularities are in evidence, solicit the assistance of the municipal constabulary.	8. If something seems to be wrong, call the police.

Correct Words

Casual and careless speaking has caused the incorrect use of many words that sound alike but are spelled differently and have distinctly different meanings. While these words may get by in rapid speaking, when they appear in your writing, the reader depends on you to give the meaning you intend. Your words—correct or incorrect—are taken for what they say, even though you may mean something else.

The following frequently misused words are in groups that show the other words with which they are often confused. All the words are defined according to their primary meanings in good usage.

Accept:	to receive or to agree to
Except:	to omit or exclude
Adapt:	to make suitable
Adopt:	to choose or take to one's self
Admitting:	confessing; letting in
Admission:	fee for entering; acceptance
Admittance:	permission to enter
Advise:	to offer an opinion or to counsel
Inform:	to tell a person that of which he had no previous knowledge
Tell:	to express or make known
Affect:	to produce an effect upon or to pretend; to influence
Effect:	to cause or accomplish; a result
Amount:	the totality, referring to bulk
Number:	a collection of items, referring to individual units; to count
Apt:	appropriate or pertinent
Liable:	exposed to damage; responsible
Likely:	probable
As:	similarly (conjunction, adverb); not the same as like
Like:	nearly equal to (adjective); not a substitute for as
Balance:	to equalize; equality
Remainder:	that which is left
Rest:	to cease from motion
Consul:	an officer who resides in a foreign country to promote his own country's interests
Counsel:	an exchange of opinion; to give advice; one who advises
Council:	an assembly of persons met in consultation
Credible:	probable or believable
Credulous:	easily led to believe
Dependent:	contingent or conditional (adjective)
Depending:	trusting or relying for support (verb)
Due to:	payable to; owed; not a substitute for because of
Because of:	by reason of
Eager:	enthusiastic or impetuous
Anxious:	deeply concerned; apprehensive
Expect:	to wait for
Anticipate:	to look for as certain; to take beforehand
Guess:	to hit upon at random; to conjecture
Suppose:	to assume as true
Fewer:	smaller in number; not as many
Less:	smaller in size or bulk; not as much

Foreword: a preface or explanation of purpose (preceding the body of a report or book)
Forward: situated near the front (adjective)

Formally: precisely or according to rules
Formerly: some time ago

Illusion: a deceptive appearance
Delusion: deceit
Allusion: a casual reference

Imply: to insinuate or express indirectly
Infer: to conclude from what was said (the speaker implies; the hearer infers)

Its: possessive form of pronoun "it"
It's: contraction of the words "it is"

Passed: form of the verb "pass"; accomplished
Past: what has been; beyond

Per: Latin preposition meaning "by the"; used only before a Latin word

Personal: pertaining to a person or his private affairs
Personnel: the body of persons employed by a company

Practicable: capable of being practiced; feasible
Practical: pertaining to action or use; sensible

Principal: occupying the first rank
Principle: fundamental truth or doctrine

Provided: on condition
Providing: furnishing or making ready beforehand

Respectfully: with respect
Respectively: singly considered

Same: identical in kind or degree; not a substitute for the pronoun "it"

Site: ground plot; local position
Cite: to summon officially or to quote from
Sight: seeing or perception; view

Suspect: to distrust or presume; one who is believed to be a criminal
Suspicion: a feeling of mistrust

Therefor: for that; for it
Therefore: for that reason

Think: to have the mind occupied on some subject; to imagine
Feel: to be influenced or moved by; to sense by touch
Believe: to accept as true

Unique: only one of its kind

The following words may also be confusing, especially when you dictate. By spelling them when you dictate, you can make the meaning clear to the transcriptionist. Remember: sound-alike words are difficult to enunciate clearly.

accede, exceed	canvas, canvass
accept, except	coarse, course
access, excess	competent, compliment, complement
addition, edition	correspondence, correspondents
advise, advice	council, counsel, consul
affect, effect	decent, descent, dissent
allusion, illusion	disapprove, disprove
assistance, assistants	eligible, illegible
brake, break	formally, formerly
cease, sieze	forth, fourth

farther, further　　　　　　　　　practical, practicable
has, have, had　　　　　　　　　　precedence, precedents
incidence, incidents　　　　　　　principal, principle
incite, insight　　　　　　　　　　residence, residents
its, it's　　　　　　　　　　　　　respectfully, respectively
legislator, legislature　　　　　　stationary, stationery
loose, lose　　　　　　　　　　　their, there, they're
medal, middle, metal, mettle　　　through, threw
passed, past　　　　　　　　　　whose, who's
personal, personnel　　　　　　　your, you're

Technical Words and Jargon

In writing about any subject you know well, you may easily lapse into the jargon common in that field, but even a familiar word used in a technical context may baffle a reader who has never used it in that way. If you want to be plainly understood and believed, make your reader comfortable by defining any common word you use in a technical way. A synonym or short phrase in parenthesis after the technical term gives the reader instant insight with minimum loss of reading time. Here is an example.

> For best appearance, reports may be typed so as to justify (make even) the right margin also. Readability of report pages is optimum when the document is prepared on pale yellow paper in pica (ten points to an inch) type.

WORK PROJECT 2

Using the Right Words

Rewrite each of the following items in the space provided, wording each example to convey a clear meaning to the reader. Correct wording and add punctuation as needed.

1. The grill plate should give you many years of satisfaction.

2. We will send the merchandise to you as early as possible.

3. This house is quite roomy and modestly priced, with many trees and a sizable patio in the rear.

4. In the majority of instances, you will find a person will cooperate without any trouble.

5. Will you attempt to finalize the situation relative to the matter of new patents prior to the time that Mr. Franklin arrives?

6. Under the aforementioned circumstances, it will be possible to make an extension of time on the amount of the loan until the end of the month of January.

7. I matriculated in a typing class in my freshman year, and could possibly produce a respectable paper if time were of any unlimited quantity.

8. Please reply your intentions for submitting a proposal by November 15. Proposals must be in this office by November 23.

9. Once fired shotshell cases of the size chosen are used most due to the decrease in cost.

10. I do feel that I do possess enough agility in the oral and written use of language to qualify me for such a position.

11. The purchase of this machine would be of great savings cost-wise and a great service customer-wise.

In the remaining exercises, mark out the incorrect words in each group shown in parentheses. Be prepared to justify your choice.

12. A decision of this importance makes (its, it's) own results.

13. He evidently (feels, thinks, believes) that further investigation would uncover unethical actions.

14. Her work will be (acceptable, exceptable) (providing, provided) she checks it carefully.

15. (Due to, Because of) the (foreword, forward) in the annual report (illuding, alluding) to the new practices in the industry, the board of directors is (eager, anxious) to learn all the details.

16. This machine is the most unusual one I have seen for the economical preparation of company (stationary, stationery).

17. Our company is (eager, anxious) to help establish your next offices in our city.

18. The (personnel, personal) director has instituted a (practicable, practical) new method of computing merit points on the (principles, principals) of age, education, and experience.

19. I (advised, informed, told) him not to (adapt, adopt) the new procedure until he was sure what (affect, effect) they would be (apt, liable, likely) to have on the (personal, personnel) in the accounting department.

20. The younger executives act (like, as if) they are (dependent, depending) on the (consul, council, counsel) of their superiors in the organization, instead of taking charge of their responsibilities in each of the three departments (respectfully, respectively).

16

21. Once the gate is electronically locked at 8:00 p.m., nobody gains (admittance, admission) even though the person may have paid the (admitting, admission) charge.

22. (As, Like) you said, the plot was entirely (credible, credulous) until the official view of Dave's alibi explained why the (cite, site, sight) of the crime was his own basement.

23. The house detective was inclined to (suspect, suspicion) a woman who (formally, formerly) worked on the night shift.

Do you know the meaning of the sound-alike words listed earlier? Circle the correct word in each pair of sound-alike words used in the sentences below. If you are not sure of the meaning, check your dictionary.

24. After careful discussion, we (acceded, exceeded) to his request.

25. The judge's order provided (access, excess) to the company's accounts, seven of which contained funds in (access, excess) of a half-million dollars.

26. The law firm provided legal (consul, counsel) to the import company, which had been contacted by the foreign (consul, counsel), and his staff.

27. The plane began its (decent, descent, dissent), although (decent, descent, dissent) arose between the pilot and copilot about the possibility of bad weather near the airport.

28. The handwriting on the application was (eligible, illegible). Therefore, the committee could not determine if the application was (eligible, illegible).

29. We received a (compliment, complement) on our financial statement, which (complimented, complemented) the annual report.

30. The test results did not (disapprove, disprove) the theory, but the division manager (disapproved, disproved) of the whole procedure.

31. The tax notices will be mailed after November 1 or as soon thereafter as (practical, practicable).

32. The speaker made several (allusions, illusions) to legal (precedence, precedents) that had been established by the court's ruling. After his remarks, none of us had any (allusions, illusions) about the matter.

33. The molding on the car is so (lose, loose) that you may (lose, loose) it.

34. If you are going to be a (resident, residence) of the state, you must establish a local (resident, residence) requirement.

35. Forty years have (passed, past), and the problems associated with the lawsuit hopefully belong to the (passed, past).

36. The voters' league decided to (canvas, canvass) the voters.

37. He showed he had courage and (meddle, metal, mettle) by his actions during the crisis.

Formal Definitions

Any time you are not sure that your audience will understand specific terminology you are using, be sure to define these terms in a formal definition. The formal definition requires a specific structure: it places the term defined in its class (genus) and then lists the differences (differentia) between the term and other objects in the class.

term	class	differences
A *chair is*	a *piece of furniture*	that has four legs, a single seat, and back.

All formal definitions should follow this example, even though the level of language should be adjusted to fit the needs of the reader:

Advection (for a general audience): a weather process causing large amounts of heat to travel near the earth's surface from the equator to the North and South poles.

Advection (for a meteorology student): the large scale, low-level atmospheric transport of heat, characterized as horizontal convection, from the equator to the poles.

Dermatitis (for a preveterinary student): a disease of the skin, characterized by an inflammation affecting both the epidermal and subcutaneal layers.

Dermatitis (for a pet owner): a disease of the inner and outer layers of the skin causing a reddened and inflamed appearance.

When a writer determines that the reader will need definitions, several methods of including definitions are available. Definitions, if there are a number of them, may be placed in a glossary. (See Chapter 5). Or, words may be defined at the bottom of the page on which they occur. The following excerpt from a report on virtual storage in computers shows how definitions can be effectively integrated into the report context (definitions are italicized). Generally, this method is preferable, as the reader's attention is not drawn away from the content of the report.

Tables used for dynamic address translation during program execution are built to identify the segment and page locations. *These tables are known as page frame tables.* The page frame table size depends upon the number of page frames in the system. Each table entry has four parts:

1. page frame number (*index to the table*)

2. program ID (*name of the program currently using the page frame*)

3. segment and page number (*item that specifically identifies the page in the page frame*)

4. status (*item which indicates whether a page frame is available or being used*)

The paging supervisor is a special process that is programmed into the computer to perform various process-management functions within the page frame tables. The paging supervisor used the page frame table to record allocation of page frames of real storage to the user for programs for real storage management. The paging supervisor also takes care of table maintenance and functions such as page replacement strategy.

Expanded Definitions

Frequently, a formal definition may not provide sufficient information about a particular term. When this situation occurs, the writer can use the following organization devices to "expand" the definition:

Explication:	further defining words used in the formal definition
Operational definition:	description of an object in use
Description:	physical characteristics (size, shape, finish, etc.)
Division:	partitioning an object or concept into subparts
Analysis:	explanation of interior functions or operations
Comparison/Contrast:	similarities and/or differences between the term defined and another more familiar concept
Analogy:	simple comparison using "like"
Elimination:	separating the terms from other related concepts or objects; stating what the term is not
Cause/Effect:	description of relationship between results and the factors producing those results
Pictorials:	visual aids (drawings, diagrams, pictures, etc.)
Illustration:	verbal examples
History:	background information of a term
Etymology:	history of the meaning of a word

The following examples show how several of these devices can be used to expand a formal definition.[1] Shaping information about these devices will help produce a clear, structured definition. The expanded definition should proceed either inductively or deductively. As in any writing, the writer should keep the audience and purpose clearly in mind. See first the deductive expanded definition, followed by the inductive expanded definition.

"Using the Extended Definition Paper to Teach Organization," *Journal of Technical Writing and Communication,* 10 (1), 1980, 3-10. Reprinted by permission of © 1980, Baywood Publishing Company, Inc.

A Definition of an Annelid

Audience: second-year biology major

Procedure: deductive

Simple Definition Classification Division	An annelid is a bilaterally symmetric worm whose body is made of specialized segments. The word "annelid" is derived from the Latin *anulus,* meaning ring. The annelids are members of the phylum annelida, which has three classes: (1) polychaeta, (2) oligochaeta, and (3) hirudinae.
Description of Division 1 Etymology Illustration	The polychaetes are exclusively marine annelida. They either swim and crawl freely or live in tubes which they build in the sand. The polychaeta's distinctive head bears eyes and antennae. Excluding the head, the body segments are all alike. Each segment has a pair of lateral appendages, called parapodia, used for respiration and locomotion. On each parapodium are thick bristles called setae. The word "polychaeta," in fact, comes from the Greek *polys,* meaning "many," and *chaite,* meaning "bristles." These numerous bristles are characteristic of all polychaetes. For example, the fanworm, a tube dweller, has an iridescent array of green, pink, and red setae that wave in the water at the tube entrance.
Description of Division 2 Etymology Contrast Comparison	The class oligochaeta, composed of freshwater and terrestrial annelida, includes the earthworm. The word "olichaeta" comes from the Greek *oligo,* meaning "few," and *chaite,* meaning "bristles". This reduced number of setae is not the only difference between oligochaetes and polychaetes. The oligochaetes lack a well defined head and parapodia. However, like the polychaetes, the oligochaetes are segmented internally as well as externally.
Description of Division 3 Etymology Comparison Contrast Description Analogy Illustration	The class hirudinae is comprised solely of leeches, the most specialized of the annelids. The word "hirudinae" is derived from the Latin *hirudo* and *hirudini,* meaning "leech." The leech has the same external segmentation found in polychaetes and oligochaetes. Unlike its two cousins, the leech has no internal segmentation. The leech's body is flattened, lacking parapodia and setae. At each end of the body, the segments are modified, forming suckers. With these suckers, the leech can move its body similar to the locomotion of an inch worm. For example, the bloodsucker, a more familiar leech, uses the suckers to attach itself to a host. The leech is also equipped with a chemical, hirudin, which prevents the coagulation of blood. Since the blood does not coagulate, the leech can feed for extremely long periods.

A Definition of Depreciation

Audience: an introductory accounting student
Procedure: inductive

Etymology	Depreciation is derived from the medieval Latin word *depretiare,* which was formed from the prefix *de,* which means "down from," and *pretium,* which means "price." The general usage of depreciation
Contrast	refers to a decline in value of property through wear, usage, or other causes. However, the accounting meaning is more specific.
Operational Definition	A business normally acquires property for use in its operations. The amount paid for this property is a cost to the business and is recorded in its books as an asset. Over the period of time the asset is owned and used, its value usually declines. This decline in value can result from wear, usage, deterioration, or obsolescence. The portion of the value of the asset which is used up or lost during each year should be charged as an expense of running the business. In this way, the costs of an asset are allocated to expense over the period of its useful life.
Division	Assets can be classified as current or fixed and as tangible or intangible. Depreciation is used in allocating the costs of those assets
Illustration Explication	which are both fixed and tangible, such as buildings, equipment, and furniture. Fixed, or long-term, assets are those assets which are ac-
Contrast Explication Illustration Contrast Illustration Contrast	quired for use in the business rather than for sale to customers. However, some fixed assets, such as land, do not decline in value and are not subject to depreciation. Tangible assets are those which have substance, such as a piece of furniture. On the other hand, intangible assets are abstract and include copyrights, patents, and franchise rights. The process of allocating costs of intangible assets is called amortization rather than depreciation.
Operational Definition Analysis	The amount of costs to be charged to expense each year can be determined by several methods. Each usually involves estimating the useful life of an asset, the rate at which its value declines, and how much it will be worth when the business is finished with it. The straight-line method assumes that the value of an asset declines by the same amount each year of its life. Amounts charged to expense are thus the same for each period. The production method assumes the value declines relative to its use. Generally, the amount charged to expense is determined by the number of units produced. Accelerated methods assume an asset is more useful and its value decreases faster early in its life than in later periods. Expense is therefore greater in the early years of the life of an asset. These methods thus provide a systematic procedure for allocating costs to expense.
Simple Definition	Therefore, "depreciation" is defined as the process of systematically allocating the costs of a tangible, fixed asset to expense over the period of its useful life.

When you are required to "explain further," you are really giving an expanded definition. When you "explain further," be sure that you organize your explanation instead of writing whatever comes to mind. Shaping information about these expansion devices, as the writers of both examples have done, will help you organize your thoughts and present your idea logically. Planning your explanation by proceeding either deductively or inductively will also help you organize your message.

WORK PROJECT 3

1. Select five jargon words from your field. Define each word for two audiences. Choose two audiences which differ significantly in their knowledge of your field.

2. Write an expanded definition of a technical term in your field. Use as many of the expansion devices as you can in developing the expanded definition. Before you begin, stipulate your audience, your purpose, and your method (deductive or inductive).

3. Examine the following two extended definitions. What method (deductive or inductive) is used to develop each? What organizational devices has each writer used to present information about each topic? Write the name of the expansion device in the space provided on the left.

Marketing

Audience: freshman business students

Purpose: introductory information about marketing

The term "marketing" is derived from the Latin word *mercantus,* which means "to trade." The history of marketing dates from the time men began to trade items they had grown for items they needed. Bartering was advantageous to both the buyer and seller, since no currency was used. However, marketing assumed new meaning when trade volume began expanding, as transportation improved.

The Marketing era, which we have today, was preceded by the Production era and the Sales era. During these two eras, business believed wholeheartedly in increasing human productivity and promoting the product without considering the consumer expectations. But by the early 1950s, when competition stiffened, marketers began asking the housewife what she wanted and needed. This approach produced the Marketing era, because it placed emphasis on consumer needs and satisfaction.

Marketing is a function of the total business system, along with accounting, finance, and management. It is not to be confused with any of the three because it is a total system in itself. Marketing encompasses numerous business activities that deal directly with the flow of goods and services from producer to consumer. Business activities include product planning, pricing, distribution, promotion, and product management. All these activities are required to market the product effectively.

Marketing can be found in non-business organizations as well as in business areas. Non-profit groups like the political, social, religious, cultural, and civic organizations, employ marketing knowledge to be more effective in reaching people, by understanding their interests and attitudes. Whether conducting a local political campaign or testing a new floor wax for the national market, the skilled marketer and volunteer are both required to present want-satisfying products and services to potential customers or voters.

Marketing can now be defined as a total business system of interacting business activities designed to plan, price, promote, and distribute want-satisfying products and services to present and potential customers.

Computer Hardware

Audience: freshman electronics student with a speciality in computer hardware

Purpose: to give introductory information on computer hardware

Hardware is the computer's physical equipment which is directly involved in communication or data processing. The physical equipment consists of three components: input units, central processing unit (CPU), and output units.

Input units are devices which feed computers with data and information. This data and information is transferred to a memory unit, where it is stored until needed. Examples of input units include card readers, keyboards, tape drives, magnetic character readers, CRT displays, teletypes, and remote data entry devices. The central processing unit is an electro-mechanical device which performs computational and logical activities for the computer. The CPU directs the operations of all the basic components. It consists of three elements: memory units, arithmetic/logic units, and control units.

The memory units are devices which store data, instructions, and results of arithmetic operations for the computer. These units supply information and data to the output units. Memory units are of two types: main and secondary.

The main memory is a device which temporarily stores the data and instructions with which the computer is working. The storage is called the working area of the computer. For example, a list of and a run of a program are temporarily stored in the main memory until erased. The secondary memory is a device which stores information, like the main memory does, but it stores the information permanently. For example, computer programs and group data files are permanently stored in the secondary memory.

The control unit is a device which takes instructions from the memory unit and interprets them. It then sends signals to the other units to cause the execution of the instructions. For example, the control unit converts computer language to machine language, so it can understand what the instructions mean.

The arithmetic/logic unit is a device which does the mathematical calculations and decisions of the computer. These calculations and decisions are sent to a memory unit for storage. For example, the square root of a number is calculated in the arithmetic/logic unit.

The output units are devices which take data from the memory units. They print out the information for the operator. Examples of output units include line printers, CRT displays, teletypes, and plotters.

You soon become aware of the power of words, for they may be arranged in an almost limitless variety of ways to create changes in meaning. But do you sometimes have trouble understanding a written sentence even though you recognize each separate word in it? The average reader is conditioned by education and by language background to expect certain word patterns called sentences. By definition, a sentence is a group of words including a subject and a predicate and making a complete thought. Anything short of this is not a sentence—it is a fragment.

Fragments Versus Full Thoughts

Not every word group that begins with a capital letter and ends with a period or question mark makes a true sentence. One or more of the three essentials may be missing—the subject, the verb, or the complete thought. If you omit the subject or the verb, you have a phrase (a group of related words); if you include subject and verb and add other words to give meaning, you have a clause (a group of related words, including a subject, and a verb, but not necessarily making a complete thought). If the added words complete the meaning, you can use the clause as a sentence; otherwise, you put two or more clauses together to make a sentence that establishes your full thought.

You want each sentence to carry full value in the thought you give the reader. Arranging the parts of your sentence in their proper relationships assures a clear, complete thought. Awkward arrangement and incorrect punctuation account for much of the confusion found in written messages.

The following examples show some groups of words that appear to be sentences, but the italicized parts are only fragments.

You can express complete thoughts, as the writer probably intended, by revising them as shown at the right.

Original Version	Revised Version
1. Our plan is to be in Sacramento for the spring meeting and would like to see your new plant. *This being the first opportunity to visit.*	1. This being our first opportunity to visit the state capital, we would like to see your new plant when we are in Sacramento for the spring meeting.
2. *Your inquiry about the annual sports equipment sale.* The sale was not held this year as usual.	2. The annual sports equipment sale about which you inquired was not held this year.

Misplaced Words, Phrases and Clauses

A reference word, phrase, or clause should be as near as possible to the word it modifies; otherwise, your sentence may not give the reader the idea you have in mind. Anyone reading your sentence naturally assumes that you intend a close relationship between the words you place together. The following examples show how word placement changes the meaning of a sentence:

1. This plan was *only suggested* to the planning committee. (Not more than suggested.)

2. *Only this plan* was suggested to the planning committee. (No other plan.)

3. This plan was suggested to the *planning committee only.* (To no one else.)

Misplaced phrases such as those in the left column would puzzle the reader. The sentence would have to be reread, and perhaps a line or two before and after it, to find the real meaning.

Original Version	Revised Version
1. The section prepares a record tabulated of all credit sales *on the first of the month.*	1. *On the first of the month,* the section head prepares a tabulated record of all credit sales.
2. Please enclose your representative's names and *telephone numbers in charge of this proposal.*	2. Please enclose the names and telephone numbers of your representatives in charge of this proposal.
3. With the engineers, they wrote mostly technical reports for *management containing line charts and graphs* to furnish details.	3. To furnish details to management, the engineers wrote mostly technical *reports containing line charts and graphs.*

Clauses beginning with "which" or "that" are especially troublesome because the first word of the clause *must be* next to the word it refers to. Plan your sentence before you start writing. Otherwise, you may confuse the reader by such misplaced clauses as these.

Original Version	Revised Version
1. A cross-section blueprint is enclosed with this letter *that gives complete and accurate details.*	1. Enclosed is a cross-section blueprint *that gives complete and accurate details.*
2. Saline Oil Company would now like to be able to tell Forest Transmission to divert their gathered crude to another company which would remove it from this line.	2. Saline Oil Company would now like to be able to tell Forest Transmission to remove their gathered crude from this line by diverting it to another company.

Incomplete Clauses

You can flash some rather distorted pictures upon the mind of the reader by omitting the subject from a minor clause. Actually, the reason for calling it a minor clause is that it contains a minor theme and depends on the rest of the sentence for its meaning; therefore, the minor clause needs to have all its parts. Be especially watchful when you begin a clause with a verb ending in *ing* or *ed* (the participle). Remember to show the reader the subject of every verb in your sentence. Here are a few examples of confusion resulting from incomplete clauses.

Original Version	Revised Version
1. When examined carefully, *you* will see some interesting new points in the program. (Are "you" examined?)	1. When you carefully examine the new program, you will see some interesting new points in it.
	or
	1. When examined carefully, the new program will reveal some interesting points.
2. Having been built of the best materials, *we* believe the structure will outlast any other in the area. (Are "we" built of the best?)	2. As it was built of the best material, we believe the structure will outlast any other in this area.

26

or

2. Having been built of the best materials, the structure will outlast any other in the area, we believe.

3. Obviously, not everyone invited can be present; but, by inviting more than are needed, *alternates* will be available. (Are the "alternates" doing the inviting?)

3. Obviously, not everyone invited can be present; but if we invite more than are needed, alternates will be available.

or

3. . . . but, by inviting more than are needed, we will be sure to have alternates available.

Run-On Sentences

Decide on the main theme of each sentence you are about to compose, and make sure it carries only one complete thought. When you put several complete thoughts (or some complete and some incomplete ones) into one sentence, the reader has to take the trouble to untangle them and reassemble them in separate thought units. Run-on sentences always confuse readers and put an unnecessary burden on their time and patience. In clear writing, no two unrelated ideas are crowded into one sentence, no matter how brief the thoughts may be. Here is a typical closing sentence that is so worded as to contain two unrelated ideas.

Original Version

Thank you for your letter (1) and do not hesitate to call on us if we can be of further help. (2)

Revised Version

Thank you for your letter. Call on us again whenever we can be of further help to you. (One sentence of thanks, the other about helping.)

or

We appreciate your writing to us and shall be glad to help you again whenever you call on us. (Two parts of one thought about help, now and later.)

The worst type of run-on sentence stretches into several lines, or even a paragraph, with clauses adding to the confusion.

Original Version

This division has been requested to assemble considerable information which is needed in regard to a safety hazard problem which might arise from operation of the plant which is proposed for the Eastex area and in connection with this an attempt has been made to secure certain data relative to detection instruments and devices providing reliable warning.

Revised Version

This division has been asked to describe the complete safety plan to be used in the operation of the proposed Eastex area plant. We have therefore tried to find the best possible devices for detecting and eliminating hazards.

In an effort to write simply and to avoid long, involved sentences, you will sometimes be tempted to break your thought into such small pieces that the reader gets the impression he is going through a set of flash cards. A strong, simple sentence is very effective for calling attention to a summarizing fact or to a point of decision, especially when you set a short sentence into a passage composed of long sentences. This practice is quite different, however, from making a whole paragraph of short sentences, many of which contain incomplete ideas related to the other sentences in the passage. Your writing is more interesting and shows clearer relationships if you combine some of the short sentences for smoother reading and more logical thought groups. The newly employed engineer reading the following original version must have felt like a child receiving instruction about his first day in school.

Original Version	Revised Version
We wish to tell you about the usual plan for orientation. This orientation plan takes one week. During this first week, you learn about the organization. You also learn the type of business we are in. Also, you will talk with some of the management people.	The first week of your employment will be spent in orientation. During this time, various members of management will tell you about the electronics industry and describe our firm's organization.

Another writer with a striking idea about saving his customer's money, chopped the idea into small pieces and spoiled the effect of his thought.

Original Version	Revised Version
Our economy of operation is achieved through intensive work simplification. It has eliminated high cost of production. This has been passed on to our customers.	Through intensive work simplification, we have eliminated the high cost of production and are able to pass this saving to our customers.

WORK PROJECT 4

Making Clear, Complete Sentences

Write a concise, acceptable revision of each item in the space provided. Try to retain the meaning that was probably intended in the original version. Hand this sheet to your instructor for review.

1. If conveniently possible, we would appreciate your examining the April report.

2. There is no equipment involved which makes setting the dial very simple.

3. Action to correct these situations and install efficient methods have been taken.

4. Reviewing the results of the Greenpoint Plant, the situation seems to be under control.

5. It is the responsibility of headquarters to see that it gets reports promptly; to do this, it is necessary to have their report writers properly trained.

6. 40 acres are located in back of our building that can be used to place equipment necessary to complete your job.

7. It is necessary, therefore, that you have the three carbons signed by you and your wife, notarized, and keeping one for your files return one to us and send the other to the bank which is the trustee along with the certificate which must be signed by you and sent preferably by registered mail.

8. We have been carrying on conference sessions with the travel and transportation department relative to their procedures for entering these costs, and it is our expectation that they will fully agree with your suggestion as of July 1, 19____.

9. By raising the salary of these men to compete with other companies, FLORCO could have retained their work experience and actually saved money when compared to the salary paid for new and unproductive help.

10. While a part-time employee with the state highway department in the summer, I discussed the possibility of permanent employment upon my graduation from the university as a highway engineer in training with a member of the highway department's personnel division.

11. Mr. Crosby's precise work would be hindered by his poor health which could result in production troubles.

12. I would be glad to act as company representative. This would be a job I could work in with my regular business obligations and time schedule. I would like this.

13. The case, measuring 12 × 4 when closed, opens with a roomy 4-section file on top and a hard, flat surface for writing on the bottom side.

14. By signing the enclosed, already addressed card, we would send you a 10-lb. bag of rye grass seed and two boxes of gladioli bulbs now.

15. Let us help you in maintaining your good credit rating by sending your check for the full amount in the enclosed envelope.

16. Internal threads occupy one inch of the bottom of the funnel that are used to secure the pump.

17. The wires are guaranteed to take normal usage and after a thorough examination the wires rusting occurred when it was stored in a damp place or submerged in water.

18. This form of denotation is called rectangular coordinates. The X component being the reference axis and the Y component the quadrature reference of the phasor.

19. Speaking as a student of junior standing many students wait until two weeks from taking the final to begin studying the courses; the final in this instance measuring nothing but two weeks of cramming.

20. The machine is now ready to clean the floor which can be done by pushing it around the desired area.

21. As a member of Northwest Credit Association it is our duty to our fellow wholesalers to report all accounts that have not been paid in 90 days or more.

22. A sales meeting found me out of my office this morning when you phoned and upon returning my secretary told me of your call.

23. This unit consists of a pulley exerciser, a chest pull or expander, a rowing machine, an abdominal developer, and with patented foot holders you can practice weight-lifting movements.

24. By sending us a check for $79.16, we will ship your order at once.

25. After replacing the condenser, the A-C will give you years of service.

26. We are requesting proposals from ten firms, each of which will be evaluated according to the quality and portability of equipment described.

27. Heyne Company will construct a 100′ cooling tower on the roof of the building which is sufficient to cool each floor.

28. After the merchandise is received, it lies on the floor in the aisles for days which obstructs traffic.

29. When the distance between stations is great, relays or repeaters are used to boost the current.

30. Standing behind the handle of the mower, the throttle should be put on the choke position.

31. Being a leading supplier of steel for the United States, I would like very much to be a part of U.S. Steel.

32. This area has had my attention for the past couple of months and I too would be interested in finding out the reason why we have not had the output we expected to have, and how we can go about getting it.

33. This morning I received the expected shipment of paper from your company which shows a slight mistake.

34. My Bachelor of Science with a major in Technology and a minor in Business will aid each other greatly.

35. Give a full record of your inspection trip that was reported on your expense account in detail and arranging the steps in chronological order.

36. Papers of various sizes are needed. Each paper should also be a different texture and grain. Tests should be made on all sample papers. Sample papers should be left in the testing bin.

37. We may be able next week to remove some of the extra paper stock from the warehouse that will not be needed before it mildews.

38. Turning the knob to the right, the copy moves through the machine faster exposing the paper to a lighter heat intensity.

39. Specialized equipment has attracted cargo to our railroad which previously moved by private motor transport.

40. There is a newer table model sold by Monogram-it Co. which other stores are using.

Concise writing is a highly desirable quality in business and technical writing because it wastes no time and shows proper reader consideration. If you write concisely, you save your own time, the reader's time, and the time needed to prepare the typed page. In addition, you save the money which time represents. Well-worded, concise communications are an important means of achieving goodwill. In contrast, wordy writing can make the message confusing and create hostility in the reader, who often lacks the time, interest, and desire to decipher a wordy, dense message or report. Basically, concise writing has three goals: clarity, brevity, and directness. To learn to write concisely, you must practice developing sentences that avoid the following pitfalls.

Wordiness

Always avoid phrases which can be replaced by one or two words. In the following examples, using one or two words rather than four, five, or even six words produces conciseness without changing meaning.

Instead of	Use
according to our records	we find
at a later date	later
at the present time	now
by means of	by
despite the fact that	although
due to the fact that	since, because
during the time that	while
for the purpose of	to, for
for the reason that	since, because
in accordance with your request	as you requested
in order that	so
in order to	to
in the event that	if
in the neighborhood of	about
in the normal course of procedure	normally
in the near future	soon
in this day and age	today
it is our opinion	we think
on a daily basis	daily
on the grounds that	because
prior to	before
pursuant to our agreement	as we agreed
the reason is due to	because
until such time as	until
we are not in a position to	we cannot
will you be kind enough to	please
without further delay	now
with (reference, regard, respect) to	about

Avoid "fad" or "buzz" words. The following words have lost any precise or clear meaning because they have been overused in too many contexts:

time frame	time-saving, money-saving, labor-saving
hard data	in-depth

input
output
feedback
interface
matrix
ongoing
seminal
viability
integrated
functional
logistical
contingency factors
flexibility
dynamic

multifaceted
broad-based
grid
infrastructure
monolithic
participatory involvement
role playing
systematized
synchronized
hardware
programming
capability
far-reaching

Avoid phrases that are clearly redundant:

Doublets	Two-Word Patterns
advice and counsel	absolutely free, complete, essential
advise and recommend	background experience
agreeable and satisfactory	basic fundamentals
consent and approval	close proximity
courteous and polite	complete absence
due and payable	completely eliminate, unanimous
each and every	consensus of opinion
earnest and sincere	entirely possible
fair and equitable	exactly identical
first and foremost	final end
full and complete	first begun
help and cooperation	mail out
hope and trust	past experience
if and when	personal opinion
opinion and belief	quite unique, very unique
permanent and lasting	rarely ever
prompt and immediate	rather likely
ready and willing	seldom ever
right and proper	reduce down
thought and consideration	repeat again
	summarize briefly
	true facts
	very latest, complete, unique

Other redundant phrases are ludicrous:

green in color   (as opposed to shape?)

human volunteer   (who else volunteers?)

period of time   (as opposed to space?)

past memories   (as opposed to future ones?)

twenty in number   (as opposed to height or depth or shape?)

Writers often use strings of empty words which can be eliminated from the sentence without changing its meaning:

to the extent that	with reference to
in connection with	in view of
as a matter of fact	in order
relative to	as to
by means of	such that
as regards	in a manner of
as far as _____ goes	in view of
as a matter of fact	beg to inform
contents duly noted	thanking you in advance
awaiting your favor	replying to yours of

Note that many of the above phrases are associated with traditional business language. Omit these archaic phrases and use simple language.

Instead of:	Use:
according to our records	we received
acknowledge receipt of	thank you for your letter
allow me to thank you for	thank you for
attached please find	you will find enclosed
at this present writing	now
we regret to inform you that	we are sorry
we wish to say	(just say it)
we wish to inform you	(just do it)

Repetition

Many times wordiness comes from unnecessary repetition of ideas:

Original Version	Revised Version
This particular division's work consisted of three projects; that is, three different projects were worked on by this division.	This division worked on three projects.

The repetition of words usually results from careless and hasty writing. The annoying overuse of "that" is common practice because the word can serve as several parts of speech.

Original Version	Revised Version
In the accident *that* Mr. Blake described, we found *that* it was true *that* the foreman had overlooked the safety check for that day, and for *that* reason, the company thought *that* it was best *that* claim not be presented.	The company decided not to present a claim for the accident Mr. Blake described, because the foreman had not made a safety check on *that* day.

When you write, "Will you please return the plans to us so that we may, in turn, return them to the drafting department," your reader has a right to think you should have used a synonym somewhere. One of the most common types of repetition is the needless use of two or more phrases of about the same meaning, presumably to emphasize the idea.

Original Version	Revised Version
We wish to cooperate fully in every way possible.	We wish to cooperate fully.
Registration of trainees and supervisors is under way at the present time for the seminars.	Trainees and supervisors are now registering for the seminars.

When you repeat words or ideas for emphasis, you deliberately place them in points of your message where they will receive the best attention, and you try to choose words that will maintain the interest of your reader.

The writer of the original version of the report below was earnestly hammering away at the reader with two important ideas, one the cause of the other. The writer had reason to believe that the gauges were unreliable (idea 1) and recommended their not being installed on any type-B plants, such as Hilldale (idea 2). The writer could have convinced the reader in about half the time and space by presenting each idea only once and in its appropriate order.

Original Version

There is now considerable question as to the reliability of fixed gauges. (1) It is recommended that their installation be discontinued as a matter of routine. (2).

More specifically, it is recommended that we do not install these gauges at the Hilldale station, soon to be opened. (2) It is extremely doubtful that these instruments give any protection whatsoever. (1)

Although we have made an industry-wide survey in order to obtain the best instruments available, our experience to date indicates that these instruments are unreliable and cannot be entirely depended upon to perform the function intended. (1)

In view of the present reliable system and the other reliable protection devices that have been and will be installed on type-B stations such as Hilldale, it is recommended that the fixed gauges not be installed. (2).

Revised Version

Our experience with fixed gauges and the facts furnished by others in the industry convince us that these gauges are unreliable for the safe operation of type-B plants such as Hilldale. (1)

I recommend, therefore, that the use of fixed gauges be discontinued in all type-B plants in our company. (2)

Even when you repeat for emphasis, you must plan carefully to prevent the reader's becoming bored or irritated. When wordiness comes from unnecessary repetition of ideas, the reader unconsciously resents the implication that he is too stupid to understand your first reference or too absent-minded to realize that you are saying the same thing.

Dead Phrases

While redundancy—either of words or ideas—always produces wordiness, "dead" phrases can frequently make unnecessarily long sentences. The following are common dead phrases that should be eliminated:

It is interesting to note that . . .

It should be pointed out that . . .

It should be remembered that . . .

It is significant that . . .

It has been demonstrated that . . .

It is essential that . . .

It is evident that . . .

Note how the following sentences which use dead phrases can be more directly stated when these phrases are omitted:

Original Version	Revised Version
It is essential that the requirements of all switching systems be recognized. (12 words)	The requirements of all switching systems must be recognized. (9 words)
It should be noted that the quality of cable was increased. (11 words)	Note that cable quality was increased. (6 words)

Another kind of opening dead phrase is the common "there is" or "there are" which are roundabout ways of beginning sentences. Eliminating these routine beginning phrases saves words and makes your sentence more direct:

Original Version	Revised Version
There are six steps necessary to administer CPR. *These are:* . . .	To administer CPR requires six steps . . .
There is a city parking lot which is used by the bank during the week.	A bank uses a city parking lot during the week.

Eliminating dead phrases has two advantages. First, words which fail to add meaning to the sentence are pruned. Second, the important part of the sentence is presented to the reader immediately.

Uncommon Words

The writer must be sure to consider his audience when deciding how technical the jargon can be. Aside from this basic premise of effective writing, the writer should choose the short, familiar word rather than the longer, less common word. Longer words produce longer sentences which are harder for the reader to process. Therefore, use words which will seem natural to your audience. Never use a cumbersome word when a short one will do:

Instead of:	Consider using:	Instead of:	Consider using:
accelerate	speed up	explicit	plain
accumulate	gather	facilitate	make easy, help, ease
acquaint	tell	indebtedness	debt
additional	added	indicate	show
aggregate	total	initial	first
ameliorate	improve	initiate, inaugurate	begin
anticipate	foresee	locality	place
apparent	clear	maintenance	upkeep
approximately	about	materialize	appear
assistance	aid	modification	change
attributable	due	objective	aims, goals
cognizance	knowledge	obligation	debt
commence	begin	optimum	best, most
commitment	promise	participate	take part
compensation	pay	proceed	go
consequently	so	procure	get, buy
construct	build	purchase	buy
contribute	give	reimburse	pay
correspondence	letter	subsequent	next, later
demonstrate	show	sufficient	enough
encounter	meet	terminated	ended
endeavor	try	transmit	send
equivalent	equal	utilize	use
expedite	hasten	voluminous	bulky

Long, vague, "beautiful" words and phrases can frequently defy precise definition and meaning. However, these wordy, meaningless phrases are all too common in reports and business documents:

integrated management options

total organizational flexibility

responsive organizational capability

total logistical time-phase

Because the best writing helps the reader to visualize the message clearly, you should avoid using abstract nouns which, from overuse, tend to mean little to the reader: activity, condition, connection, extent, method, nature, policy, position, quality, reason, relation, result, situation, standpoint, utilization.

Passive Voice

Usually, sentences lack directness and brevity because they are written in passive voice rather than active voice. That is, the sentence uses an object–verb–agent word arrangement (o–v–a) rather than the more natural subject–verb–object (s–v–o) arrangement. The following passive voice sentence contains eleven words. Rewritten in active voice, the sentence contains only five words:

Passive	Active
A weight loss of ten pounds was *experienced* by the trainee.	The trainee lost ten pounds.

The writer should use active voice whenever possible. It produces shorter, more direct sentences; and it preserves the rhythm and natural quality of spoken English, a characteristic that is desirable in business writing. The following example shows how strange a simple sentence can become when it is written in passive voice:

Passive	Active
The home run was hit by Pete Rose.	Pete Rose hit a home run.

Clearly, the active voice version is shorter and easier to read.

Furthermore, when a writer uses passive voice, the sentence gains length from prepositional phrases. Too many, particularly those that occur between the subject and the verb, can dissolve meaning:

$$\overset{s}{\text{The existence of frictional resistance}} \mid \overset{1}{\text{to relative motion}} \mid \overset{2}{\text{between material sub-}} \overset{3}{}$$
$$\overset{4}{\text{stances}} \mid \text{in contact} \mid \overset{v}{\text{was concluded.}}$$

In addition, the subject of the sentence, the agent responsible for the action, disappears from its expected place, the beginning of the sentence. The following passive sentence (twenty-six words) contains eight prepositional phrases. The real subject—agent of the sentence (automobile owners) is bottled up in two prepositional phrases:

$$\overset{s}{\text{The uncertainty about an improvement}} \mid \overset{1}{\text{in the manufacture}} \mid \overset{2}{\text{of steel frames}} \mid \overset{3}{\text{is of}} \overset{v}{}$$
$$\overset{4}{\text{concern}} \mid \overset{5}{\text{to owners}} \mid \overset{6}{\text{of automobiles due to}} \overset{7}{\text{increases}} \mid \overset{8}{\text{in insurance and}}$$
$$\text{repair costs.}$$

The active voice version (twenty-one words) contains no prepositional phrases and places the subject and verb close together at the beginning of the sentence:

$$\overset{a}{\text{Automobile owners}} \overset{v}{\text{\textit{do not know}}} \text{ if steel frame manufacturing} \overset{a}{\text{improvements}}$$
$$\overset{v}{\text{will be great enough to offset increased insurance and repair costs.}}$$

Perhaps the best structure recipe for good, clear, direct sentences is to maintain agent–verb–object as consistently as possible. A–v–o sentences are hard-hitting and economical because they do not produce excessive prepositional phrases, the major enemies of conciseness. Always try to build sentences by using a–v–o clauses rather than phrases. The following example illustrates this point. The original passive sentence contains twenty words, six prepositional phrases, and one verb:

$$\overset{1}{\text{In their designs}} \mid \overset{2}{\text{for buildings,}} \mid \overset{s}{\text{brick}} \overset{v}{\text{is}} \text{ usually stipulated by} \overset{3}{\text{architects}} \mid \overset{4}{\text{because}}$$
$$\text{of its resistance} \mid \overset{5}{\text{against the effects}} \mid \overset{6}{\text{of weather.}}$$

In active voice, using agent–verb–object structure—two dependent and one main

41

clause (three verbs) instead of prepositional phrases—the sentence requires thirteen words and no prepositional phrases:

a   v   o   a   v   o   a v

When they design buildings, architects usually stipulate brick because it resists weather effects.

Essentially, the main argument for active voice is as follows: the heart of the English sentence is the *verb*. Active sentences emphasize verbs, while passive sentences emphasize nouns as they occur in prepositional phrases. In short, the more verbs the sentence has, the stronger and more direct the sentence is. The following passive sentence is built around seven prepositional phrases. The sentence has twenty-seven words and only one verb:

s   1   2   3

The attorney's attempt at an investigation | into the club's handling | of the project

4   5   6   7

was met by a refusal | to allow an examination | of its expenditure | of funds.

Rephrased into active voice clauses, the sentence becomes more direct, more concise, and easier to understand. The sentence still has twenty-seven words, but it now has four verbs:

a   v   a   v

The attorney attempted to investigate how the club handled the project, but the

a   v   o   a v   o

club refused to allow the attorney to examine the way it spent its funds.

Consider one further example:

1   2   3

Aside from the value | of changes | to the organizational structure | to achieve

4   5

better personnel usage, | the restructure | of all levels | of the company | and ade-

6   7

quate utilization of good planning | will result in improved performance | in

8

major company departments. |

This sentence requires thirty-eight words and eight prepositional phrases. It has only one verb. Rephrased into active voice clauses, one independent and one dependent, the sentence requires twenty-four words, one prepositional phrase, and three verbs. The meaning of the sentence now focuses sharply:

dependent   independent

If the board votes to restructure the company (the new organizational structure will use personnel better and improve planning and performance in major departments.)

Beginning a sentence with a "dead" phrase will frequently produce a passive sentence, as in the following examples:

Original Version	**Revised Version**
It is believed by the committee that *there are* too many unqualified persons trying to claim professional status. (19 words)	The committee believes that too many unqualified persons are trying to claim professional status. (14 words)

It is suggested at this time that purchase be made of the two vacant lots now available. (17 words)	We suggested purchasing the two vacant lots now available. (9 words)

Concrete Agents as Subjects

When you compose a sentence, try to choose a subject or agent that is concrete, either a person or an object. That is, whenever possible, try to avoid using abstract words such as the following: ability, condition, degree, extent, nature, position, problem, purpose, question, reason, relation, result, situation, utilization. The more specific your words are, the clearer your sentence will be. In many passive sentences, abstract words are the subjects of the sentences. Then, if no agent is given, the sentence loses clarity and directness. Frequently, the sentence is awkward:

> s
> The *position* of John Smith with respect to the other candidates was felt to be of the highest order.

> s
> The *nature* of the enrollment pattern was confusing to the board of directors.

Phrased in active voice and using a concrete agent as a subject, the sentence becomes more direct and concise:

> s
> *John Smith* has a better position than the other candidates have.

> s
> The *enrollment pattern* confused the board of directors.

However, even in active voice, an abstract subject ("reason") rather than a concrete one ("John") produces an awkward, less concise sentence:

Original Version	**Revised Version**
The *reason* John lost the election was due to the fact that he became ill.	*John* lost the election because he became ill.

An abstract subject can often lead to an incorrect meaning—that is, the subject, which is only an abstraction, cannot perform the action the remainder of the sentence assigns it:

> s
> The *purpose* of this part of my study is to increase the amount of deductible expense.

Obviously, the purpose might be to *discuss* ways of increasing the amount of deductible income, but "purpose" cannot "increase the amount of deductible income." The true subject of the sentence is "study":

> s
> My *study* will show ways to increase the amount of deductible expense.

FINAL CONSIDERATIONS

As will be discussed in Chapter 5, many times writers must use passive voice to describe process. However, when building sentences, use active voice whenever possible. Every writer should be aware of the syntax problems that can result from passive structures. No matter what sentence order you choose, eliminate unnecessary words and phrases. Use concrete, vivid words to help your reader visualize your message. Because verbs are the heart of the English sentence, build sentences around action verbs rather than "is," "are," and other forms of "be" verbs. Basically, you should decide specifically what you are trying to say and then present your message as directly and concisely as possible. However, conciseness at any cost is not desirable. Because your message is written for another human being, you must achieve conciseness and preserve good tone—the subject of the next section.

> **Wordy:** We wish to assure you that we have given your request full and due consideration and that we have made a decision to hold a meeting with the representatives of the petitioning group sometime in the course of the next week. (41 words)
>
> **Concise but curt:** In view of your request, we decided to meet the leaders next week. (twelve words)
>
> **Concise and pleasant:** After considering your request, we planned to meet with your representatives at a convenient time next week. (seventeen words)

APPLICATIONS

Examine the following wordy memo to see how conciseness improves clarity, readability, and message appeal. In the revision, note how the author states the important points only and phrases each point as concisely as possible.

Original Memo

```
Memo to:  All Flat-Salaried Personnel

Subject:  English Compositions for Effortless Interpretation

It has been observed with increasing dismay that already-complex written
material emanating from this division continues to develop even greater
complexity to the point that some of subject material can be interpreted only by
persons with college educations and some such material is completely
unintelligible. For this reason it is considered advisable that steps be taken to
reduce the amount of verbiage with which we must daily contend almost without
exception.

In line with a trend throughout almost all industry to improve written
communications an intensive program will be initiated at Compresi-Faircross in
which all flat-salaried personnel will be afforded an opportunity to enroll in a
course designed to maximize each subject employee's efficiency in the writing of
material that can be rapidly and easily read and understood.

Subject instruction will be available on company time and each department is
assigned the responsibility of arranging for instructors for its own personnel
and scheduling such personnel so as to obtain maximum effectiveness in this effort
while at the same time creating a minimum of interruption in normal work
assignments.
```

Subject of this effort to encourage unmuddied understanding throughout all levels of the line and staff organization will be "English Composition for Effortless Interpretation."

Upon successful completion of the course which will meet one (1) hour each day for a month all personnel who achieve a score of 90 or higher in the test will be repaid by an increase of five (5) per centum in their bimonthly wage rate with the exception that U.S. income tax will be deducted in an amount commensurate with the individual's salary as established by the Congress of the United States.

Instruction sessions will be held in two sections with persons bearing names beginning with the letters A thru L meeting at 2:00 p.m. and personnel bearing names beginning with the letters M thru Z meeting at 3:00 p.m. Such instruction sessions will be held in the cafeteria.

The usual cooperation of all personnel concerned will be sincerely appreciated.

Manager

Concise Revision

Memo to: All Flat—Salaried Employees

Subject: Course in "Writing for Easy Reading"

Want a 5 percent pay increase?

All you have to do is take a course on "Writing for Easy Reading" and score 90 or better on a final exam.

You and all other flat—salaried employees may take the course on company time.

Classes begin June 6 in the cafeteria. They will meet one hour a day, Monday through Friday, for four weeks. People with names beginning A—L will meet at 2:00 p.m. People with names beginning M—Z will meet at 3:00 p.m.

Each department will have charge of its own course and will obtain its instructors. Your department head will give you additional details.

We are making this offer because we must take a bold step to improve our written material. Some of the writing turned out at this division is understandable only to college graduates, and some of our writing is understandable to nobody.

We hope that this course, dealing with the principles of writing for easy reading, will get rid of most of this unintelligible written material.

Manager

Insurance policies are legal documents that have been most strongly affected by the "plain English" laws now in force in many states. These laws require insurance policies to be written in layman's language. The following excerpts are taken from two life insurance policies written by the Connecticut Mutual Life Insurance Company. One policy was written in 1941; the other, in 1979.[2] Notice the differences in style and word choice as well as format:

[2]Policies provided by and used with the permission of Connecticut Mutual Life Insurance Company, Hartford, Conn.

Table of Values (1941)

Assuming that premiums shall have been duly paid in full for the number of years elapsed and that there shall be no indebtedness to the Company or outstanding paid-up addition, the Values guaranteed by this Policy for the end of the years specified appear below. "Years Elapsed" in the following table shall be reckoned from the due date of the first annual premium. The Loan Values are the maximum amounts available at the end of the years specified. Loans may also be obtained at any time during such years as set forth in the above clause entitled "policy Loan." Guaranteed Values for other years, if any, as provided in this Policy, will be computed upon the same basis and stated upon request.

Table of Values (1979)

The values shown in the *Table of Values* on page 3 apply if premiums have been paid to the end of the policy year specified and there is no indebtedness.

The loan values are the maximum loan values available at the end of the policy year shown.

Values will be increased by dividend credits and by paid-up additions only as specifically provided in this policy.

No value is provided under this policy until premiums are paid to the time the value is first shown in the *Table of Values*.

All values are greater than or equal to those required by a state statute.

On request, we will furnish values for any policy year not shown in the Table of Values.

Policy Loan (1941)

At any time after due payment of two or more annual premiums hereon, while this Policy is in force otherwise than as Extended Insurance, on proper assignment and delivery of the Policy to the Home Office of the Company for endorsement and is the sole security thereof, the Company will loan any sum up to the limit secured by the Cash Value of this Policy less any existing indebtedness on or secured by this Policy and less any unpaid balance of the premium for the then current policy year. Additional policy loans may be made without further endorsement. Unless the loan is for the purpose of paying premiums to the Company, the Company may defer the making of such loan for a period not exceeding two months after application therefor; or if such period is in excess of the maximum period permitted by law, then for the maximum period permitted thereby. Such loan shall bear interest at the rate of 3 percent per annum, payable annually, not in advance, on the due date of the annual premium, principal and interest to be payable at the Home Office of the Company. The Company will credit upon such indebtedness payments made at any time.

Any interest when due and unpaid shall be added to the principal of the existing indebtedness and shall bear the same rate of interest, but failure to pay either principal or interest shall not void the Policy until the total indebtedness to the Company secured herein, including accrued interest, shall equal or exceed the then Cash Value when this Policy shall immediately cease and become void, but not until thirty-one days after notice shall have been mailed by the Company to the last known address of the Insured, or of such persons as may have been designated to receive such notice, and of any assignment of record at the Home Office of the Company.

Policy Loan (1979)

At any time after this policy first has a cash value and while it is in force other than as extended term insurance, we will loan you any sum up to the policy's maximum loan value less existing indebtedness.

The loan will bear interest at the rate specified on page 3, payable on the policy anniversary.

The maximum loan value is the amount which, with interest at the policy loan rate, shall equal the cash value on the next policy anniversary, or the next premium due date if earlier.

We will make the loan when we receive a written request. We reserve the right to inspect or endorse the policy before making the loan.

We may defer making the loan for a period not exceeding six months after application unless the loan is to be used to pay premiums under the *Premium Loan* provision.

Any premium due when the loan is made will be deducted from the loan amount.

The policy will be the sole security for the loan. Lack of endorsement will not indicate that the policy is free of loans.

Any interest not paid when due will be added to the loan and will bear interest at the same rate.

The indebtedness may be repaid in whole or part at any time before maturity if it has not been deducted from the *Automatic Extended Term Insurance or Paid-Up Insurance* benefit.

Both principal and interest are payable at our Home Office.

Whenever indebtedness equals or exceeds the cash value, this policy will terminate and have no further value thirty-one days after we mail notice to the last known address of the insured (or the person designated to receive such notice), and of any assignee of record at the Home Office.

WORK PROJECT 5

Achieving Clarity and Conciseness

Write a more concise revision of each item in the space provided. Correct any errors you find in spelling, punctuation, and grammar.

1. We hope and trust that we can collaborate together to eliminate complete repatitious effort among departments that work in close proximity.

   Revision: We hope to work together to eliminate repetitious effort among departments that work in proximity.

2. In the normal course of procedure, we would not ask you to send the information at the present time, but due to the fact that a change of management is about to occur, it was my suggestion that we request all information be sent at the earliest possible moment. Our first and foremost desire is that this arrangement will be agreeable and satisfactory with you.

3. Please give immediate effort to insure that the pages of all reports compiled for distribution are numbered sequentially and in a position to insure optimum visibility.

   Revision: Please number the pages clearly and correctly.

4. Alternative courses of action is a major decision that must be made by managers. They must decide which alternative to take. The number of alternatives must be reduced by examining many other alternatives and picking the most appropriate one.

5. The possibility of delay in manufacturing the experimental transistors is of concern to the buyers of radio component parts due to an increase in the rate of inflation.

   Revision: Radio component buyers are concerned about possible delays in manufacturing experimental transistors because of increased inflation.

6. In the case of gasohol research, it was found that total use of gasohol was ineffective on the engines tested.

7. It is an evident indication of effective organization when personnel esti-mates are correct.

Revision: Correct personnel estimates indicate good planning.

8. It should be noted that the final report is the most important.

9. It is my suggestion that the company adopt the current scientific test administered in the selection of new employees for the firm.

Revision: I suggest the company adopt current scientific tests to select new employees for the firm.

10. In efficient organizations, usage of personnel to attain maximum produc-tion times are attained.

11. There are six steps in administration of CPR. They are: (1) getting medical help, (2) placing victim on back, (3) external cardiac massage, (4) relax hands, (5) mouth-to-mouth respiration, (6) continue process.

12. Reallocation of land resources were achieved by better planning.

13. In an earlier estimate, a new timetable was presented, and a new budget was suggested.

14. In order to become a successful intern there are certain demands that need to be taken into consederation.

15. It is important that the intern can be relied on at all times.

16. This type of measurement is very useful in deciding that once a product is on the market should it be discontinued.

17. Using these cashier's hours along with the Customer Distribution per Hour Report, it is possible to predict how many cashiers will be needed each hour to cover the number of customers.

18. After studying the old and new methods, it is clear that the new methods outlined above are much more productive for the store and the shopper. There will, however, be some problems which will arise until the system has been operational for a period of time.

19. Brands may not be specified unless there is no equivalent product at the present time. The reason for this is that all purchasing is based on product comparison and competative bidding. This insures cost and quality control on the grounds that it avoids vendor favoritism.

20. The reason for the silence vary, but the most common reasons are fear of reprisal, particularly of an economic nature, is a formidable deterrent to "blowing the whistle" on sexual molesters.

21. Turnovers in companies should be avoided not only because they are costly, but also because the loss of an honest, responsible, and hard working person could account for the reduction in productivity.

22. A common source of delay is the fact that department heads do not follow this procedure.

23. This circuit allows additional fuel to flow into and mix with the air passing through the carburator. This causes a richer fuel mixture to be delivered to the engine for full power operation.

24. Another reason problem solving guidelines are needed is due to the fact that a manager is constantly under pressure, and it is precisely during this time, when people are clamoring for action, that he needs a systematic approach to follow.

25. The most important time that a manager needs an efficient method for handling problems and making decisions is when his time is short.

26. The fuel nozzle is located at the front-end of the combustion chamber through which fuel is sprayed into the high-pressure air.

27. Since the subject of real estate tax shelters is a vast and ever changing topic, my purpose is to orient the potential investor about what tax shelters are, some types of real estate investments available that shelter taxes, and how the investments reduce the tax payers taxes.

28. It has long been my desire to be a contractor and through past experience my talents have been found to be in that area.

29. People enter the tool business to make money, and for the purpose of serving the consumers.

30. When discrepancies occurred and / or ambiguities existed, it was necessary for me to communicate orally by telephone and by written memo.

31. The delivery of the 24 cases will be trucked directly to your home office.

32. The motor is a simple electric motor which runs on any 120 volt source. The motor is capable of putting out 40 watts of power at a speed of 1000–2000 revolutions per minute. The motor turns the blade by means of a drive shaft. The speed of the motor is determined by the speed switch located on the handle.

33. If you would like to establish credit with us, we have enclosed our application for credit form. If you do not wish to establish credit with us, we will credit your account with the extra $20 of your check. But if you do not wish to establish credit, we will send you the balance of the $20.

34. Before placing the distributor cap on the distributor housing, it is important that it be dust free which might cause it to malfunction.

35. There were several meritorious ideas which were presented at the meeting for consideration by the advisory committee . It was believed by the committee members that such suggestions should be made in written form so as to make possible the awarding of small but morale-building sums of money in cases where such awards seemed to be justified by the utility value of the suggestions offered.

36. Recommendation is made, therefore, that payment be made on this claim and that the company be assured of no further responsibility.

37. Here we see true two-way communication operating to narrow the gap between employee and management attitudes and action and then attempting to merge them to achieve the unity of purpose requisite for attaining the objectives of the business and the satisfaction of employee needs. We attempt to accomplish this through good downward communication by management to gain employee confidence and trust and through truly effective upward communication by means of which management may be kept informed of employees' needs and desires in order to readjust its planning.

38. I checked with our billing department in Atlanta, Georgia and they cannot list all the invoice numbers on one voucher per month. The reasons for this is they bill repairs continuously. If they listed all the repair invoices and numbers on one voucher they would have to hold all repair billing for a whole month which they dont want to do and I'm sure the company doesn't want to do since it would put the billing even further behind. As per the meeting, all invoices will go to you with vouchers. Dan Brown is also to send three copies of all repair order tickets to Mr. Thomas. This will be done every friday. The mechanic will also be leaving a customer copy on the job site when he makes a call. I've also notified Memphis that when they invoice the company they are to put the date the work was done on the invoice. I would appreciate your passing this information on to the people in your division who need to have this for their reccords.

39. Revise the following letter to achieve clarity, correctness, and conciseness. After studying Chapter 4—Graphics—examine this letter again. Can you develop a suitable graphic to display the important price information contained in the letter?

January 18, 1980

ABCD Corporation
P. O. Box 1330
Houston, Texas 77001

Attention: Robert Howe

Dear Robert,

As you know on January 11, 1980 we wrote you a letter explaining what your billing rates were for mechanics, helpers, and teams for regular time, time and a half, and double time.

This letter is to explain when we will bill you these different labor rates. As you know your company is covered for regular time call backs. If we answer a trouble call during the week or on saturdays on over time and it is a normal trouble call we will bill the company $16.88 for every hour the mechanic spends on that job, which is at the time and a half rate. If the mechanic answers this trouble call on a holiday or sundays the charge is double time and we will bill the company $33.76 for every hour the mechanic spends fixing this call.

If a trouble call occured monday through friday during the regular work hours and it is a trouble call not due to vandalism then the company is not billed for any portion of this work. If it is a vandalism call and we do bill the company during the normal work day, then the company will be billed 31.75 for each hour the mechanic spends on the job. If it required a team of men to repair the problem, then it would be $55.25 per hour. There are many vandalism calls that occur monday through friday 8–5 that we do not bill for. The types of vandalism calls that we have been fixing and not billing for are the ones that do not involve a lot of extra parts cost and labor on our part.

If we answer a normal trouble call day or night, then the mileage the mechanic charges us will not be billed to the company. If however, we answer a trouble call that involves vandalism, then we will bill the company for the mechanics mileage cost.

Sincerely,

Michael T. Harris
District Manager

---

40. Rewrite the following memo to achieve clarity and conciseness.

FROM: Douglas H. Johnson, District Director
          Office of Planning and Evaluation
          ABC School District

DATE: May 7, 1979

SUBJECT: PROGRAM EVALUATION QUESTIONNAIRES

TO: All ABC teachers

As the dual stresses of increased accountability and restricted funding have come to the fore in public education, so has discussion of the appropriate means to evaluate an institution's instructional programs. The results at those institutions which have implemented formal processes for conducting program evaluations have been mixed.

A pivotal factor which seems to separate the successful process from the expensive failure is the degree to which the process is attuned to the needs and expectations of those using it. Goals of an evaluative process frequently have been poorly defined, and the process itself designed in such a way as to be incapable of providing the kind of information required to meet diverse sets of needs among its users and participants.

There is little room for doubt that external pressures to account for the ways in which resources are being used, and internal needs to know more about the potential benefits of using these resources in alternative ways, will require the ABC School District to implement some formal mechanism for the evaluation of its instructional programs in the near future. (Investigation of adjunct processes for evaluating administrative and support services is moving apace on another front.) The attached questionnaires are an initial attempt at better understanding the potential benefits and limitations which might be ascribed to a process of program evaluations at this school.

The objectives are twofold. The first objective is to give definition to the goals and expectations of the various groups who would participate in, and use the results of, formal program evaluations. Secondly, we hope to develop the framework for a standardized process which will be facilitative of these goals and expectations while utilizing to as great an extent as possible existing resources of the institution. Because different groups have different goals and expectations, a broad sampling of faculty and administrators has been selected to receive these questionnaires.

You are asked to respond as clearly and candidly as possible to both questionnaires. Additional input will undoubtedly need to be developed as decisions are contemplated about the appropriate role and scope for program evaluations in the conduct and management of campus affairs. It is hoped that this first effort will shed light on the form further developments should take, and will help to avoid some of the costly fits and starts which have characterized more insular efforts at other public school districts. Your responses, expressing the unique set of experiences which you bring to your job, will provide a singular contribution to this effort. I hope you will choose to make this contribution by thoughtfully answering each of the questions posed.

I would appreciate having your completed questionnaires by Monday, May 28. This return date should allow analysis of the closed-end questionnaire results to be completed and ready for distribution by the end of June. It is hoped that analysis of the open-end questionnaire can be completed by the end of August.

41. Bring to class a poorly written memo, such as the one above, that you have received. Then, using the criteria for bad style, explain why the writing in the memo is bad. Rewrite the memo to achieve clear, concise sentences. (You may wish to examine a selection from a textbook in your field. Analyze the passage. Then rewrite it to achieve clarity and conciseness.)

Whereas all your on-the-job writing is produced to be read by another person, you need to give memorandums and letters a distinctive tone not found in reports and technical papers. The "tone" of what you write means the way it sounds to the reader. Your message may be clear and concise, but its tone may be offensive or cause the reader to doubt your sincerity. This person understands what you say all right, but does not like the way you say it.

Courtesy Comes Naturally

Courtesy is contagious. Although you would never knowingly be discourteous, the reader can easily misjudge you on the basis of a hasty message that sounds terse or egotistical or insincere. Merely saying "please" or "thank you" is not the essence of courtesy. A good tone in your message will come from your attitude—from remembering that a human being will read what you write.

When this person reads your memo or letter, will it bring the reaction you want? Will it make the reader believe what you say? Will it show you as a pleasant individual and your company as credible people?

As you observe the following examples, notice how the writer's poor attitude shows in each original version. Then read the better version for a "lift" in tone.

Poor Attitude	**Better Tone**
1. We are sorry your shipment was late but we have been so rushed with an extra large order from an overseas customer we could not get to the regular orders until now.	1. We appreciate your business and regret the delay in shipping this order. More space and personnel have been added to care for an exceptionally large volume of shipping, and we believe your next order will get to you within a week, as usual.
2. We have checked our records for the payment you say you sent last month, but the computer shows no such amount in that time segment.	2. The payment you wrote us about last month still has not arrived and we are trying to trace it. Meanwhile, you may want to warn your bank to stop payment on it.
3. If you feel that you cannot afford to contribute this large an amount to the fund this year, just tell me how much you will donate and I will make up the difference.	3. The amount of each individual gift is a personal matter and all gifts—larger and smaller—are much needed and greatly appreciated. We just hope you will take a part.

The Sweet Sound of You

Naturally, the reader is more interested in himself or herself than in what you want or think or believe. Sometimes writers are surprised to realize how many times they use I, me, my, we, us, our, and all the other first-person references. By using six first-person pronouns, the writer of the following original version gave the message a selfish, peevish tone.

Original Version	Revised Version
We feel that we have every reason to expect the Commission to give us a favorable ruling after our letter of October 8 in which we itemized our third-quarter expenditures.	You can reasonably expect the Commission to give a favorable ruling after they analyze our October 8 letter itemizing third-quarter expenditures.

The better version puts the reader into the picture and emphasizes the action of the Commission by using only one first-person reference.

An application letter naturally tends to use several first-person references, but the selfish tone of the following original paragraph would disgust a possible employer.

Original Version	Revised Version
I think your company would provide me an excellent opportunity for advancing in my chosen career. I hope you will call me for an interview at my home phone number where I am always at home after 3:30 p.m. (7 first-person pronouns)	Kraemer Corporation's excellent opportunities for well prepared technologists make me eager to talk with you about my qualifications. I can come for an interview at any convenient time, and can be reached at 432-0123 any day after 3:30 p.m.

The company official reading the revised version, however, would envision a well organized young technologist who thinks in terms of company need and gives a phone number and time for easy contact.

Good tone, then, is not achieved by inserting at least one "you" for each first-person pronoun in your message. Rather, it depends on an attitude—on acknowledging that what you write is to be read by another person, one with self-interests and company priorities much like your own.

Flattery

If you resort to flattery to obtain the reader's goodwill, you will probably accomplish the opposite effect. Any sensible reader can tell when the *you* viewpoint is overdone. Too many adverbs such as "indeed," "extremely," and "exceptionally" also make a person think all you say must be taken with reservations. Here are samples of obvious insincerity that make the reader suspect the writer's motives.

Original Version	Revised Version
1. Our company considers it a great privilege to have the opportunity to offer you, the leading manufacturer of the entire southwest, a proposal regarding the landscaping of your acreage in Fremont.	1. We sincerely appreciate the opportunity to present a design for the landscaping of your Fremont property and assure you that landscape architect Frederick Cash will make an on-site study as a basis for the proposal.

2. It is indeed a pleasure
   to have the privilege
   of serving on the com-
   mittee with such a
   capable chairman as
   yourself.

2. I shall be glad to serve
   on the committee with you
   as chairman.

Writing Person-to-Person

To avoid using too many first-person references, some writers try an artificial, detached style that makes their messages sound rather like "The Voice of the Company" or even of the Supreme Court. This device actually emphasizes the writer's self-consciousness and pushes the reader away. By using the passive voice almost exclusively, a self-conscious writer may avoid all personal references, but the letter sounds stilted and cold. When business correspondents have occasion to meet in person or to talk to each other over the telephone, they may be surprised to discover that the "stuffed shirt" who writes those letters and memos is actually a very warm and cordial human being.

Expressing appreciation would surely give anyone an excellent opportunity to show courtesy and consideration, yet many writers end their letters with such cold wordings as these.

Original Version	**Revised Version**
1. Your immediate reply will be appreciated.	1. We shall appreciate having your reply some time this week (or before Monday).
2. Your cooperation in making this meeting a success will be appreciated.	2. I shall be grateful for your cooperation in making the meeting a success.

The writer of such cliché closings probably does not think he is discourteous, but consider how they sound to the reader. Who (if anybody) would actually appreciate the quick reply or the cooperation? Appreciated by whom? Gratitude is such a warm human quality that you will want to use the active voice and identify the one who will be grateful. Anything less is a trite and insincere gesture.

Writing Tactfully

Although letters and memos usually accomplish their purpose more effectively if you use the active voice, you will find that the passive voice can soften criticism or veil an accusation quite diplomatically. The following original phrase is "brutally frank," and even though the true facts are given, the writer needs to be careful about the way they are expressed.

Original Version	**Revised Version**
Mr. Smith reports that your statement to the Board was misleading and that they were made to see the case in the wrong light because you refused to tell them of the White Company's prior contract.	It is believed that the Board received an inaccurate view of the case, especially as the White Company's prior contract should have been recognized in the account.

The more tactful wording of the revised version points out the reader's action, shows an understanding of the motive, but does not tell who believed this account. This lack of direct accusation in the passive revision does not lighten the reader's moral obligation, but it does avoid the possibility of a suit against Mr. Smith or his company. Also, the writer of the original passage would be hard pressed to prove such statements as "you refused" and "they were made to see." Although this is an extreme example, it does illustrate how the passive voice can soften and obscure a harsh situation, yet retain the facts.

Delicate situations that demand honest discussion and calm decision require that you choose your words most carefully. You can handle such a problem better by writing than by face-to-face communication in many cases, because when you write you can deliberate, weigh your words before you use them, rephrase, and present a final message in the best tone. Oral communication is likely to be hasty, and sometimes it opens the breach for angry words and violent actions.

Here is another example which is sarcastic and takes for granted that the reader received an instruction manual that may not have been received.

Active Version	Passive Version
If you had read the instruction manual which you received the first day the machine was installed, you would have seen that it specifically states you are to oil the cable track every day.	The cable track should be oiled every day. On page 28 of the instruction manual is a diagram on which the oiling points are marked and numbered.

In any case, the purpose of the message should be to explain the cause of the problem and to tell the user how to avoid a recurrence of the trouble. The passive voice in the revised version does both these things tactfully.

Words with Negative Tone

Certain words and phrases frequently used in company writing seem invariably to create a negative reaction. These expressions give the impression that you consider the reader careless, stupid, or untruthful. Anyone is likely to be repelled by such accusations as "you failed to include," "if, as you claim," "you neglected," and "your complaint." Here are some typical examples designed to put the reader in his place.

Original Version	Revised Version
1. You neglected to confirm the details of the Louisiana incident; consequently, we had no way of knowing who was responsible.	1. We needed your confirmation of the details in the Louisiana incident so as to know who was responsible.
2. If the property is as desirable as you say, we would be interested in having our man appraise it for possible purchase.	2. Your description of the property interests us in having it appraised for possible purchase.

Disciplinary phrases, such as "we will allow (grant, permit) your request," belittle the reader. Stereotypes such as "surely you are aware" and "it should be obvious" make a person appear somewhat dim-witted. If a writer says, "It must have been obvious from my last letter that this office has no jurisdiction over field personnel in the Mid-State territory," the reader bears the burden of misinterpreting the previous letter, even though the letter may have been confusing. Rather than quarrel about the past, the message would accomplish more and have a better tone if you told what progress has been made toward answering the reader correctly, in this way, "Your inquiry of October 3 has been sent to the personnel section of the Mid-State territory, and you will be hearing from them in a few days."

The tone of the following original version builds a wall of formality and restriction between the writer and a scholarship applicant.

Original Version	Revised Version
After we have investigated your statement, we will be able to determine whether we can act favorably on your request or not.	As soon as the customary check has been made, we will send you a full reply to your request.

The revised version obscures who is actually doing the "check" and does identify "we" as the one who will give him complete news.

Another kind of wall is the one the writer sets up by using the phrase, "company policy forbids." Though this may be the exact truth, the reader feels that policy is not an acceptable reason, and a good writer will learn to soften this word by calling it a custom, practice, or usual procedure, or by some other inoffensive term.

Thinking Negatively	Saying It Positively
1. It is not a question of our willingness to grant your request, in this instance; it is the fact that we cannot go against company policy.	1. Under agreed company provision, your leave could be extended only if it were for illness or family death. The same regulation affects all full-time employees.
2. Company policy forbids granting the use of the exhibit hall to anyone under 18 or not a citizen of Crawford County	2. To assure that the exhibit hall will be used by our local residents, it is made available to anyone at least 18 years of age who is a citizen of Crawford County.
3. Our company's policy forbids return of equipment that has not been cleaned for full credit. A $50 deposit is required but that does not mean you get it all back.	3. The $50 deposit paid by anyone borrowing the equipment will be refunded on return of the equipment, provided it is clean and in working order. Otherwise, charges for cleaning and repairs will be deducted before the balance of the $50 is refunded.

Then there are the sad words; the reader gets the blues when he reads a message emphasizing ideas such as "we are sorry," "we regret," "unfortunately," and "disappointment." When you have to include such a low note in your letter, it sounds much better somewhere in the middle between more cheerful and optimistic themes. Also, one low note is enough; expressed clearly and sincerely, one regret or apology is more believable than many repeated protestations.

Thinking Negatively	**Saying It Positively**
1. We are sorry we cannot cooperate with you, but you neglected to include the six Hillside stations in your estimate.	1. If the six Hillside stations had been included in the estimate, we would have been glad to consider it.
2. Regrettably, we do not allow reimbursement for such expenses.	2. The accounting office can reimburse you for travel expense only; hotel bills belong in a separate category.
3. We are very sorry to disappoint you but unfortunately, the coat you returned cannot be replaced free because you bought it three years ago and naturally it shows wear.	3. The worn spots on the elbows of the jacket you returned for replacement show that the coat has given you good service since you bought it here three years ago.

Positive Words for Negative Ideas

Of course, day-to-day letters and memos include many in which you have to convey a negative idea—a refusal, a disappointment, or delay. As a persuasive writer, you can do much to improve the tone by the words you use and the way you arrange them. The reader may not realize the effort you have made to spare his feelings, but he will know you are sincere and your message will leave no scars. Because negative words naturally spring to mind when you think of negative situations, you will probably have to review and revise your messages until you get accustomed to the technique of stating a negative thought in positive words.

Instead of obviously negative expressions, you can rely on such limiting words as "only," "limited to," "requirement," "instead of," and "rather than." Your plan is to convey a clear message which says no in a way that sounds better to the reader because it tells him what you can do instead of what you cannot do.

Perhaps it would be too much to claim that you can always say no and still keep the reader happy; but, if you develop the finesse of wording a negative idea in positive terms, you can be more confident of keeping the reader open-minded to your alternate proposals. It would go something like this:

Thinking Negatively	**Saying It Positively**
1. You failed to sign your name in the proper place on your application for membership. We are returning the blank.	1. We are ready to process your application as soon as you return it with your signature on the second page.

2. We cannot grant your request for a list of company positions and annual salaries, as nobody but company executives are allowed to know this information.

2. The list of positions and salaries you requested is confidential information, limited to use by our company personnel only. For your research, however, we will be glad to send you related information on industry-wide trends in similar positions.

WORK PROJECT 6

Creating an Appealing Tone

In the space below each item write a revision improving its tone. To make it concise, too, you may mark through and change words in the original.

1. Much as we regret to do so, we must refuse your request for funds, as our company receives so many such requests we find it impossible to fill them all, worthy as they might be. Unfortunately, we cannot make an exception in your case.

2. The accounting department failed to advise me of the new system until this week, resulting in the unfortunate delay in the distribution of our monthly report.

3. In making his statement to the magazine, Mr. Blake neglected to say that the company expansion program is budgeted for five years.

4. We are investigating the whereabouts of the papers you claim you sent to us on September 30.

5. Because you have evidently overspent your income for the past six months, we are sorry to inform you that the credit manager will not grant you a credit account.

6. In submitting the transfer of equity papers, you failed to put the correct amount on your check.

7. Your attention to this matter will be appreciated. Thank you.

8. Your gracious reception of Mrs. Jackson and myself was deeply appreciated by the writer.

9. As our guarantee covers defective workmanship and materials, we cannot be expected to repair the fan free unless we receive proof that the blades have not been tampered with by other than our repairmen.

10. As one of the stockholders, I know you see why I would like you to serve as a committeeman this year.

11. I recently collected some interesting information when I was on a panel of ten discussing"Management of Managers" that I think would be helpful in my new assignment.

12. If, as you stated, the suit still does not fit properly after being altered in our store, we would certainly prefer you to bring it in again, as we would rather deal with the customer direct than ignore.

13. We have sent you two reminders of your overdue bill, but you evidently choose to ignore your debts.

14. When you receive the repaired luggage clasp in a few days, kindly read the attached guarantee and the warning against overloading the case.

15. Your talk was tremendously inspiring, and we all felt extremely honored to have had you at our meeting.

16. We would like to send the copper plate you saw in Hayer's, but unfortunately our company does not sell directly to the customer, but through gift shops and department stores.

17. In reply to your letter about fixing my wall lamp that will not light, I am returning it today by express collect and hope your promises are better than your products.

18. The Frobush Company is pleased to have you on their long list of satisfied customers.

19. We are sorry that we cannot cooperate with you but our company policy forbids extending credit to companies with less than the 2 to 1 ratio of assets to liabilities.

20. If you had taken the trouble to preview the film in advance of the meeting, the union members would have been aware of the controversial subject content—that is, if you had seen fit to let them in on it. By the way, have you read the training manual on use of films?

21.   Rewrite the following memo to improve the tone.

TO: Marketing Division Staff

FROM: Harrison K. Rand, Division Supervision

RE: PROPER SUBMISSION OF TRAVEL REQUESTS

It is likely that a cry of despair will emanate from the Marketing Staff soon. The source of this untoward occurrence will be someone who failed to submit a travel request soon enough for it to be approved before departure, resulting in nonpayment of travel expenses.

At the moment I am looking at the umpteenth late travel request from you people in the last three months. If I approve it, the individual in question may receive reimbursement, but not without irate notes and calls from the fiscal department and other assorted functionaries.

You folks really should cure yourselves of this habit of submitting late travel requests. First of all, it's impolite. In addition, it doesn't endear us to others to request permission from them to do something that we've already done. Second, it's dangerous. You may get to the well after the water is gone. Without the ingenious maneuvering of your stout district manager, many of you wouldn't have received a penny. It's foolish to assume that his powers approach that of Moses at the rock.

Also, I'm tired of this problem. I realize that part of my job is to take "flack," and I'm more than willing to do so when it will help us. But I do not enjoy taking "flack" that could easily have been avoided. And there's another result——your late submissions and the trouble they cause tend to spill over to other issues and affect our ability to resolve them in our favor.

So knock it off. O.K.?

---

22.   Many times poor tone results when the writer does not consider either the reader or the goal of the message. By carefully defining (1) your reader and his attitude toward the subject and (2) your goal in writing the message, you can initially avoid an approach that may produce a callous, hostile, or indifferent response from the reader.

In the following memo, the writer wants his staff to attend a company social function, although many had not attended the previous company function. Every employee who had not attended that picnic received the following memo. What do you think the effect on the employees will be? What is the writer's apparent attitude? What specific words and phrases create the tone?

```
TO:

SUBJECT:

I am at a loss to know why attendance was so poor at the last company picnic. You, of
course, know that employee attendance is not mandatory, but these outings are
planned to improve our team spirit. Many of you have claimed that company morale is
a problem for us. Your failure to attend has been observed.

To facilitate planning for the picnic, it is imperative that you report to me
before 12 noon on Wednesday, your attendance plans. Your prompt cooperation will
be appreciated.
```

Assume you are the individual who wrote this letter. Revise the letter. If you want all employees to attend the picnic (and be in good spirits about doing so) what should you say? What tone should you use?

3

Letters and Memorandums

To write an effective letter, you must first decide on its exact purpose; that is, you must have a clear idea of what you want to happen when your reader gets the message. Actually, the purpose depends on whether you wish to give information, to get information, or to do both of these things. Therefore, before you write the first words, think through your whole message and sum it up in a brief statement:

> Letter to persuade the Interstate Commerce Commission that the present classification of company's rate is correct. (Give information—draw conclusion—ask for agreement.) Expected result: ICC will agree that the present classification is correct.

> Memo to (1) give details on Sonor line capacity and (2) request report on toll charges. (Give information—ask for information.) Expected result: The persons concerned will understand data on line capacity and will be alert to notify us of toll charges.

> Report to (1) present new facts to justify installing remote copiers in this office and (2) recommend purchase of three copiers. (Give information—draw conclusions—make recommendations.) Expected result: The board of directors will authorize purchase of remote copiers under the next budget.

CONSTRUCTING YOUR MESSAGE

Not every letter can be built by the same plan because the sequence of ideas depends on the specific outcome you desire. While the basic outline of (1) introduction, (2) middle, and (3) conclusion can serve as the general design, you must carefully select the ideas that go into each of these parts.

Following a suitable plan is the key to building a successful message. The several plans in this chapter can guide you as you put together various routine and special messages you can use for personal reasons and on-the-job responsibilities.

All except very short messages need to show paragraphs, both for logical thought breaks and for easier reading. Of course, some paragraphs are only one sentence long, but usually a group of related sentences is needed to enlarge the core thought completely.

By placing your core thought first in the paragraph, you can add details until you fully develop the paragraph by deductive logic. Here is such a paragraph from a firm's welcoming letter to a young engineer they had just hired.

```
        The 16 to 20 months of planned job experience is a flexible program intended to
        broaden the employee's knowledge of our technical operations. The assignments
        usually last from 3 to 6 months. We make an effort to have the employee assist on
        projects from start to completion, thereby engaging in productive work while
        learning a phase of the pipeline technology in detail. All rotating assignments
        are expected to be here, except toward the end of the program, when we contemplate
        an assignment to a field location. As the availability of suitable projects has
        great influence on the rotating job schedule, we probably shall not be able to give
        you definite information about these assignments for some time yet.
```

Another convincing way to present your ideas is to start with an attention getting detail and add others until you complete the paragraph with a summary sentence. This arrangement, known as inductive logic, is used by a commercial realtor in the following example. The letter began with this paragraph of good news to an out-of-town client, concerning a suitable property for lease.

```
        In the heart of the city, the Weller Building offers you 125,000 square feet of
        fireproof storage space. Its two freight elevators, each 10' x 12', are
        self-operating and serve all floors from the loading platform on the Texas Street
        side of the building. At the rear of the building a spur track permits easy handling
        of rail shipments in and out by fork-lift trucks. In fact, the facilities and
        location of this building make it ideal for an industrial warehouse.
```

Keeping in mind the person who will probably read and react to your message, build it with paragraphs in a planned sequence that is suited to your purpose. Here is how a training director built a successful letter for the purpose of getting a corrected shipment within a week.

At the left is a list of sentences expressing ideas the training director wanted to include. Apparently they were just written down as they came to mind. The completed message in the center of the page shows that related sentences were placed in logical paragraphs, with needed details added for complete ideas. Then the paragraphs were arranged in a sequence, planned to lead the reader to act as the writer wanted.

Ideas to Include	Successful Claim Letter	Plan
Please send the replacement tables by April 28 to allow time for unpacking and assembling.	Dr. Mr. Adkins:	
	The typewriter tables we received this morning from your Pasadena warehouse have several broken parts. When our receiving clerks opened the apparently undamaged cartons, they discovered a splintered top on one table and two broken legs on another.	1. Calmly give the facts.
The typewriter tables we received from your Pasadena warehouse this morning had several broken parts.		
These tables were to be set up in our new training room, with the first class scheduled for May 1.	These tables were to have been set up in our new secretarial training room, with the first class scheduled for May 1. Without them, we have no work stations for two clerks who have registered for instruction, so as to qualify for promotion this summer. You can see our dilemma.	2. Tell how the trouble affects you.
When our receiving clerks opened the apparently undamaged cartons, they discovered a splintered top on one table and two broken legs on another.		
Because previous dealings with your company have been entirely satisfactory, we are relying on a prompt replacement.	Because our previous dealings with your company have been entirely satisfactory, we are relying on a prompt replacement. Please send the tables by April 28 to allow time for unpacking and assembling.	3. State what you want as redress for the grievance.
Shall we return the damaged tables by collect truck freight?	Shall we return the damaged tables by collect truck freight?	4. Confidently expect the reader to agree.
You can understand our dilemma.	Yours sincerely,	

Starting with a clear account of the facts, the training director then tells how this situation adversely affects the company, requests specific action, and ends with confidence that the reader will follow through.

While each sentence carries a related thought, the opening one is especially important in launching the message clearly. Also, the closing sentence is important in order to leave the reader in the mood to act favorably.

Before you compose a whole message, take a close look at these sensitive parts of a plan.

BEGINNINGS AND ENDINGS

Much of the tone of a letter is determined by the way it begins. Start with the best idea for the particular purpose and think about the specific reader. In a concise, courteous opening, tell the reader something he or she does not already know about the subject at hand. Any sensible person would resent the time-wasting clichés in the left column below. The better wordings actually tell the reader something new.

Obvious	Informative
1. We have your letter of June 1 in which you request . . .	1. We are glad to give you the information you requested in your June 1 letter.
2. This is to inform you that your report has been filed with the tax department.	2. Thank you for sending your report; it has been filed with the tax department.
3. This will acknowledge receipt of your letter of April 30 in which you stated that you wished information on the company's position.	3. Your letter of April 30 gives us an opportunity to explain the company's position.

To specify the reason for writing, many companies use a reference or subject line plus a short, informative first paragraph. Here are some helpful examples:

1. Reference: Merit Award Records, File 54-F42A

   The company records have been adjusted as you suggested in your letter of August 7. You were right about those dates.

2. Subject: Specifications for storage systems

   Revised specifications for storage systems in the mapped flood table are expected from the county engineers. These new figures will supplement our own studies.

Standard in-house memo forms show a subject place as part of the heading, and any letter format may use a reference line, inserted as the copy is prepared in the Word Processing Center or by the typist in a smaller office. See the typical memorandum format and subject line on the standard letter.

CHIMNEY ROCK OIL COMPANY

Opalousas, Oklahoma

R-5

Chemical Research Division

TO: Mr. Mangum Hutchinson, Vice President for Sales   DATE: August 25, 19

FROM: R. L. Carso

FIRM NAME AND PERSONNEL CONTACTED:
>   Topperco, Inc.
>   Mr. Fred Cotterby, Technical Director
>   Mr. Anson Fischer, Assistant Technical Director
>   Mr. Clarence Martin, Chemist

PURPOSE OF CALL: To ascertain the results of their tests on Plyds 501 and 501-X34 samples.

Discussion

Martin, Fischer, Cotterby, and I discussed the samples and method of application. Topperco wanted answers to treating oven time and temperature, percent weight solids, and solvent system used. Cotterby explained that they had been waiting a long time for a plastic manufacturer to come up with such an idea. I pointed out that the necessary B staging had already been accomplished and that oven treating time should be reduced to a minimum, as the purpose of oven treating was to drive off the solvent in the system. As for high temperature laminating systems, I explained that Topperco should find XFL-200 equal to or better than competitive materials because of its refinement.

Cotterby was interested in XFL-200 and asked about its chloride content. I recalled discussing with Frank Sayers, the former Technical Director, the fact that the systems Topperco has used were called to their attention by Chimney Rock Oil and the CRO personnel had recently given them samples and other aid. With this background, I told him that we believed we would be included in Topperco's ply-solids purchases.

Cotterby said he had reviewed these facts with Frank Sayers and fully agreed. He asked Martin whether there was any objection to purchasing Plyds 501 immediately; Martin hesitantly said no. Cotterby said he would instruct the Purchasing Department to order the next material from CRO.

Recently, Martin has spent his full time on a problem in copper clad laminates which he has partially overcome. He is now evaluating 501-X34, and if the tests are successful, Topperco will purchase 501-X34 instead of Plyds 501.

Conclusion

CRO can now take over all Topperco's ply-solid purchases. We have overcome the prejudices developed when a problem in Plyds 501 caused Topperco to change to purchasing a 501 equivalent from Vacks-Mendol.

Next Action

We shall appreciate your help in meeting Topperco's requirements of Plyds 501. Please keep up with and let us know of any action that will help us to compete with Vacks-Mendol.

ADVANCED LETTER WRITING SERVICE
5001 Market Drive
Beaumont, Michigan 48902

May 19, 19__

Angelus Food Processing Company, Inc.
3043 Natchez Trace
White Mountain, WV 25701

Attention of Mr. Harvey R. Taylor, Manager Office Services

Gentlemen:

Subject: Full Block Form with Special Parts

Here is a letter in the block style. The reason I addressed it to the company was that I wanted to show you how to use an attention line. It is inserted between the inside address and the salutation and has a double space before it and after it, thus directing a matter of company business to the individual notice of the proper official.

As the letter is addressed to the company, the salutation is Gentlemen: the salutation always agrees with the first line in the inside address. Instead of the word of in the line, you could use a colon or even a dash.

A subject line usually appears between the salutation and the first paragraph, with a double space before and after it. The word SUBJECT or REFERENCE (or RE) designates the place to write in the wording. To get special attention you may put the subject in the large blank area between the letterhead and the inside address. Break a long subject into a block of very short lines and attract the reader's eye at once. This block of the reference matter is the only part not starting at the left margin in this letter form.

In the block style, you will see that all parts begin at the left margin except the letterhead. Not having to indent makes the typing job easier and faster when you are putting out a volume of mail. That is why I am sending Miss Bertie Hersh a sample for her files in the word processing center.

Below the reference initials is an enclosure notation to remind me to send you a new booklet which is small enough to put into the same envelope. If I wished to send you something too large to enclose, I could type the words Mailing Reference: New Catalog in the same place as the enclosure notation to remind the mail clerk to send the catalog in the same mail.

Sincerely yours,

L. Marion Burns, President

LMB/hm

Enclosure: Style Booklet

copy: Miss Bertie Hersh

The end of the message is also an especially influential part, as the reader then begins to process mentally what you have said.

Think how you want this person to feel and act, then use a strong statement or a stimulating question that specifically ties in with your whole message. Notice that in each of the following good closings, the tone does not offend. Reader interest is maintained to the last word.

Strong Final Statements

1. As soon as we receive your signature on these papers, we will send the revised plans for your approval.

2. This routine plan should keep all offices posted on proposals and changes.

3. The January 30 agreement still provides an adequate basis for our working together in the new field.

Prompting a Response

1. What is the first possible date that you can attend such a conference here in Houston?

2. Could you send your thoughtful analysis of this proposal by next Tuesday, in time for the general staff meeting?

3. When may we expect to receive your new price sheet?

Open-Door Endings

1. Your opinion of their report will be interesting to the committee.

2. Let us know any way we can help you to prepare for the April meeting.

3. Come to see us again when you are in our town.

4. Your ideas for developing this project will be most welcome.

Avoid the traditional traps, such as the participial closings, fragmentary sentences, and tiresome clichés in the left column below.

Weak and Trite	Strong
1. Thanking you in advance for your usual fine cooperation, we are,	1. We will sincerely appreciate your cooperation in starting the new schedule this week.
2. Trusting you will appreciate our position in this instance,	2. Thank you for giving us this opportunity to explain our views.
3. Please do not hesitate (please feel free) to ask us if you have any questions.	3. We will be happy to send you any new information we get on these imported fabrics.

Basically, the letters and memos produced and received in business either ask for information or give information or do both. Here are some typical plans, with letters written by the planners. As you observe these examples, notice that the plans vary with the stated purposes. Select a suitable plan for each writing problem you study in the project at the end of the chapter.

Routine Letter to Get Information

Plan	Message
	January 18, 19—
	Mrs. Marge Manning, Instructor Metropolitan Professional Institute Oklahoma City, OK 53539
	Dear Mrs. Manning:
1. State your request or ask a forth-right question.	Will your department offer the Records Management course in the first term this summer?
2. Specify when and why you will need the information. The "why" may be omitted if it is obvious, but a timed response is more effective than "at your earliest convenience "by return mail," and similar clichés.	That is the only course I have not completed for a Supervisor's Certificate, and I am trying to make plans that will allow me to finish the work this year, if possible. My employer will agree to my driving in for the two-hour class, provided I can be back at work by 1:00 p.m. A similar course is being taught at Woodlake Junior College, three nights a week for eight weeks this summer; however, I would much prefer your course, both for its content and for the daytime hours.
3. Explain how the information will be used. (optional)	
4. Include a word of appreciation at either the beginning or the end of your message.	As my department head has asked for summer plans to be on file by February 1, I would greatly appreciate an answer before then.
	Sincerely yours,

Requesting a Special Favor

Plan	Message
	April 12, 19__
	Dear Mrs. Manning:
1. Explain the need for information or action, enlisting your reader's interest by at least one idea of reader benefit. Make no apology; indicate no possible reason for a refusal.	By completing your Records Management course last summer, I have qualified to receive a Supervisor's Certificate. The company has offered to reimburse me for the cost of my last three courses, provided I present a letter from the teacher of each course verifying satisfactory completion of the work. Would you please write a short letter to that effect?
2. State your request or ask a forthright question.	You will be pleased, I think, that my title is now assistant to the director of records for my company, and the chances are good for a promotion to a specialized records center by next year. The work is enjoyable because I know how valuable it is to the whole company, too. Thanks to your course, I am now confident of being able to handle its many details.
3. Give as much detail as is necessary to show the importance of the response to you and to the reader.	I would appreciate your sending a statement of verification to my immediate superior:
	Mr. Thomas E. Kelly Director of Records Bravo Chemical Company Angleton, OK 53530
4. Show sincere concern about the answer, and suggest a time for it. Make your expression of appreciation in conditional terms; say "We should greatly appreciate having your consent" rather than "Thank you in advance."	He has asked me to have all letters in before May 1, as the next budget period begins on that date.
	Sincerely yours,

Saying Yes

Plan	Message
	Mr. Frank Boysen Boysen Farm & Dairy Mill Creek, CO 73737
	Dear Mr. Boysen:
1. Respond in the first sentence; show as much pleasure as the case warrants, but never reveal reluctance. If you seem to be acting contrary to your better judgment, you become vulnerable to further demands.	We certainly will replace the lawn furniture that rusted, as the guarantee is still in effect. Just use the enclosed card to check the frame color and style number of the pieces, so that we can enter the order right away.
2. Explain your decision if it sets a precedent; otherwise, treat it as a routine matter. If the reader would be surprised at your consent, you could comment that it is in line with company practices. Give enough details to be clear, but not so many pros and cons as to appear to be debating with yourself.	When your new furniture arrives, please return the other pieces freight collect.
3. Use a firm, confident close. Courteously assume that the reader is pleased with your message. You weaken your action by expressing doubt through the use of such clichés as "If there is anything further we can do, please do not hesitate to call us" or "I trust (hope) this meets with your approval."	Thank you for writing us so that we could make this adjustment. Cordially yours,

Directing a Change and Justifying It

Plan   Message

Date: 4/18/___

TO: Department Heads

FROM: Ralph Goodman, Purchasing
        Manager

1. Recall something the reader knows
   about the situation or something
   similar in another well known
   situation.

Moving into the new building is now
only about 8 months away, and we are at
a point of making final selections on
the furnishings. Everyone is looking
forward to updating the office equipment, especially as the individual
offices are, on the average, 8 by 10 ft.

2. Introduce the new or more complex
   matter into this familiar setting.
   Use some connecting word or expression, such as "similarly," "in this
   way," "the next step," "at the same
   time," "on the other hand," or
   "for this reason."

For this reason, much attention has
been given to the choice of simple,
space-saving storage facilities, such
as filing cabinets and shelving. In
looking at the original requisitions
received from each staff member, I
notice that nearly everyone listed "two
5-drawer file cabinets" and a
"6-shelf bookcase."

3. Show parallels and contrasts between the simple (or old) and the
   complex (or new) ideas.

If the two 5-drawer files of the traditional type were put in an 8 by 10 ft.
office, they would be very inconven-
ient to use, as they use 40 in. plus
the space where you would stand in
order to pull out the drawer.

4. Develop the new or complex ideas
   confidently and extensively enough
   for the reader's complete
   acceptance.

In searching for a way to save space
and still have enough file room, I
investigated the desk-height file
case made by Rollafile and found it to
be the kind we need. It occupies a 72 by
9 in. floor space, with a 36 in. height
that leaves desirable wall space for
decorating. The most convenient
feature, though, is that the two
drawers are light, roll easily on
steel bearings, and pull out from the
long side of the cabinet. Thus, it
uses only 28 inches of space when
fully opened.

An order for 23 of these Rollafiles
has been placed, so as to assure their
delivery before the move-in date. A
scale drawing of an individual office
with this file and other furniture
is posted on the conference room
bulletin board. Take a look and let me

5. Leave the way open for the reader's view to be expressed.

know how you want the file placed in
your office. I believe this new-style

6. Use a confident, courteous close
   that credits the person with being
   willing to carry out the directive.

equipment will not only save you space
but will be more convenient.

Getting Help with a Problem

Plan   Message

                                                  Date: 5/7/___
                                            Dear Steve:

1. Show the reader's connection   Your remark about busy people being
   with the problem.   the ones you can always count on set me
                                         thinking as I drove home from the meet-
                                         ing. You are right, and that is why I
                                         would like your help with selection
                                         of a site for next year's conference.

                                         The planning committee is not plan-
                                         ning. I checked with Frank today and
                                         he seems to think next year will never
                                         come! It is already too late to get
                                         the Ridgeway-Shelton, the best place
2. Describe the problem with clearly   in St. Louis, for a group the size of
   stated facts. Point out the crux   ours. Parking, shopping, transporta-
   of the difficulty.   tion––all these aspects must be
                                         worked out, in addition to adequate
                                         meeting rooms and food services. Try-
                                         ing to budget ahead is also a problem,
                                         with prices spiraling as they are. The
                                         site must be nailed down and some
                                         commitments made as soon as possible.

                                         Frank was appointed chairman of plan-
                                         ning under your administration as
                                         president, and I would not want to in-
                                         terfere with what he may possibly do.
                                         The trouble is he is either not plan-
                                         ning (no committee meeting) or not
                                         saying.

3. Specify what you would like the   Could you suggest a way to move him
   person to do about it, or   off dead center? Any help you can
                                         give him will certainly help me and
4. Request an alternate plan for   the chapter. Please urge Frank
   solving it.   and his committee to get the site
                                         selected and confirmed before next
5. Indicate confidence that the   month's chapter meeting.
   reader will respond willingly, and
   suggest a time for action.

The same plan is often used for in-house directives because good management recognizes the need to explain why something must be done before requiring it to be done. The wide geographic spread of many companies' activities calls for more careful and better quality written messages to their own personnel, as well as telephonic and electronic communication.

With adequate identification in the usual memo heading, the message itself should be especially brief and clear. While the wording can be more technical than that of a message to an outside reader, the tone should be both courteous and sincere.

Plan to Obtain Cooperation

1. Get the reader's attention to the problem by at least one specific fact involving the person's interests.

2. Clearly recount the facts that make the problem.

3. Specify what you want done or ask for the reader's solution.

4. Indicate confidence that the reader will respond, and specify a time for the action.

The following example shows how a logical plan and clear wording corrected a communication problem involving an entire department. The original directive was so repetitious and confusing, it likely caused the lack of cooperation in the first place. By contrast, Mr. Cannon's well organized revised memo is concise and clear, with a tone that firmly and courteously expects compliance.

Wordy and Confusing	Logical and Clear	Points to Notice
TO: Sid Maresa, Nogales Division Superintendent and Staff	TO: Sid Maresa, Nogales Division Superintendent and Staff	
FROM: Contract Sales Manager	FROM: P. R. Cannon, Contract Sales Manager	
SUBJECT: Instructions on Procedure	SUBJECT: Instructions on Addressing Omega Industries	1. Subject line about a well known customer, name repeated in first sentence.
As you know, all sales to the Omega Industries are to be routed through the Sales Department of the Pushbutton Appliances Department and specifically to the attention of Mr. Williams.	Since January 1, standard company procedure has made it necessary to address all sales contracts and correspondence to the Omega Industries through Mr. Avery Williams in their Pushbutton Appliances Department. Occasionally, however, correspondence and other records are improperly addressed, especially those concerning electronics. These errors have caused misunderstanding and embarrassment.	2. Problem described as "improperly addressed" and "caused embarrassment and misunderstanding."
There are occasional lapses in this procedure in the conduct of correspondence and in other details in regard to this matter, especially with those that deal with electronics.		
Would you please emphasize to all your people that correspondence and official contracts with the Omega Industries are to go through the Sales Sub-Department, Pushbutton Appliances Department, Attention: Mr. Williams. Mr. Williams will see that all such matters receive prompt and adequate attention.	Will you, therefore, make sure that all your correspondences, sales records, and other official contracts going to Omega are addressed exactly as follows: Attention: Mr. Avery Williams Sales Sub-Department Pushbutton Appliances Department Omega Industries Houston, TX 05673	3. Clear, specific instructions.
This is not meant to discourage informal contacts with any department with Omega Industries. However, where any such informal contacts develop to the point where correspondence is initiated or sales are made, the correspondence or sales must be routed through the Pushbutton Appliance Department, Attention: Mr. Williams, as outlined above.	We shall expect and appreciate your cooperation in following this procedure without exception.	4. Firm but courteous closing.

When you write a letter or memo to persuade someone to accept your views or to act in a certain way, your plan must be more psychological (emotional) than logical (intellectual). To overcome natural reader resistance and motivate the person to do what you want, your message must show reader benefit from beginning to end.

This principle is especially important when the situation requires that you say NO or NOT NOW. A mild and related idea at the beginning, followed by at least one strong, factual reason for the impending negative, will give you a chance to show consideration for the reader. In such a message, you are actually trying to make a substitute sale; that is, you will not do what was asked of you but will try to convince the reader to accept an alternative.

The human relations problem is obviously to retain the goodwill of the person while you reject the person's request. Of course, nobody likes to be rejected; it does something to one's ego. Therefore, the plan and the tone of the message must show that you are not rejecting the *person* but are doing your best to open another way to solve the problem.

Here is a plan for saying NO while salvaging the relationship with the reader.

1. Express suitable interest, concern, or thanks in discussing the matter with the reader, but do not sound as if you are saying YES when you know you are not. In the first sentence (second clause possibly), begin a bridge for the reader's thoughts to cross from the neutral opening to the strongest reason for the impending NO. A word or phrase such as *nevertheless, however, if it had been* can give the proper turn toward the next thought.

2. Give all the facts causing the NO as specifically and impersonally as possible. Here is a good place to use the passive voice to prevent an accusing tone.

3. State the negative decision unless you have built such clear evidence by now that the reader can plainly see the NO. At this point, a word of regret may be in order, but not an apology—if this is the right decision.

4. Quickly offer an alternative—something you can do instead of what you were asked to do. Point out how the reader can benefit from this substitute action. Name all the alternatives you consider reasonable.

5. Close optimistically and courteously, showing that you believe the reader is still your friend. Avoid ruining the whole case by clichés such as "If you have any questions, please do not hesitate, etc," or "We trust you will understand our policy does not allow, etc."

In the two letters analyzed below, you can see how consideration of the reader's self-value guided the writer in each case. Refusing a petulant request for free repair or replacement of a briefcase on which the lock had evidently been broken open by a sharp tool, the company that made the case was tactful but firm.

<table>
<tr><td>

Good NO Letter—1

Dear Miss Kent:

Thank you for returning the briefcase described in your letter, as our lock specialists have been able to examine it thoroughly. The original guarantee against defects in material and workmanship is still valid, subject to normal usage of the case.

In the workshop, the locksmiths who install and test the locks on our hand-made cases such as yours went over the plate and mechanism. They report that the lock shows scratches from instruments and that the mechanism has been sprung by being forced open, damaging it beyond repair. While such abnormal usage would cancel the guarantee terms, we can install a new lock, making the case as good as new. Charges for this replacement would be only $17.50 for parts and labor, and the guarantee would be renewed for six months.

You have a fine briefcase, Miss Kent, and we realize you need it returned as soon as possible. The sooner you send us your check for $17.50 the sooner we can replace the lock, stamp your initials in gold on the case, and return it to you.

               Sincerely yours,

</td><td>

Points to Notice

1. Pleasant opening. Bridge words are "specialists . . . examine it," and "subject to normal usage."

2. Facts are given in detail and strongly described.

3. NO is stated as "abnormal usage would cancel guarantee."
4. Alternative is replaced lock and renewed guarantee for reasonable charge.

5. Even a would-be cheater can save face in this confident close.

</td></tr>
</table>

Here is a soft answer in which a credit union officer turns down a loan request. Inasmuch as the reader is a fellow employee of this writer, the human interest features are especially keen.

Good NO Letter—2

Dear Mr. McKinney:

Your application for a loan of $3,000 to purchase the boat and trailer rig has been carefully studied and analyzed. The members of the Loan Committee have been especially concerned, as you doubtless are, about the excess repayment time.

As was explained in our conversation when you visited our office, repayment time for loans is established by the charter committee for Federal Credit Unions and is a stated number of months for each class of loans. For the $3,000 you wish to borrow, the stated time is a maximum of 36 months. Your present financial uncertainty, shown by the information on your application, would make it difficult for you to plan on a shorter repayment time than the 48 months you offer.

Would you, therefore, consider making your request for a lesser amount that could be handled within the required 36 months? Or would you prefer to wait a while until your financial picture is improved? If your present debts could be decreased by, say, $1,500, your application would be more likely to receive approval.

We shall be glad to work with you in obtaining the loan as soon as you have qualified in either of these two ways.

Points to Notice

1. Interest and concern shown. Bridge thought is the "excess repayment time." The wording tactfully assumes he also recognizes the problem.

2. Reason is stated in factual terms. "NO" implied.

3. Statement of NO is unnecessary.

4. Alternate plans are given.

5. Confident close that indicates he had a choice of ways to act and they await his choice.

While the use of direct mail for selling products and services has traditionally been a strong factor in the nation's business, it has given place somewhat to other direct media such as television and radio. Catalogs are increasingly popular with sophisticated urban consumers who find shopping a tiring and time-consuming chore. In many of these slick-page booklets with highly colored photographs and artistic design, you will find an opening letter from the company management, attempting to personalize the appeal to their prospective customers.

Elaborate mail campaigns are frequently supported by other media—telephone calls, TV and radio "spot" advertisements. All these expensive efforts are planned to do whatever is necessary to increase the company sales, brighten the company image, and boost the company profits. With all the mass media striving for the consumer's attention, the sales letter to an individual reader, recognizing the person's particular needs and desires, still gets results.

Poorly conceived and planned sales letters are so prevalent they are generally ignored and classed as junk mail. It takes ingenious effort to obtain a response that justifies the trouble and expense of special sales mailouts. Such messages are usually prepared by advertising professionals as part of a larger promotional campaign. Even solicitations for charities and community funds are created and executed by experts in the psychology of such appeals.

Basically, the letter that succeeds in selling a product or a service uses the well known four steps: (1) get attention, (2) create interest, (3) establish desire, and (4) stimulate action. The plan can be adapted somewhat like this:

1. Attract the reader's favorable attention at once by piquing his curiosity, by boosting his ego, or by sympathetically touching some basic human emotion such as love or desire for security and success.

2. Build the reader's interest in your product, service, or idea by showing how he can benefit by using it to fill a present or potential need. Emphasize the main attraction (central selling point) of what you are trying to sell, and give enough other detail to establish his interest. Include such factual proof as testimonials, statistics, guarantees, and vivid description to arouse desire.

3. To assure his desire to have the thing he now realizes he needs, give him a preview of the satisfaction he will experience if he makes the desire a reality. Confidently picture him enjoying its benefits.

4. Tell the reader exactly how and when to act so that he can obtain the product, service, or idea he now realizes he must have, and make it easy for him to get it.

Here is a letter, mailed in late October, that obtained several thousand new savers from a list of the bank's small-account depositors.

Successful Sales Letter	Points to Notice
Suppose this letter contained a check for $500, what would you spend it for? Christmas presents for the family . . . a new refrigerator or washing machine . . . that special vacation you're planning . . . or maybe something big like the down payment on a car or a home?	1. Attention-getting question opens the letter. Desire for Christmas money. Several emotions.
A lot of people are going to get checks like that in the mail next week. They are members of our Christmas Club who have found an <u>easy</u> way to save for the things they want.	2. Interest created by "easy way to save" and "people . . . get checks." Central selling point: "you can do it too."
You can do it too. You can save as little as $5.00 a week and as much more as you like, and you can do it so easily you won't miss the money. It will surprise you to see how fast "little money" grows into "big money" through Christmas Club savings.	
The Christmas Club for next year is forming now. It will be nice for you to open an envelope like this <u>next</u> <u>year</u> and find in it the money to make it a really Merry Christmas.	3. Desire to "open an envelope like this," "find . . . the money."
Why not drop in at Rio Grande National at your next coffee period or noon hour —come to windows 28 and 33 and let us explain the simple details and open your account.	4. Specific times and places to act. "Simple details."

Although you may never be responsible for direct-mail selling of your company's products or services, the principles apply equally well to the important task of selling yourself. When you submit your credentials for membership in an honor society or professional organization, you include a letter "selling yourself." If you try for a scholarship, fellowship, or research grant, you are asked for details about your qualifications, accompanied by a letter explaining your goals and purposes.

You can modify the "sales letter" plan to serve as a guide for effectively presenting yourself and obtaining a personal interview. While this plan may also be used for a job application, you will find more details about that important activity in the next few pages.

1. Give the reader a favorable first impression of yourself by showing that you understand the requirements of the job, the school, or the society, and make a sincere effort to fill these requirements. Avoid labeling your letter by the use of such wording as "Please consider me an applicant" or "I am writing to apply."

2. Describe your qualifications for the position. If you arrange complete data attractively on an easy-to-read second page, as preferred by most personnel departments and qualifications committees, you can make a general state-

ment here calling attention to the attached sheet. In so doing, point out the most significant items on the data sheet.

3. Show that you know enough about the activities and philosophy of the firm or society to want to become a working part of it. Tell what you have learned from your working experience, education, or cultural background that would be useful to the organization. Let the reader see that you would fit well into the whole group.

4. Request a personal interview to discuss further your qualifications for the position and request a reply, or

5. Express appreciation for the opportunity to be considered for the scholarship or membership, and request a reply.

Summary of Procedures for Dictating or Writing a Standard Letter

Organization

1. State the subject (or point) of the letter in paragraph 1.

   In the middle paragraphs, develop the subject. Give specifics to support the major point.

   In the last paragraph, make clear to the reader what will happen about the subject or what the reader should do.

Style

2. Cover the necessary points and stop.

3. Keep sentences to 15–24 words. Longer sentences are harder for you, the originator, to control and harder for the reader to follow.

4. Try for one idea in each sentence. To avoid unwieldy sentences, put a period after each idea.

5. Keep paragraphs 5–7 sentences in length.

6. Emphasize "you" rather than "I" or "we."

7. Watch tone. Always present negatives by using statements that are as positive as possible. Always remember to build good will.

WORK PROJECT 7

Letters and Memorandums

Write an acceptable revision of each item in the space provided. Hand this sheet to your instructor for review. The letter's theme is given in parentheses at the end of each item.

Openings

1. This is with reference to your letter of June 1, 19_____, requesting that we review our position regarding the tariff ruling. (our position is unchanged)

2. This is to acknowledge your inquiry of May 26 with regard to the company's eligibility for changes in rates. We have petitioned for further hearing on this. (account of past action and future hopes)

3. In your letter of April 16, 19_____, addressed to Mr. John White, you asked about plans to extend service to the Bayfront area. (service to be extended)

4. Per your recent inquiry, the plan now in effect is to continue for the rest of the summer. (plan for temporary job fill-ins)

5. The report of your inspection trip has been received and we are pleased to inform you that it is acceptable. (confirmation of new supervisor's report)

6. Reference is made to personal data form X5010 for Joe Doe, covering his employment in the statement department. (form being requested again)

7. Pursuant to your report on the employee meetings, we wish to verify our approval of the schedule. (approval needed before schedule begins)

8. We have before us your letter dated September 25 which is in reply to our letter of September 21, in regard to the variation in the stock at your station for the month of August. (acknowledging explanation of stock variation)

9. Reference your order for unfinished pine boards which were out of stock when order received. (boards still out of stock)

10. Subject: C. R. Smith's letter of April 17.
For your information, we are attaching a copy of the letter we received from C. R. Smith, dated April 17. (transmittal of a resignation letter)

Closings

1. Thank you in advance for showing the interest needed to give us your opinion. (request for opinion on packaging change)

2. We regret it is not possible to fulfill your request, as the matter is extremely confidential. (reply to student's request for wage scale)

3. Will you kindly advise if this proposal is feasible. If such is feasible, will you kindly tell us how much expense would be entailed. (proposed change in club's serving hours)

4. Please feel free to contact us, if you desire further information on this. (reply explaining price increases)

5. In the meantime, if you have any questions about the foregoing, please do not hesitate to write. (details of proposed convention program)

6. It would be appreciated if you would let me hear from you regarding the above. (request for refund on shipping charges)

7. Looking forward to your advice on this matter, we are, (request for help in selecting a conference leader)

8. We trust you will understand our position in this case and that the suggested course of action will be acceptable. (refusal of order to give an extra discount on a large order)

9. Please do not hold this instance against our record of errors. (company at fault in late shipment)

10. We shall be awaiting your reply to this letter at your earliest convenience. (urgent request for payment of account)

Routine Letters and Special Problems

1. In the space below, revise the following poorly worded letter, giving it all the good qualities you have learned to use in business messages. As it is a collection letter to an old customer, maintain good will. Organize the message as a routine inquiry. Hand your revision to your instructor.

Dear Sir: We haven't received your payment of $416.32. As you have always paid your bills promptly, we wonder why this one is late.

Could it be something wrong with our product or service? Or is it something on your end? If you will let us know, we can get together on some solution.

If your payment is on the way, ignore this letter. If it is not, we expect to be hearing from you soon.

Yours truly,

2. In the space below, rewrite this poor reply to a man who inquired about a new light he saw advertised in *Popular Mechanics*. When he got the letter, he concluded the company must not be very good and dropped the matter. Leave out the clichés and negatives and make the tone cause the man to be glad to prepay the order for the new light. Hand in your revision for review by the instructor.

This will acknowledge your recent note, asking us to send you one of our new compact lights on a C.O.D. basis. We regret to advise that we do not handle this in this manner and would suggest that you send us either your check or money order, and we will make early delivery.

This compact light is in the process of being distributed and will probably not be available in your area at the present time. We would be glad to mail you one of these lights upon receipt of your check or money order in the amount of $11.98 each, which includes postage.

3. Analyze the letter below and write your observations on this page beneath the letter. While the writer is amply justified in declining the request from Mayor Justis of Littleburg, he fumbles the job of presenting his case. Point out the strengths and weaknesses of this NO letter, especially in wording, sentence structure, tone, and sequence of ideas. Submit your analysis to your instructor.

Dear Mr. Justis:

It was an honor that you thought of me for the position of local chairman of your Big Helpers Community Fund Drive. I would like to help in this drive.

Having just started in business in Littleburg I am not acquainted with many people that live here. I also have plenty of work because as you know a young business has many problems when it first starts. I am working constantly on these problems so I'll have a business that will be able to give its best to this great little community.

Being as things are, I don't think I can serve as chairman of the Big Helpers Community Fund Drive however I would be able to serve in some lesser capacity in this worthy cause. I believe there are some in this town who are older and more qualified people who could do a much better job as chairman.

Sincerely,

4. On the basis of your critique of problem 3, revise the letter and set it up on a simulated letterhead of the young man's company stationery (8½ × 11). Make up the address, etc. and include all other appropriate parts of this letter that would be mailed to the mayor. Use the plan for a NO letter. Assume the letter is typed by the writer's wife, who is the secretary in the new business.

5. Revise the content of the following letter of special request to improve its form and tone. Correct any errors in punctuation, spelling, and usage that you find.

Dear Dr. Smith:

I am writing to you to try to establish some ground rules for our panel on "Computer Application in the Engineering Communication Program." Since our panels three papers will probably be discussing material that most of the audience will be unfamiliar with, I would like you to send me a list of relevant definitions that we can prepare in advance. If you are going to need any special equipment for your talk will you also send me that information.

I would like to keep our individual presentations to 12–15 minutes maximum and entertain questions only at the end of the session. I advise you that I intend to be strict about this time and I expect you to do everything possible to cooperate willingly.

I also hope that you will not read your paper. I am at a loss to know why anyone would do this.

Send me a copy of your paper as well as the answers to my other requests as soon as you can. This will expedite problems.

Sincerely,

6. On a separate page, revise the *special request* of this program chairman to sound less like a high school sophomore. Organize the message to get a YES from this excellent speaker. Use a complete format for a personal letter and hand it to your instructor.

Dear Mr. Jenson:

The annual installation banquet of the Aspiring Managers Society will be held this year, as usual, and it will be the one occasion of the year when a social theme will be carried out, as AMS is a student group of serious purposes and the other programs are always very beneficial. The meeting will be on the evening of October 8 at 7:00 p.m. in the Green Room of Taub Hall.

The emphasis during the past year has been on the qualifications of a good management trainee, and next year it will be "How Management Is Changing with Automation." This is the keynote of the speech we would like to have made at this meeting, and this is where you come in, Mr. Jenson. Won't you do us the favor of making a 30-minute talk on that subject and also giving brief remarks of instruction to the new officers who will be installed at that time?

Probably, you have heard of other AMS chapters or maybe even of this chapter, as the picture of our president was in the paper last year. A man with your interest in young men who wish to become members of the management profession would mean much as the toast master and guest speaker for our annual banquet. We would also like to invite your wife, as this is the one meeting when wives and girl friends are admitted.

We certainly hope to hear from you very soon that you will come, as we are trying to complete all our plans before summertime. Thank you.

                    Respectfully yours,

7. On the memo form below, write a good solution to this situation. Use the plan for getting cooperation and make yourself a rough draft of the message before putting it on this sheet to hand in. Be careful of your tone.

As general manager of the MacKay Dress and Fabric Company, you have been authorized to issue building keys to the members of the designing staff and the art department. Several times lately, the building superintendent has reported that the outside doors have been found open by the watchman in his rounds at 5:00 a.m., but that no one was found in the building at that time. The superintendent threatens to change all the locks unless this stops, as he is responsible for the security of the building and its contents. Write a memo to the possibly guilty ones, assuming that any member of the named departments might have left the door unlocked. Point out that regulations make it necessary to lock the door even while in the building after 6:00 p.m., and especially upon leaving. Although you cannot discipline these artists, you are responsible for what they do with the issued keys.

```
                       MACKAY DRESS AND FABRIC COMPANY
TO:                                                   date:
FROM:
SUBJECT:
```

8. You are Steve Williams, owner of Steve's Appliance Service in Jasper, Alabama. You have been in business three years operating your appliance repair shop in the oversized two-car garage on the premises of your parents' home. Having returned from the service several years ago, you and your wife and small son accepted the offer to live in your parents' home until your finances became more stabilized. Thus you were able to invest your modest savings and your exceptional talents in repairing and servicing electric equipment and appliances, at first for friends, and then for more and more satisfied customers among the townspeople.

The first year's business netted you about $8,400 and you now have 200 customers—all cash payments and no credit to anyone. Your supplies, parts, and work tools and equipment have been purchased for cash with a 2 percent discount from E-Tex Electric Company, Lufkin, Alabama. Last year you paid income tax on $36,754.

You think it is now time to expand, stock more parts, use better tools, put in a section for resale of some supplies, and get ready for more customers. Working alone, you have been forced to turn away much business that you wanted; therefore, you are considering a larger building and a possible working partner. Also, you realize expansion would mean buying equipment, supplies, and parts in a quantity that would require credit.

The largest and most prominent supplier to the electrical repair trade in your part of the country is Southern Supply Company, 435 Ashford Street, Huntsville, Alabama 54615. Write to this company (on one of your letterheads) to inquire about possibly holding the Jasper franchise for SSC brand name products—electrical supplies, parts, and tools.

Say you are enclosing a copy of your financial statement for the past year, revealing your net income and current assets, including a bank balance of $1,854. Ask what credit arrangements you can make with this firm. Would they sell you as much as $5,000 worth a month and on a 2/10, N/30 basis? If not, how much? Enclose names of three character references, businessmen in Jasper who have known you a long time. Ask for a quick reply, as you need this information in order to make further decisions.

9. As credit manager of Southern Supply Company (problem above) you consider the letter from Steve Williams. You cannot accept a $5,000 order for your merchandise on a 30-day basis because he does not have enough cash or substantial credit experience. Your credit policy would limit him to $1,800 or less at one time. Point out that a franchise to handle SSC brand products is issued only to companies of long-time substantial reputation. As you admire the young man's ambition and ability, you wish to avoid discouraging him in his plans, which seem to you a bit too vague at this time. Show him that his space limitations might make a large shipment a real problem and that it could be better for him to obtain your fine brand of goods in smaller lots. You can deliver by truck on one day's notice. Besides setting up an $1,800 credit line for him, you can also offer him a new-customer discount of 3% for cash and thereafter give the usual 2 percent.

10. As an electronic meter specialist at the Tuftek Instruments Company, you design modified meters, verify product quality, and advise customers on their needs and purchases of equipment. Your company manufactures, sells, and services several kinds of meters for scientific and industrial instruments and installations. Your catalog lists an array of 18 types of electronic meters, most of which come in various sizes. Some models can be modified to exact customer specifications.

An order arrives from Falmouth Equipment Company, Oxford, Miss. (the first customer from that part of the country) asking for six of "the latest model electronic meters for hydrothermal equipment such as that used by physical therapists and hospitals in treatment of circulatory ailments." Although you are pleased to receive this new business, you have all kinds of questions about it. Such vague and incomplete orders occur often enough that a form letter has been devised to save dictation time, but you think this new customer would need a more personal message to clarify his order. Avoid implying that he is ignorant; your inquiry letter is also to establish good will. You will ship immediately after you receive his clear order. You are assistant sales manager.

11. You are employee relations representative in the personnel division of a local industrial firm located in the channel area. Most of the 56 office employees (82%) have voted to request the company to provide a bus for the three-quarter-mile ride from the front gate to the office building. Cars must park in the lot near the front gate, making it necessary to walk the three-quarters of a mile along a wide macadam path that winds among the buildings occupied by the production and storage departments.

    Write a memo to your company vice president of industrial relations (give the individual a name) requesting that such a bus be provided. It should accommodate at least 45 persons (all but seven are women). You recommend that each rider be charged 50 cents in either direction, as the persons involved said they would prefer to pay to ride instead of getting paid time and a half for their walking time before and after their working hours.

    This group's hours are 8:00 a.m. to 5:00 p.m.; therefore, the bus would not be a hazard for the day shift workers, whose hours are 7:00 a.m. to 4:00 p.m. The bus would have to travel the same macadam pavement used by walkers.

12. Write a memo to the director of employee development in your company, Universal Space Enterprises, asking for some special training classes in advanced techniques of your special kind of work. It seems that when you began work here two years ago, this kind of training was being given, either in plant or in selected schools and colleges. For some unexplained reason, no such program has been in effect for over a year and some of you are getting rusty on techniques that may be needed to qualify you for promotions and raises.

    The reason for your memo is to make the man aware of your interest and your desire to keep ahead of needed work skills and knowledge. Also, you are puzzled as to why training has been discontinued, as it was considered a fringe benefit at the time you were hired. Ask for a reply so that you can make personal plans related to further training for yourself.

13. Write a memo to the head of the shipping and receiving department of your company, Technical Enterprises, asking that their personnel be especially careful in checking arriving shipments, to detect possible damage of enclosed apparatus. Several times recently, seemingly unmarred boxes showed dents and scars on outside surfaces exactly where the damaged items were located inside. Although replacements can be and have been obtained in all cases, this procedure delays use of the apparatus and all the red tape is a nuisance.

    If the shipping department employees would carefully check the outside for any evidence of possible inside damage and refuse the shipment, it would be returned by the same carrier immediately. This procedure would prevent having to make claims and would speed up the replacement. Of course, you want to know of any refused shipment, when it has been refused, company shipping it, and carrier transporting it.

Put this request on the basis of improving the efficiency of the company and saving time and money involved in the claims procedure. Request a reply showing how he reacts to the idea. Your title is purchasing agent.

Everything that has been said about creating good tone in letters and memos applies doubly to the letter of application. Perhaps in no other letter you will ever write will good tone be so important. Every sentence, every paragraph of the letter of application contributes to your personal portrait which emerges from the letter itself. Even one carelessly worded sentence or paragraph can suggest to the reader that you are patronizing, incompetent, overconfident, anxious, pessimistic, lazy, or indifferent. Therefore, as you prepare the letter of application to accompany the resume, do so with scrupulous care, keeping in mind that the total impression your letter and resume make on the prospective employer will determine whether or not you receive an interview.

The letter of application is not just a "cover letter"—it works with the resume. While the resume records essential facts about your background, the application letter develops particular items that will be of interest to your reader, giving these items life and meaning. Therefore, in planning your letter of application, consider what particular parts of your education and experience (selected from your resume) will be of greatest interest to the prospective employer. Then organize your letter to display these points as positively as possible.

Opening Paragraph

For the letter of application to be off to a good start, its good tone should be established immediately, in the first sentence. The opening sentence should be forceful enough to catch the reader's attention and encourage further reading. Always avoid opening sentences such as these:

> This is in reply to your ad for a civil technologist in the April 18 *Houston Post*. [flat—trite]
>
> Replying to your ad for a civil technologist, I am writing this letter to submit my qualifications. [more trite phrasing]
>
> I just happened to be reading the Sunday *Dallas Morning News* and noticed your ad for a bookkeeper. [job search not planned; writer not seriously looking for a job]
>
> I will be receiving a B.S. in mechanical technology in May and am wondering if your company will be interested in hiring anyone in my field. [no knowledge of company; job search is a "fishing" expedition]

To develop a good opening paragraph, you can always use one of the following forms:

> **Summary Beginning** (emphasizing qualifications for the job): Four years' experience as a receptionist-bookkeeper and three years of courses in business administration and accounting at Texas A&M University make me confident that I am qualified to fill the position you have open for a part-time receptionist-bookkeeper. I learned of the opening from your ad in the *Eagle*, Friday, October 8.
>
> **Name Beginning:** Dr. John Adams, Professor of Recreation and Parks at Colorado State University, told me that you have a naturalist position open. May I familiarize you with my qualifications?
>
> **Question Opening** (good for unsolicited letters): Do you have any summer job openings for student workers majoring in agriculture? Dr. Curtis Howard, As-

sociate Dean, College of Agriculture, suggested that I contact you to see if you planned to add students to your staff during the coming summer.

The "original" opening can also be used, but be sure that in trying to sound original you do not sound bizarre:

> **Poor Original Opening:** "We're ready when you are!" your firm's advertising slogan is most attractive. No doubt an indication of one of the most successful airlines' effective use of the media. I am also ready when you are to make my career with Delta. Either an aircraft/pilot support position or one with airline management would utilize me to the fullest. Are you ready for me?

> **Good Original Opening:** I am a biomedical science student at Howard College, with the qualifications to become a lab technician and general assistant in your company's research division.

Sometimes you can combine elements of these four types of openings to create an opening that is both original and effective:

> At a recent meeting of the IEEE Communications Chapter, I learned from Mr. Joe Smith of Western Electric that you are planning to hire two telemetry systems engineers. I have the qualifications for that position, based on my education and experience in communication systems.

Middle Paragraphs

The middle paragraphs of the application letter—either two or three—should discuss particular aspects of experience and/or education that will interest the prospective employer. The order of presentation here should follow the order of the resume: if you list experience first in the resume, then you should discuss experience first in the letter. In discussing either education or experience (or both), shape the particular ideas to show how your background meets the company's needs. In the following sample experience paragraph, the student, who is applying for an assistantship in a biochemistry department, describes laboratory techniques she can perform:

> Working for the USDA Veterinary Toxicology and Entomology Research Laboratory has given me three years of valuable laboratory experience. My work involves insect biological oxidative systems. I routinely prepare and analyze insect and rat microsomes. For example, I determined the extinction coefficient of microsomal P-450 in houseflies. Through this work I have learned invaluable techniques involving UV Spectroscopy and differential centrifugation. I raise the houseflies which are used in the experiments. My work has also included applying insecticides and insect growth regulators to houseflies and stable flies. To determine the effectiveness of the compounds, I kept careful records of enclosure rates. Purifying compounds by thin-layer chromatography is another part of my duties. This involves making the tlc plates, streaking the compound, and extracting the purified band.

Other suitable topics for the middle paragraphs of the application letter might be social or community activities in which you have excelled. However, you should include these only if these activities would interest your reader and help form a positive judgment about you. In short, the middle paragraphs are not to be a chronological recital of your past, but a highlighting of specific points selected from your resume and presented with your reader in mind. In the following example paragraph, an honor student applying for an accounting position in an oil company shows how his academic activities provide a meaningful experience that would be valuable to an employer:

> I believe that my scholastic activities and honors reflect my willingness to participate and to work diligently. I am an active member of the Accounting Society and Beta Alpha Psi, an honor society for accounting majors. In these organizations, I have worked to serve both students and the community through such activities as career awareness conferences, tutoring, and tax information booths. This spring, for the second year, I will receive the Thomas S. Gathright Award, an academic achievement award presented each year to the top sophomore, junior, and senior from each college at Texas A&M.

When building these middle paragraphs, remember to choose and shape information that will be informative and interesting to your reader. Instead of sending the same application for every job, custom-design your message for each prospective employer to insure its being reader centered.

Concluding Paragraph

The concluding paragraph of the application letter should request an interview. Write the paragraph as forcefully as possible to try to elicit a response from the reader:

> *Example 1:* May I come in and talk with you or another member of your firm? I believe I can assure you of my value. I will be available to begin summer employment after May 14.

> *Example 2:* I will be in Houston from December 14–18 and would be happy to come in for a personal interview at your convenience. If another date is more convenient for you, I can be reached at the temporary address shown on the resume until December 31.

> *Example 3:* Because of my engineering education and practical experience dealing with machines and people, I believe I am able to meet your requirements. Will you allow me to have an interview at your convenience? I can be contacted at the address given in my resume.

In contrast, avoid endings that do not encourage a specific response from the reader or sound as if you are not eager or confident about arranging an interview:

> *Example 1:* I am looking forward to hearing from you. Thank you for your time.

> *Example 2:* I was wondering if I could possibly get an interview with your people in one of the aforementioned departments.

RESUME

The resume is usually divided into at least four major sections: (1) heading, (2) education, (3) experience, and (4) personal data. Other divisions, such as references, may be included, depending on the prospective employer's preferences. Remember: every resume is different. As in the application letter, design your resume to display the details of your qualifications as clearly and effectively as possible.

While "tone" does not actually apply to the resume, the format and wording of your resume can give the reader an unfavorable impression about you or discourage the reader from wanting to read the resume. Effective formating—appealing use of type, spacing, and arrangement of content—can encourage the reader. The resume should be visually appealing. Content should be easy to see, easy to read, easy to follow. However you may develop your resume, avoid a cluttered, disorganized appearance and omit extraneous, trivial information.

Heading

Your resume should begin with an appropriate title. Do not use RESUME as a title. Word the heading appropriately for the kind of job for which you are applying. Include your address and phone number so that the prospective employer can find it immediately:

```
                EXECUTIVE SECRETARY CREDENTIALS OF MARY ANN SMITH

                            1410 Suncrest Hollow
                            Houston, Texas 77036
                            713-555-6272
```

```
                            WINSTON H. CARROLL, C.P.A.
                         MANAGERIAL ACCOUNTING CREDENTIALS
                                      for
                                IBM CORPORATION
    2224 Belmont Drive           Houston, Texas              713-555-2123
```

Education/Experience

The next section of your resume should document either your education or your experience, depending on which you are emphasizing in your job search. In either case, list the data chronologically, beginning with the most recent experience or educational background.

For education, give inclusive dates, names of institutions attended, degree or kind of study taken at each. Consider using the following format if you are relying heavily on your education to appeal to the prospective employer. Under education you may want to list honors received and your grade point ratio (only if good). However, if you have earned enough honors, you may wish to save these for a special section that would include other distinguished achievements.

CONSTRUCTION MANAGEMENT QUALIFICATIONS

STEPHEN JAY WILLIAMSON
918 Old Lake Road, Houston, TX   77057
468-1998

EDUCATION

Bachelor of Science in Technology with a major in Civil Technology (Building and Construction) from the University of Houston, May 1979

Houston Baptist University, majored in Business Administration, 1974-1976

Construction Courses:

Building Materials and Methods	Mechanics of Structures
Plans and Specifications	Structural Steel Construction
Surveying	Soil Mechanics
Water Technology	Fundamentals of Concrete
Transportation Technology	Reinforced Concrete
Construction Management	Technical Drawing
Statics	Architectural Drawing
Strengths of Materials	Structural Drawing

Related Courses:

calculus	(6 hrs.)	statistics	(4 hrs.)
business law	(3 hrs.)	speech	(3 hrs.)
economics	(12 hrs.)	electronics	(3 hrs.)
management	(12 hrs.)	computer science	(3 hrs.)

Special Educational Courses:

Certification in Structural Steel and Concrete Detailing, 360 hours. Texas A&M University Engineering Extension Service, 1973
Steam Engineering, 30 class hrs., Rice University NROTC, 1975.
OSHA Certification in Construction and Fire Safety, 30 class hrs., University of Houston, 1977

Jack F. Davis
1601 Holleman Apt. G-7
College Station, Texas 77840   MANAGEMENT PROFILE

713/846-2671

PERSONAL

Age: Date of Birth: March 4, 1954

Family: Married

Education: Bachelor of Science, Horticulture, Texas A&M University,
                        19__, Cum Laude
                        Emphasis was placed on Ornamental Horticulture, Plant
                        Pathology, and Business.

OBJECTIVE   To obtain a challenging position dealing with nursery
                        production or management.

EXPERIENCE

June 1975 to   MONROVIA NURSERY COMPANY, Azusa, California
August 1975
                        Participated in Monrovia Nursery's Summer Training
                        Program. During the ten-week program gained valuable
                        knowledge and work experience in all phases of nursery
                        production and management.

May 1974 to   GREEN THUMB CORPORATION, Apopka, Florida
August 1974
                        Organized and directed the planting and care of four acres of
                        Philodendron oxycardium stock plant area. Acquired
                        firsthand experience in managing labor.

December 1973 to   GREEN THUMB TROPICAL PLANT RENTALS, Houston, Texas
January 1974
                        Consultant on care and maintenance of foliage plants.
                        Instructed maintenance crews on correct watering,
                        fertilization, and pest control practices.

June 1973 to   GREEN THUMB CORPORATION, Apopka, Florida
August 1973
                        Assisted in all phases of greenhouse production of several
                        species of tropical foliage plants.

December 1970 to   GARDENLAND, INC., Houston, Texas
June 1972
                        Experience in direct sales and operations in a retail
                        nursery business.

ACTIVITIES   Texas A&M University Horticulture Society
                            President, 1974-1975
                            Vice President, 1974
                        American Society for Horticultural Science
                            Treasurer, Southern Region, ACB, 1975-1976
                        Texas A&M University Agriculture Council, 1975
                        Alpha Zeta National Agricultural Honor Fraternity
                        Laboratory assistant, Nursery Production course, Texas A&M
                            University, 1976

SCHOLARSHIPS   Burpee Award in Horticulture, 1975
AND AWARDS   Texas Association of Nurserymen -- Gardenland Scholarship,
                            1975
                        Houston Men's Garden Club Scholarship, 1975

REFERENCES   Furnished on Request.

When describing your experience, begin with your current or most recent job and list other pertinent jobs in reverse chronological order. Work experience is very important, so make a working list of every job you have had. Then select the jobs you will list, choosing the ones that the prospective employer will be most interested in. You should be able to relate valuable experience associated with these jobs in the experience section of your application letter.

In listing a job, give the beginning and ending dates, name of the company, location of the company, and your job title. Then, using phrases beginning with action verbs (organized, directed, implemented, led, planned, developed, supervised, coached, etc.), list your duties. Remember that you want to appear as positive and assertive as possible. Avoid using sentences to keep the description as brief and readable as possible. Examine the following entry:

```
1972 to          Eagle Management and Trust Company, Houston, Texas
1973
                 Acted as an executive secretary for this investment
                 company. Drafted and checked all company correspondence
                 made travel arrangements, calculated expense accounts,
                 ordered company supplies, maintained personal accounts
                 for company officers, updated weekly stock reports, and
                 served as editor of company brochure.
```

Personal Data

For your brief section on personal data, choose those items that distinguish you as an individual. Professional affiliations, social organizations, civic activities, language expertise, avocational accomplishments, special skills, and military records are good items for the personal section. Giving your place of birth (if outside the United States) can be an asset if the company might be considering you for a foreign assignment. Avoid giving race, religion (unless these might specifically interest a reader), hair, and eye color. While most employers still expect age and marital status to be included in personal information, you are not obligated to furnish this information if you believe these facts would discriminate against you. Do not give height and weight if you are grossly overweight. In short, consider the positive and negative implications of every item you might include under personal information. Choose those items that will help your application, but do include some personal data, as employers usually expect to see some.

References

If you have a substantial and impressive section on experience, you are less likely to need to list other references. Because previous employers may be requested to furnish information regarding your time with them, you do not repeat their names in the reference section. Whether to include references on your resume depends upon the preference of the company and the nature of the specific job. Generally, do not include references on your resume. State, instead, "References furnished on request." A good kind of reference is a person of integrity and some accomplishment who knows you well enough to answer questions about your character and personality. As a matter of

108

courtesy, be ready to submit such persons' names (three to five) only after asking and receiving their consent to be used as a reference.

Format Suggestions

Length. Many resume consultants stress that a resume should be only one page. However, to be on the safe side, develop two resumes—one that is two to three pages and one that is one page, drawn from the material listed on the longer resume. If the resume is your only chance to sell your qualifications, you are probably better off sending a full-length resume, one that you believe gives a complete view of your potential. However, experiment with developing a one-page resume. With careful formatting and by using elite type, you can include a great deal of information on one page.

Resume and Letter of Application

1. For the application letter, use semiblock. Generally, the application letter should be kept to one page. (See the following letters for format examples.)

2. For both resume and application letter, use 20-lb. (heavyweight) nonerasable bond paper. Consider buying a higher quality 24-lb. bond paper in an attractive color—light gray, off-white, beige, or celery. Avoid colors like pink or blue. Check with a stationer who can show you brands and samples.

3. Both the letter and resume should be typed error-free. Corrections are permissible if they are invisible, but absolutely no misspelled words, punctuation errors, or usage errors should be present. Even one such error suggests that you are either careless or unable to handle your language.

4. Type the resume and letter using a carbon ribbon, as cloth ribbons make uneven, fuzzy characters.

5. Experiment with various formats, typing styles, and spacing. Use adequate spacing to insure an uncluttered page. Experiment with headings that use both all caps and mixed case. A resume that is all mixed case with no underlining or variation in spacing is unattractive, boring, and discouraging to the reader. Therefore, plan the layout so that your resume is visually accessible and appealing.

6. Use elite type if you have a great deal of information to include in the resume.

7. When preparing to mail the resume and letter, mail them in a 9″ × 12″ envelope. Do not fold and mail them in a standard-sized business envelope. Be sure that the label on the envelope is properly and neatly addressed and correctly spelled. Do not include with your letter and resume transcripts, letters of recommendation, or work samples. Send these only when requested.

CONCLUSION

College students who have little work experience frequently complain: "I don't have anything to put on a resume." Yes, you do! Note the following resume written by a college freshman applying for a summer job. The student does an excellent job of displaying his high school background, which is all he has. No matter how limited your background, you *can* develop a resume and letter to display your background and abilities to their best advantage.

Remember, however, that a good resume and application letter take time to plan, write, format, and type. An excellent resume and letter take even longer. Allow yourself plenty of time for the project. List every item about your education, work experience, social activities, hobbies, skills, and interests. Once you have the information, then you can begin to decide which data you will use, how you will group it, and finally, how you will display it on the typed page. Inevitably, a "rush" job will always produce mistakes you cannot afford to make—sloppy format, typographical errors, poorly worded sentences, poor organization of ideas, even lack of important information.

In the example letters and resumes that follow, observe how effectively each letter works with the accompanying resume. Then, examine the resume formats to see the various ways that data can be effectively displayed. Since everyone's background is different, every resume will be different. Again, allow sufficient time to experiment with format.

Letter of Application

```
                                        378 Penland Hall
                                        Baylor University
                                        Waco, Texas 76703
                                        February 20, 19__


        Mr. Bill Alley, College Recruiter
        Personnel Department
        Brown & Root, Inc.
        P.O. Box 3
        Houston, Texas   77001

        Dear Mr. Alley:

            I am a student at Baylor University in the electronic engineering program.
        During the summer, I would like to work for your company as an electronic
        engineering apprentice to earn my tuition. Mr. Robert Varnadoe, a civil engineer
        for your company, tells me that you hire college students for summer employment.

            The enclosed resume sheet shows special areas of study which have
        contributed to my qualifications. I have excelled in the field of mathematics,
        obtaining a perfect score of 36 in math on the ACT exam. While in high school I was in
        Mu Alpha Theta, an honorary math society, and on the math team which participated
        in tournaments around the state. Having completed a study in computer math in high
        school and a computer science course during the first semester of college has given
        me a good background in Basic and Fortran IV computer language.

            The applications of mathematics in electronic engineering would be an
        exciting field of work, and I would certainly try to fulfill any position you
        offered me.

            I will be in Houston during the week of March 10-15. Would it be possible to
        have an interview with you during that week? If so, you may contact me at the address
        on my resume.

                                        Sincerely,


                                        Clifford B. Martin

        Enclosure
```

110

CLIFFORD B. MARTIN

Statement of Employment Assets for
Summer Work in Electronic Engineering
Available: May 12, 1980

School Address
378 Penland Hall
Baylor University
Waco, Texas 76703
(817) 555-2135

Permanent Address
19614 Shinwood Dr.
Humble, Texas 77338
(713) 555-2776

EDUCATION

Currently a freshman in the Honors Program at Baylor University, working toward a
B.S. degree, majoring in Engineering Science.

Graduated: Jefferson Davis High School, Montgomery, AL, in June, 1979
Class Ranking: 18 in class of 711   GPA: 3.94 on a 4.0 scale
ACT Score: 31 overall; 36 in math   SAT Score: 1260

Outstanding Academic Honors and Awards

National Honor Society   National Math Honor Society
National Spanish Honor Society   Mr Alpha Theta (Honorary Math Society)
Recipient of Walter W. Ross Memorial Scholarship awarded by Beta Sigma Phi

Courses of Value

High School

Computer Math
Analysis and Trigonometry
Physics

College

Calculus
Computer Science
Chemistry

Skills

Typing—60 WPM
Computer—Basic and Fortran IV

EXPERIENCE

Fall & Winter
1978–1979

Wuv's Hamburgers, Montgomery, AL
Worked part–time during senior year
Cooked hamburgers and cleaned restaurant

Summer
1978

Wiggin's Lawn Service, Montgomery, AL
Mowed lawns and edged grass at apartments and business
complexes for professional lawn service

Summer
1977

Glenn's Furniture Repair and Refinishing,
Montgomery, AL
Repaired, sanded, stained, and refinished furniture
Picked up and delivered furniture

PERSONAL DATA

Birth: September 2, 1960
Birthplace: Ennis, Texas
Marital Status: Single

Health: Excellent
Height: 6'1"
Weight: 165 lbs.

ACTIVITIES AND INTERESTS

Boy Scouts of America during junior high school
Dixie Youth Baseball—7 years; elected to all–star team every year
High School baseball, basketball, and track teams
Church Royal Ambassador's basketball team—won Alabama state championship in
      1978; won second place in 1979; received outstanding player trophy in 1979
Intramural basketball—Baylor University

REFERENCES WILL BE FURNISHED UPON REQUEST.

2016 South Fisher Court
Pasadena, Texas 77502
November 30, 1979

Mr. Paul Raymer
DialAmerica Marketing, Inc.
6001 Gulf Freeway
Houston, Texas 77087

Dear Mr. Raymer:

Your advertisements in the University of Houston <u>Cougar</u> newspaper for part-time marketing positions captured my attention. I am very interested in working part time for your marketing firm while completing my college education.

I am presently a senior attending the University of Houston and expect to graduate in May 1980 with a B.B.A. in Marketing. I have already completed 18 hours of marketing courses at the University of Houston, including courses in Marketing Research and Marketing Administration. The knowledge obtained in these courses would not only qualify me for your positions, but also should minimize your costs in training me.

My previous work experience has consisted of various secretarial and retail positions in which my job duties included selling, supervising, training, and general office work. In all of these jobs, I proved myself worthy of promotions to more difficult positions while simultaneously working part-time and attending school.

A summary of my qualifications is given in the attached resume, and I will be glad to meet with you for an interview at your convenience. Please feel free to contact me by letter or at the phone number included in the attached resume.

Sincerely,

Donna Quinn

Enclosure

DONNA FAYE QUINN

MARKET RESEARCH CREDENTIALS

2016 South Fisher Court   Pasadena, Texas 77502   713: 555-2745

Qualifications for obtaining market research
position with successful marketing firm
while completing B.B.A. in Marketing

Educational Background

University of Houston, B.B.A. in Marketing expected May 1980. Grade point average
since entering in August 1976 is 3.0 out of 4.0.
San Jacinto College, completed 60 hours of general business core requirements
between 1976 and 1978, with grade point average 3.4 out of 4.0.

Marketing Courses
Elements of Marketing Administration
Contemporary Issues in Business & Society
Marketing Research
Advertising Management
Retailing Management
Industrial Marketing

Working Experience

Senior Secretary, Dean's Office, Cullen College of Engineering at University of
Houston. Conducted general secretarial duties for deans, plus handling and
processing graduate school admission applications and undergraduate
scholarship applications. August 1979-present.
Secretary, Adkins Personnel Service, Inc. and Certified Personnel Services,
Pasadena, Texas. Handled general secretarial duties for firms such as
Continental Emsco, Exxon Chemical Co., USA, and the University of Houston.
June 1979-August 1979.
Salesclerk, Foley's, Pasadena. Sold merchandise from all areas of store on
extra-on-call basis. January 1979-August 1979.
Trainer, Foley's, Pasadena. Taught training classes on all basic store policies
and NCR terminal operations to new Christmas hires. October 1978-December
1979.
Night Supervisor, Foley's, Pasadena. Supervised all night staff and functions
including: scheduling, employee reviews, inventory maintenance, floor
merchandising, and displays. April 1978-October 1978.
Salesclerk, Foley's, Pasadena. Sold merchandise and maintained floor displays
for departments, including: costume jewelry, handbags, watches, and fine
jewelry. October 1975-April 1978.

Honors and Activities

Dean's List
American Marketing Association,
    Secretary

REFERENCES WILL BE
SENT UPON REQUEST

Personal

Date of Birth: 8/12/58
Height: 5'4"
Weight: 110 lbs.
Health: Excellent
Enjoy music, sewing, reading,
and camping

5614 Darnell
Houston, Texas 77096
November 28, 1979

Mr. Jack Kelly
Director of Corporate Personnel Services
Tenneco, Inc.
P.O. Box 2511
Houston, Texas 77001

Dear Mr. Kelly:

Mr. Ken Clevenger, president of Allied Bank, told me about the position as administrative assistant to the senior vice president of Tenneco, Inc. I am excited about the opportunity to apply for this job.

My working experience and education, as well as my social and family responsibilities, have prepared me well for the job of administrative assistant to Mr. Carpenter. For the last five years I have worked as one of the secretaries to the senior rabbi of Temple Emanu El. This position demands discretion, tact in dealing with people, and the ability to keep information confidential. Office skills must meet a very high standard. I've had the opportunity to train on and operate many types of equipment, including the new IBM Memory 100 Typewriter. This facet of my experience has given me an appreciation of how to get things done efficiently in an office.

As the wife of someone who is involved in civic activities, I have been placed in many situations that have broadened my expertise in dealing with people. While my husband served as District Governor for Lions International, I worked with him to encourage members to participate fully in this charitable organization. During a two-year period, I met several thousand people, spoke before many groups, and developed opportunities for involvement by the member wives. During my husband's three-year tenure as board president and managing director of The Houston Pops Orchestra, I served in the capacity of administrative assistant to him. This work involved planning and executing all phases of the orchestra's performances, including public relations, advertising and promotions, ticket sales, fiscal management, and physical setup of the rehearsals and concerts. Since The Pops is a nonprofit group, an important part of the work was developing new sources of individual and corporate funding. During this time, applications were made to and grants received from many large companies and foundations here in Houston. The number of individual contributors quadrupled. The orchestra's tremendous growth in that period was very gratifying to me.

Working with Mr. Carpenter would be a challenging opportunity. Please let me know when it will be convenient for you to interview me. You can contact me at the address or phone number on my resume, or at 555-1201. I am looking forward to meeting you.

Sincerely yours,

Marianne Greenfield

Enclosure

MARIANNE GREENFIELD

5614 Darnell   Houston, Texas 77096   713-555-1155

To fill position as
administrative assistant to executive officer

EDUCATION

University of Houston. College of Business Administration and College of Technology. Dean's List.
GPA: job-related courses—3.8
      overall—3.7

Job-Related Courses

Personnel Technology	Industrial Communications
Operational Use of Financial Data	Distribution Technology
	Business Law
Fiscal Operations	General Office Procedures
Accounting Theory	Basic Computer Organization
Public Speaking	Microeconomics
Fundamental Business Math I	Macroeconomics
Fundamental Business Math II	Introduction to Sociology
Introduction to Psychology	Shorthand
Typing	

JOB EXPERIENCE

TEMPLE EMANU EL. Part-time secretary to senior rabbi. 1975-present.
Typed dictation, composed letters, screened calls, prepared and sent routine mailings to members. Dealt, by phone and in person, with people who were in stressful situations. Coordinated activities with other offices in congregation. Took care of all office procedures.

LYMAN I. OWEN, C.P.A. Secretary. 1960-1964.
Handled all office procedures. Typed all tax returns and financial data for clients.

JOHN JAMAIL APARTMENTS. Apartment manager. 1962-1964.
Operated 36-unit apartment project. Collected rent, leased apartments, took care of complaints, directed maintenance.

SCHLUMBERGER WELL SERVICES. Secretary. 1959-1960.
Performed all secretarial duties and procedures in Electrical Engineering Department.

MCEVOY OILFIELD EQUIPMENT COMPANY. Secretary, receptionist. 1958-1959.
Carried out office procedures and duties. Operated switchboard as relief operator and receptionist.

VOLUNTEER EXPERIENCE

Temple Emanu El—Chairman, Membership Survey Committee; member, Dues Committee, Membership Committee, Ritual and Music Committee, PTA Board.
Houston Pops Orchestra—Administrative assistant.
Temple Emanu El Sisterhood—Vice president, financial secretary, board member.

PERSONAL

Health—excellent   Married—3 children   Height—5'5"
Weight—115

References furnished upon request.

115

13718 Apple Tree
Houston, Texas 77079
February 20, 1980

Mr. C. Leroy Johnson
Corporate Services Division
Texaco, Inc.
1111 Rusk
Houston, Texas 77079

Dear Mr. Johnson:

Mr. Robert Howell, General Manager PPD, has told me of the job opportunities for graduates with the Bachelor of Science degree in the executive secretarial field. May I familiarize you with my qualifications for an executive secretarial job?

I am presently a full-time student at the University of Houston, majoring in their Executive Secretarial program. I have enjoyed my studies and have made a better than average record; my current GPA is a 3.49 on a 4.0 scale.

My degree from the University of Houston will provide me with a base from which I can develop my secretarial career. As an executive secretary, my skills in dictation, transcription, and typewriting are higher than the average person. I am also skilled in editing and proofreading. My education has provided me with the knowledge in preparation of statistical reports, legal documents, manuscripts, and other business forms that a large firm such as Texaco could utilize. My ability to operate the IBM electronic typewriter, dictaphone, electronic calculator, and various duplicating equipment will help me in planning and organizing an efficient office in the support of top management.

My skills are sharp and high-standard, and I am eager to use them. I would be glad to demonstrate them to you if you would give me an opportunity for a personal interview. Please telephone me any week day after 2:00 p.m. at 555-6189 to set an appointment at your convenience.

Sincerely,

Carol A. Seamans

Carol A. Seamans

Enclosure: Resume

SECRETARIAL QUALIFICATIONS OF MISS CAROL ANN SEAMANS

13718 Apple Tree
Houston, Texas 77079
465-6189

EDUCATION
- Bachelor of Science in Technology with major in Executive Secretarial from the University of Houston, May 1981.

UNIVERSITY COURSES OF SPECIAL VALUE
- Basic Computer Organization
- Distribution Technology
- Business Records I and II
- Administrative Management
- Records Management
- Statistics
- Office Services
- Office Systems
- Business Law
- Business and Technical Writing
- Communications Production

SKILLS IN SECRETARIAL WORK
- Dictation 100 wpm
- Typewriting 70 wpm
- Transcription 30 wpm
- IBM electronic typewriter
- Dictaphone
- Electronic calculator
- Standard Rocket spirit duplicator
- A. B. Dick and Gestetner stencil duplicators
- Offset machine

AWARDS AND ACTIVITIES IN COLLEGE
- Golden Key Honor Society (College of Technology).
- Chi Omega Fraternity—Assistant Rush Chairman, House Chairman, and Assistant Secretary.
- Honors List of the Dean (College of Business Technology)—Fall 1977, Summer 1978, Fall 1978, Spring 1979.

EXPERIENCE
- November 1978–October 1979–Joske's of Houston, worked in credit department taking payments, opening charge accounts, and balancing out the store's cash registers. Used the electronic calculator.
- January 1977–May 1977–Windmill Dinner Theatre, Houston. Receptionist; answered phones, took reservations and payments, and prepared the seating arrangements.

REFERENCES
- Will be provided upon request.

4639 Lochshin Drive
Houston, TX 77084
March 26, 1979

Mr. F. T. Welch, Sales Manager
Napko Corporation
P.O. Box 14509
Houston, TX 77021

Dear Mr. Welch:

While involved in an important phone conversation with a customer does it annoy you to see the other button on the phone blink, blink, blink? The successful salesman knows a customer kept waiting too long will probably hang up. This problem can be prevented by an experienced secretary who can either help the caller or secure enough information to put her employer "on top" of the situation before the call is returned. With ten years of experience, I believe I am well qualified for the position of sales secretary.

Presently I work part time for two manufacturers' representatives who are involved in the sale of products related to the engineering industry. Along with all secretarial and accounting duties, I quote customers and accept purchase orders by telephone. For six years I worked for Norton Company, Chemical Process Products Division. Norton Company supplies tower packings and internals to the petrochemical industries and maintains a packing inventory in a local commercial warehouse. My major responsibilities were the shipment of materials in and out of the warehouse, maintenance of all paperwork related to the inventory, and preparation of a monthly report reflecting the warehouse activity. Consequently, I worked directly with customers and purchasing agents. I also know how to trace or expedite a purchase order. My work habits are very well organized and I am an accurate and fast typist.

I am currently working on a degree in Business Technology at the University of Houston. The courses offered in this field are directly related to business and industry. My skills have greatly improved through my application of techniques I am learning. One course, of particular interest, which I will be taking this summer is Distribution Technology. This subject deals with the flow of goods and services from the producer to the consumer. If accepted for the position of sales secretary, I will continue my education at night.

With my experience and college courses I am confident that I am the secretary you are seeking. I would like to meet you and discuss my qualifications in more detail. Please contact me at the address or telephone number shown on my resume. If you wish to telephone I can be reached after 3:30 p.m. on weekdays.

Sincerely yours,

Barbara Shimaitis

Barbara Shimaitis

Enclosure: Resume

BARBARA SHIMAITIS
4639 Lochshin Drive
Houston, TX 77084
713/463-0162

QUALIFICATIONS FOR SALES SECRETARY

Significant Working Responsibilities

Sales Secretary–(June 1976–present). Kelly Campbell, Inc., Houston, TX 77024. Part time–15 hours a week. Handle all secretarial and accounting duties. Accept purchase orders. Quote prices. Expedite orders. Direct phone calls.

Engineering Secretary–(November 1974–June 1975). Hydrocarbon Construction Company, Houston, TX 77046. Worked directly for the head of the engineering department. Prepared all correspondence. Organized and typed engineering manuals. Supervised organization of conferences with clients.

Sales Secretary–(February 1969–November 1974). Norton Company, Chemical Process Products Division, Houston, TX 77042. Prepared orders and quotations. Shipped inventory from stocking warehouse. Organized and maintained all paperwork relating to warehouse. Prepared monthly sales report. Acquired heavy dictaphone experience. Prepared travel arrangements. Trained new secretaries.

Valuable Skills

Type–70 wpm   Dictaphone Experience   Ten Key Adder   Bookkeeping

Education and Training

University of Houston–(September 1978–present). Degree in Business Technology expected December 1980.

Business Courses of Value

Introduction to Business	–Grade A	Applied Business Math (taking now)
Business Communications	–Grade A	Technical Writing (taking now)
Basic Technical Math	–Grade A	Business Law (taking now)

Southwest Texas State College–(January 1965–February 1967). San Marcos, TX. Acquired 69 hours in elementary education.

Draughon's Business College–(Fall 1964), San Antonio, TX. Receptionist Degree.

New Braunfels High School–New Braunfels, TX. Graduated upper 10% class–May 1964.

Personal Picture

Birthdate:	January 16, 1947	Hobbies:	Gourmet cooking
Height:	5'6"		Plants
Weight:	125 pounds		Bowling
Health:	Excellent		Macramé

WORK PROJECT 8

Criticize the following paragraphs selected from actual letters of application. What kind of impression does each make on the reader? What are the strengths and weaknesses of each? Write your comments in the space below the item. Then revise the paragraph below the comments. Submit the corrected sheet to your instructor.

Opening Paragraphs

1. Swine production is entering a phase where the manager must be competent in a number of fields. He must have a sound understanding of breeding, feeding, nutrition, and management. For large-scale operations, he should also have knowledge of the fundamentals of accounting. If you are looking for such a manager, I can satisfy these requirements.

2. I will be graduatig from Howard University with a B.S. in Engineering Technology in May, 1979. I was wandering if your company has any openings in your microwave systems design service.

3. Your company is one of dynamic growth and continuing expansion. With a company of this calibre, you need young energetic people in management positions to grow with you. As a 1979 civil technology graduate from Jones University, I have been thoroughly and completely trained in all phases of construction management.

4. Could your firm use a Jones University engineering technology student with a limited amount of experience? If so, please consider my application.

5. This letter is in reference to the advertisement in the *Dallas Morning News*. I am very interested in joining your trust and marketing program.

6. With summer approaching, my mind has been turning to opportunities for work this summer. When Dr. Don Johnson told me you were looking for summer help in your foliage plant greenhouses, I thought I might be able to put my education and past experience as a greenhouse keeper to work for you.

7. Please forgive this xeroxed letter, but my research work, and many letters yet to write prevent me from spending the extra time required for writing separate letters. If I am to have a choice of good positions, this letter must reach as many as possible.

8. Dr. Howard informed me of your opening for a laboratory technician. Please consider my qualifications.

9. Would your firm be interested in a Smith College computer science junior to fill the part-time computer operator vacancy which you advertised in the October 12 *Daily Sun*?

10. I've slaved for four years to earn 80 percent of my college finances and gain managerial and supervisory experience. Now study at Jones University ripens into a degree: Bachelor of Science in Building Technology. Employment in a company with a real future in the Construction Industry is my next goal. Please consider my qualifications for your position as superintendent trainee.

11. I have recently graduated from Jones College, and I am now available for immediate employment. I am very interested in pursuing a career with Neiman Marcus.

12. Remembering our social meeting and discussion about summer jobs a couple of months ago, I must ask you a question. Have you considered hiring a college student majoring in accounting for your summer position working with your business records. If not, perhaps my qualifications would convince you to do so.

13. A B.S. degree in biomedical science from Texas A&M and four years of laboratory experience make me confident that I can qualify for the laboratory technician position you are creating in your hospital.

14. First of all, I would like to make a confession. This letter is being written to other businessmen. I am making each one of them the same offer. In fairness to all I shall give each one every consideration before I make my decision.

1. *Writer is applying for a restaurant manager's position.* After graduating from high school, I worked for two summers on a commissary truck selling food at construction sites and factories. I was given the responsibility of selling food at a construction site where the men were building the largest computing center in the world for the Social Security Administration, and I managed to more than double the average daily sales. I am currently employed with Mannings Incorporated as the Night Manager of the Satellite food service operation, a 350-seat cafeteria at the University of Houston. I am responsible for the total p.m. physical management of the food service and the supervision of the p.m. hourly staff.

2. *Writer is applying for a news writing job at a TV station.* I am attending Jones University and anticipate to graduate in December 1980, with a bachelor of science degree in Journalism with a minor in english. I chose these two fields because of the verbal and written skills (factors which I feel are essential in the news media).

3. *Writer is applying for a junior accountant position.* In May of this year I will graduate from Jones University with a B.B.A. in Accounting. At the present time I have an overall 3.206321 GPR. I belong to three organizations: the Accounting Society, Alpha Phi Omega, and the Uvalde County Hometown Club.

4. *Writer is applying for a technologist position.* I have majored in Industrial Technology and have a good background in Industry. I have had many courses that would be valuable to your company. Some of my important courses are labor relations, management, safety, production techniques, and psychology. I have worked during my spare time while in college, and have not been in many school activities. I have worked hard on my courses and made the Dean's List. What time I have left I try to spend with my wife.

5. *Writer is applying for a junior college teaching position.* As you will see from my resume, my teaching experience in business education has been varied: junior and senior high school, at your junior college as a part-time instructor, and as a part-time faculty member at the University of Houston. After my first year of teaching at Stephen F. Austin High School, I was selected to become Business Department chairperson where I coordinated the activities of this department and served as a liaison between the administration and business faculty. Dr. James Phillips, the principal, appointed me to serve as chairperson of two evaluation committees during our evaluation by the Southern Association of Secondary Schools and Colleges. My responsibilities in the evaluation included coordinating the discussions and written evaluations of two different areas of our school. I was chosen by the senior class as their sponsor in 1964 and worked closely with the seniors in planning graduation activities.

6. *Writer is applying for a beginning management position.* My work experience at the Randall Corporation complements my scholastic achievements. This experience helps me to understand the complexities of the construction industry. I learned to follow instructions carefully and specifically. I also read and interpreted drawings and specifications related to making quantity estimates on petrochemical construction. The knowledge I gained as a manager of a health club was invaluable in learning to deal with people. I supervised the entire operation of a health club that grossed over $75,000 a month. In addition, active participation in college organizations clearly proves my leadership talents and ability to organize and direct people.

Closing Paragraphs

1. I believe that my skills learned through education, work, and activities meet your specifications. I would like the opportunity to meet you. I will be in Dallas October 29–30. Could I have an interview with you on either of those days?

2. Mr. Brown, I would certainly appreciate the opportunity to discuss this position with you. My job experience and the courses I have taken have prepared me for a job which requires working with people as well as recording accounts. I am available at 693-8616 after 3:00 p.m. any weekday. May I expect a call from you? I am ready to work.

3. If you will have an opening of this type within the next year, please allow me to send complete credentials. If you do not, or if you are unprepared for an individual with broad experience, advanced ideas, and competence, please do not waste your time with a reply. Thank you for your time.

4. If an opening has occurred or should occur in the near future, I would greatly appreciate any consideration given to me by your Company for this engineering-related position. I will be anxiously awaiting your reply.

5. I believe my experience in the CRTI program and college education courses has made me qualified to meet your qualifications. I will be available to your convenience at the indicated phone number and address on the resume for an interview.

YOUR COMPLETE APPLICATION LETTER AND RESUME

You are within six months of graduation and now wish to launch your job-securing campaign. Line up your best prospects for employing a person with your qualifications. Compile detailed information about (1) yourself, (2) your scholarship record, (3) your work experience, (4) what you can do that a company would be willing to pay for, (5) exactly what kind of work you now want, and (6) some good character references. Prepare a data sheet with attractive layout and cover it with a letter that will secure you an interview with the proper official to discuss, in person, your capability for work with some company on your prospect list. Important to the effectiveness of your cover letter is whether you seem to know what the company does and what it wants in the person they will hire for the job. Address an envelope, also.

4

Graphics

The importance of visual presentation to the development of technical writing cannot be overestimated. Twenty-five years ago company reports were reams of unbroken print bound in drab folders. Today company annual reports are characterized by their imaginative covers, richly textured, vividly colored papers, visually appealing type styles, and extensive use of graphics, the broad category which includes all visual aids to written communication.

Graphics have become increasingly important for two reasons: (1) widespread effects of television have led to development of sophisticated visual and audio-visual methods to present information in every field; (2) effective use of graphics has been found to save words, thus making written material concise, clear, and readable. Reader response is improved. Readers now expect graphics. So great is reader aversion to extended pages of unbroken composition that the fundamental guideline for using graphics has changed completely. Where writers once used graphics if the information presented required them, writers now deliberately look for ways to use standard graphic forms—graphs, tables, charts, diagrams, drawings, charts, and photographs.

GENERAL GUIDELINES

In choosing graphics to help present your ideas, consider the following guidelines:

1. One picture may well be worth a thousand words. Therefore, the first criterion is that the graphic form should make the information immediately understandable to the reader. Any graphic expression of data should be clear and self-evident apart from the text and discussion.

2. The graphic should be suitable for the audience and purpose. Primarily quantitative ideas are more easily grasped by the reader if they are presented in a table or graph. For example, the following statement is difficult to visualize:

   In Jones Junior High School, 203 girls and 196 boys were found to have Type O blood, while 169 boys and 113 girls were found to have Type B. Only 172 girls and 159 boys had blood-type A, while 64 boys and 98 girls were found to have Type AB.

Expressed as in Table 4-1, the information becomes clear at once:

Table 4-1

Students	Blood Type			
	O	A	B	AB
Boys	196	159	169	64
Girls	203	172	113	98

However, nonquantitative information is best presented by simple drawings, pictures, diagrams and photographs.

3. The graphic should be simple. No information should be included that will not be discussed in the text.

4. The graphic should be drawn in ink with careful attention given to visual effectiveness and neatness. Color can frequently improve readability and visual appeal.

5. While the content of the graphic should be self-evident, the graphic should always be integrated with the text. Introduce the idea to which the graphic relates first. That is, explain the data and its significance; then present the graphic. If necessary, add further written analysis after the graphic.

6. Graphics should be placed within the text where they can help clarify statements. Do not compile graphics in an appendix to a report or at the end of a report section. Constant page flipping between text and graphics discourages the reader from referring to the graphic and reduces reports to unbroken pages of words. However, when graphics are mainly supplemental, they should be placed in an appendix. But be sure to refer to these supplemental graphics so that the reader will know where to find them. Otherwise, graphics stranded in an appendix may never be discovered by the reader.

Basically, graphics can be divided into two categories—tables and figures. Each type has particular conventions regarding its use and presentation.

Tables are either formal or informal.

An *informal* table is actually a tabulated list. It is introduced by an explanatory sentence followed by a colon. Informal tables have no titles and are not given numbers. Information presented in an informal table is simple, as more complex information should be structured in formal tables.

The airline gave me the following departure and arrival times for flight schedules to Boston during the morning of April 10:

Flight	Leaving Houston	Arriving Boston
307	7:30 A.M.	1:30 P.M.
521	11:55 A.M.	4:20 P.M.

Formal tables should adhere to the following conventions:

1. Every formal table has a title and a number. Both are always placed above the table, never below. Table numbers are usually Arabic, although Roman numerals are still used. Titles must clearly define the content of the table, as shown in the following example:

   Table 4

   Average Rainfall for Presidio County,
   1960–1978

2. Every column should have a heading that clearly identifies the information beneath it. Column headings have vertical reference. Line headings have horizontal reference.

Table 4-2: A Formal Table
Table (number)

Title

Stub Heading	Column Heading	
	Subheading	Subheading
Line heading →		
Line heading →		

3. Headings must not be structured so that they appear to read both vertically and horizontally, as they do in Table 4-3.

Table 4-3

Students Enrolled	Freshman	Sophomore	Junior	Senior
Technology	194	217	306	399
Business	117	202	245	461
Agriculture	230	238	212	217
Sciences	90	114	152	230

For clarity, the table may be restructured either of two ways, as in Table 4-4:

Table 4-4

(A)

Student Major	Student Level			
	Freshman	Sophomore	Junior	Senior
Technology	194	217	306	399
Business	117	202	245	461
Agriculture	230	238	212	217
Sciences	90	114	152	230

or

(B)

Student Level	Student Major			
	Technology	Business	Agriculture	Sciences
Freshman	194	117	230	90
Sophomore	217	202	238	114
Junior	306	245	212	152
Senior	399	461	217	230

4. All headings should be brief. If further explanation is required, use footnotes at the bottom of the table. Footnotes are indicated by using lower-case letters as superscripts, as in Table 4-5.

Table 4-5

Distribution of Married Full-Time Respondents' Husbands and Wives by Course Load Classification[a]

Classification	Husbands		Wives		Total	
	Number	Percent	Number	Percent	Number	Percent
Full-Time[b]	12	16.00	8	8.70	20	11.98
Part-Time[c]	7	9.33	8	8.70	15	8.98
None	56	74.67	76	82.61	132	79.04
Total	75	100.00[d]	92	100.00[d]	167	100.00[d]

[a] Married includes all respondents married at the time of the survey except those reporting married but separated.
[b] A graduate course load of twelve or more semester hours.
[c] A graduate course load of less than twelve semester hours.
[d] May not total to 100.00 due to rounding.

SOURCE: Andrew J. Thacker, "The Impact of Graduate and Graduate Professional Education on the Perceived Marital Adjustment of Married Students at a Large Urban University," (unpublished doctoral dissertation, University of Houston, 1977), p. 113.

134

5. Do not use needless lines to separate data. Space between columns can effectively separate data and eliminate visual clutter. While boxed tables can be effective, compare the following two examples (Table 4-6). (B) is much less cluttered than (A).

Table 4-6

(A)

Survey Questions		Statistical Evaluation		
	Mean	Median	Mode	S.D.
Question 1	20	22	19	2.7
Question 2	27	24	29	3.4
Question 3	24	21	26	1.9

(B)

Survey Questions		Statistical Evaluation		
	Mean	Median	Mode	S.D.
Question 1	20	22	19	2.7
Question 2	27	24	29	3.4
Question 3	24	21	26	1.9

6. A table drawn from an outside source must be acknowledged. Name the source in parentheses under the title; or use a footnote number (superscript) following the title.

Table 4

Average Rainfall for Presidio County,
1960–1978
(U.S. Soil Conservation Service)

Table 3[12]

Comparative Accuracies of the Direct Smear,
Knott's, and Filtration Methods

7. Tables should not be continued onto a second page, but if this situation is inevitable, write, "continued" at the bottom of the first page and at the top of the second page. Repeat all column headings at the top of the second page of the table.

8. In using numerals in table columns, whole numbers should be aligned on the right-hand digits. Fractions should be aligned on the decimal point:

428	2.78
72	.05
1,043	4.99
6	10.73

However, if numbers are of mixed quantities (whole numbers and decimals of differing magnitudes) they should be centered in columns:

46
12.89
9.1
.03

FIGURES

The second major type of graphic presentation, figures, includes such frequently used visual aids as graphs—bar graphs, line graphs, pie graphs, and pictographs. Other kinds of figures are drawings, diagrams, flow charts, and pictures. Like formal tables, figures must have titles and numbers, but figure numbers are always Arabic. Most conventions governing tables apply to figures also.

Bar graphs are useful in comparing static quantities. The bar graph allows the reader to see immediate relationships among quantities. Bars may run either vertically or horizontally, but some quantities, such as altitudes, should logically be drawn vertically, while distances should be drawn horizontally.

In simple bar graphs, write captions on the bars or as close to them as possible. Use keys to bar graphs only when necessary, as in the following comparative bar graphs. On any bar graph, be sure to label both the horizontal and the vertical axes. See Figure 4-1.

Figure 4-1. Comparative Vertical Bar Graph

Distribution of Married and Unmarried
Respondents by Time of Attendance

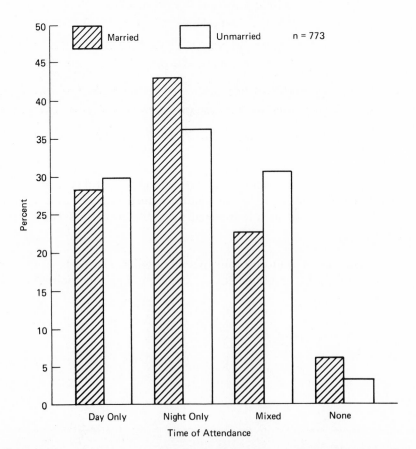

SOURCE: Thacker, "Impact of Graduate and Graduate Professional Education," p. 117.

136

Line graphs are best to present information which is not static, such as temperature, speed (mph and rpm), and voltage, all of which are operating continuously during the time they are being measured. However, line graphs may also be suitable for static quantities. See Figure 4-2.

Figure 4-2. Line Graph

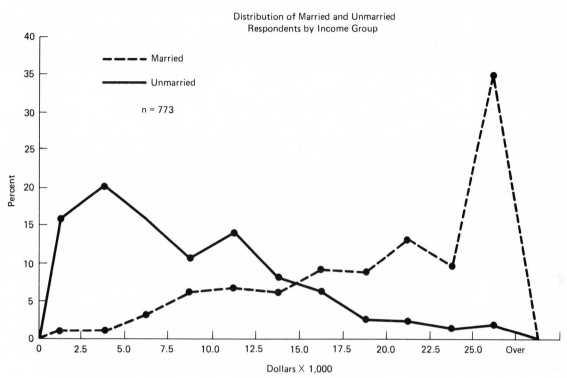

Distribution of Married and Unmarried
Respondents by Income Group

SOURCE: Thacker, "Impact of Graduate and Graduate Professional Education," p. 141.

In a line graph, the independent variable is placed on the horizontal (x) axis, and the dependent variable (y) is placed on the vertical axis. Figure 4-3, a line graph, shows changes in revolutions per minute of two engines. Imposing the line graph for engine A

Figure 4-3. Line Graph

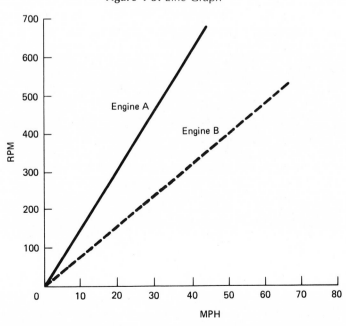

over the line graph for engine B allows easy comparison between the performance of both engines at the same speeds:

Circle graphs are used to convey proportion or percentages. In a circle graph, draw the largest segment beginning at 12 o'clock and proceed clockwise in descending size order of segments:

Figure 4-4. Circle Graph

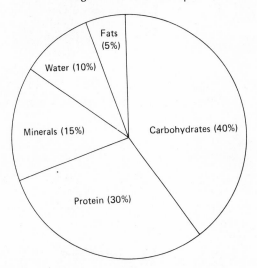

A circle graph cannot be used, however, if a large number of percentage segments must be shown. Labeling a large number of segments creates a cluttered graphic, which should always be avoided. To show how total household income is spent, as in Table 4-7, a table is the only practical choice because income is divided into fifteen categories:

Table 4-7

Salary Distribution After Annual Taxes

Item	Percentage
Rent	15%
Food	15
Car operation	12
Car maintenance	6
Utilities	7
Home improvements	5
Medical	5
Clothing	5
Lawn maintenance	5
Home insurance	5
Car insurance	5
Savings	5
Charities	2
Miscellaneous	4
Unallotted	3

Pictographs can provide effective ways of showing comparisons. However, in using pictographs, always be sure to keep symbols the same size to give the reader an exact idea of how quantities compare. For example, if a pictograph uses the same symbol in three sizes (see Figure 4-5), the reader cannot tell what ratios exist among A, B, and C:

138

Figure 4-5. Pictograph

The pictograph which uses equal size symbols, gives the reader a general estimate of the difference between rural and urban school enrollments over a five-year period in a given county:

Figure 4-6. Pictograph

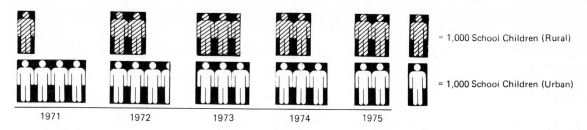

= 1,000 School Children (Rural)

= 1,000 School Children (Urban)

1971   1972   1973   1974   1975

Drawings and *diagrams* have one important advantage over photographs: they can include whatever detail the writer decides is necessary for the intended reader. Therefore, excessive visual details (inevitable if photographs are used) are removed from the visual. Sometimes photographs are desirable to give the reader an accurate, realistic view of what an object looks like. At other times, however, diagrams or drawings that include only selected parts of an object are more useful to the reader, particularly for instructional purposes. Service and specification manuals frequently incorporate drawings, diagrams, and photographs. See Figures 4-7 and 4-8.

Flow charts are an increasingly popular type of figure. Spatial arrangement of boxed information connected by lines can show relationships among various parts of an organization. Note in Figure 4-9 that the organizational structure is immediately apparent.

Flow charting is also effective in establishing and clarifying problem-solving methodology, as in the plan for a research project (Figure 4-10):

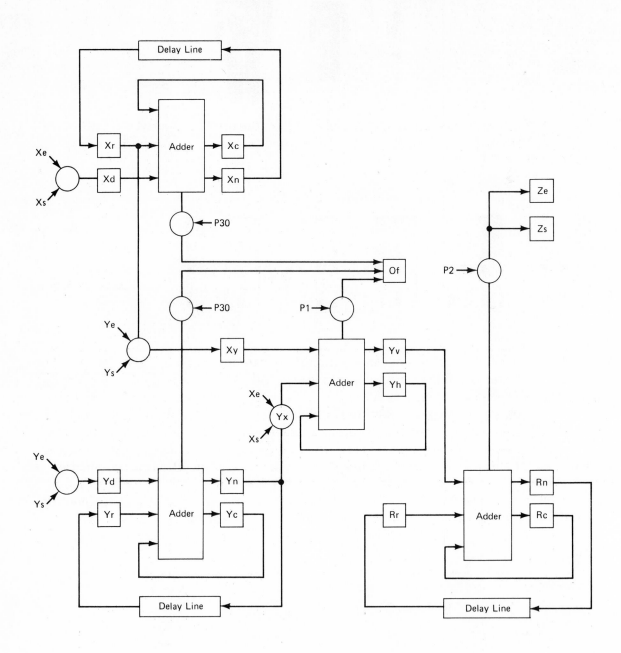

Figure 4-7. X, Y, and R Register Variable Multiplier (Block Diagram)

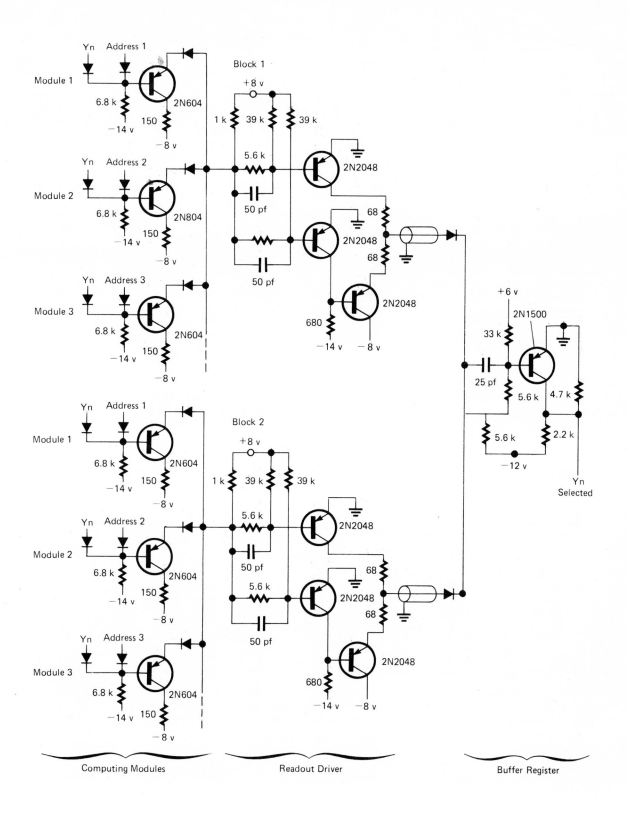

Figure 4-8. Readout Selection Gate (Schematic)

Computing Modules   Readout Driver   Buffer Register

141

Figure 4-9. Organizational Flow Chart

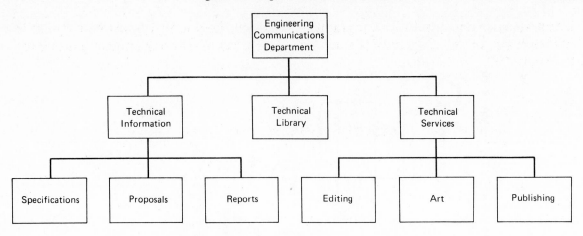

Figure 4-10. Research Project Flow Chart

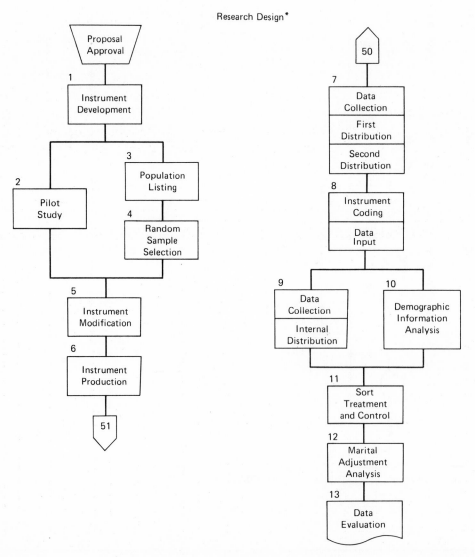

SOURCE: Thacker, "Impact of Graduate and Graduate Professional Education," pp. 50–51.

Many times, in constructing a bar graph or line graph, beginning the ordinate at zero is not necessary or not effective. For example, Table 4-8 shows average housing prices for the years 1965–1975:

Table 4-8

Average Housing Prices, Jones County
1965–1975

Year	Average Price
1965	$15,500
1966	16,000
1967	17,000
1968	18,500
1969	20,000
1970	23,000
1971	24,000
1972	26,000
1973	29,000
1974	32,000
1975	36,000

In presenting this information in a bar graph, beginning the ordinate at zero is unnecessary, as houses have never been free! In addition, beginning the ordinate at $10,000 prevents wasted area on the graph by keeping the bars from being unnecessarily tall. However, in beginning the ordinate at any point besides zero, be sure to caution the reader, to avoid seeming to be misleading.

Figure 4-11. Bar Graph

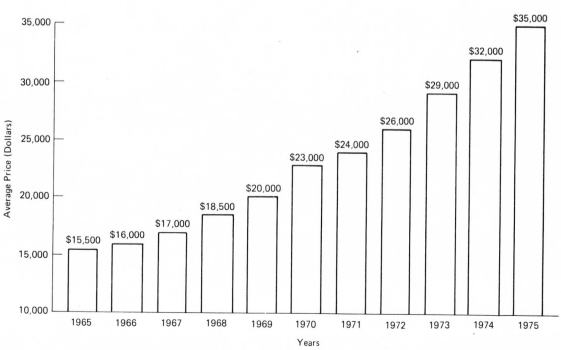

Frequently, suppressing the zero on a bar graph helps preserve the dramatic change that you want the graph to show. Assume, for example, that you want to show in a bar graph that the number of housing starts has decreased sharply during a three-year period:

Year	Number of Housing Starts
A	50,000
B	40,000
C	30,000

By *not* suppressing the zero on the bar graph, the decrease is not nearly as dramatic visually as the actual figures indicate. Remember: You want the visual presentation to reflect accurately the point you are trying to make.

Figure 4-12. Bar Graph (nonsuppression of zero)

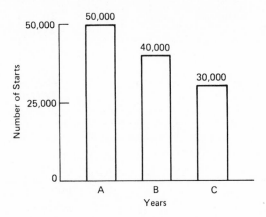

However, by suppressing the zero, you can make the decrease in housing starts appear as sharp as it actually is:

Figure 4-13. Bar Graph (suppression of zero)

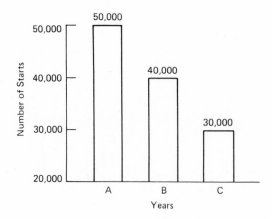

Many times you may wish to begin the ordinate at zero, but you may still wish to condense your graph, as in the table of average housing prices. In this case, you can eliminate the unnecessary area by drawing a break in the graph:

Figure 4-14. Bar Graph

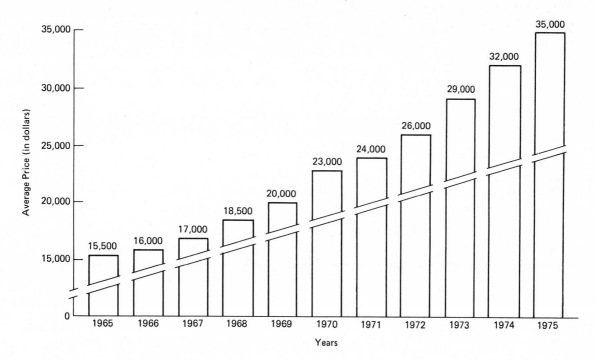

Condensing a line graph should be done as follows:

Figure 4-15. Line Graph

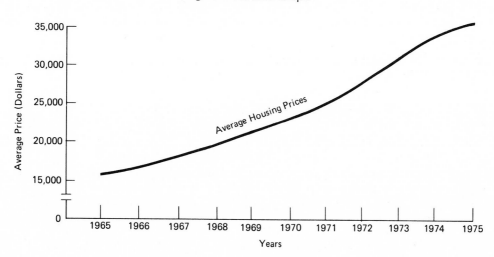

To reflect information on a line graph accurately, always choose a scale that preserves the magnitude of change you want to visualize. That is, avoid scales that either deemphasize or overemphasize changes in data. In the following example, the slope of the line can be controlled by simply adjusting the x and y axes:

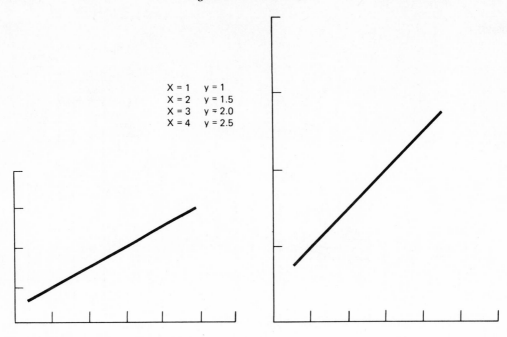

Figure 4-16. Line Graph

X = 1   y = 1
X = 2   y = 1.5
X = 3   y = 2.0
X = 4   y = 2.5

CONSIDERATIONS FOR CHOOSING
GRAPHIC TYPES

In deciding which type of graphic to use, consider three points: (1) the characteristics and limitations of each graphic type, (2) the purpose of the message, and (3) the level of the audience. Many times, as we have already seen, material can be presented in several different ways. Examine the following table and line graph, both of which show the miles per gallon recorded for three cars driven at the same speeds:

Table 4-9			
Fuel Efficiency Studies: Car A, Car B, and Car C			
	Miles Per Gallon		
Speed (mph)	Car A (390 c.i.)	Car B (251 c.i.)	Car C (209 c.i.)[a]
30	21.8	29.0	30.4
35	20.5	28.5	29.8
40	20.3	28.0	27.2
45	19.2	27.6	25.2
50	18.7	26.2	23.6
55	18.6	25.5	20.7
60	18.0	24.1	18.9
65	17.1	23.0	16.9
70	16.8	20.2	14.6
75	16.5	17.2	14.4
80	16.0	15.5	13.5[b]
85	15.1	15.1	—
90	14.4	13.1	—
[a]denotes engine sizes, cubic inches displacement			
[b]top speed capability			

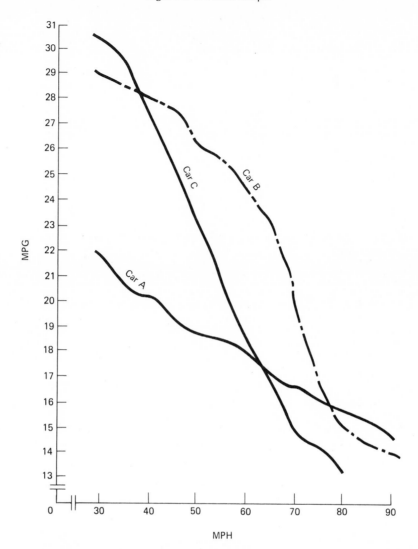

Figure 4-17. Line Graph

In these two graphic presentations of the same information, the line graph shows more quickly than the table the differences between the gas consumption of the cars at different speeds and the points at which the miles per gallon rate is the same. The same information could not have been presented in a comparative bar graph arrangement because 39 bars would have been required on the x axis (3 cars × 13 different speeds).

In other cases, the kind of graphic selected depends on the level of audience and the purpose of the entire presentation of which the graphic is a part. A technical audience generally responds better to (or even expects) line graphs, as texts in technical fields generally use linear presentation and tables. However, when giving oral presentations or writing to a general audience, use bar graphs, pictographs, circle graphs, diagrams, or flow charts, as they are more easily seen and have a more striking appearance than line graphs. Line graphs enable the writer to achieve greater exactness than do the other three types, but proportion and visual appeal are sometimes more desirable than exactness.

Frequently, tables are the only way to present information graphically because the information to be portrayed is not suitable for graphs. In such cases, plan tables to make them as effective as possible so that the audience can see at a glance the point of the graph. Table 4-10 shows how artistry affects the accessibility of material in a table.

Table 4-10

Survey of Topics Covered by Four
Technical Writing Texts

Topics Covered	Books Surveyed			
	A	B	C	D
Formal reports	Yes	Yes	Yes	Yes
Technical description	Yes	No	Yes	No
Process analysis	Yes	Yes	No	Yes
Instructions	No	No	Yes	Yes
Memos, Letters	No	Yes	No	Yes
Technical style	No	Yes	Yes	No
Audience analysis	No	No	No	Yes
Graphics	Yes	Yes	Yes	Yes
Oral presentations	No	No	Yes	Yes

The table is difficult to read because similarities and differences are hard to see. Restructured into a blocked table, the similarities and differences are easier to grasp, as in Table 4-11.

Table 4-11

Topics Covered	Book A	Book B	Book C	Book D
Formal reports	Yes			
Technical description	Yes	No	Yes	No
Process analysis	Yes		No	Yes
Instructions	No		Yes	
Memos, Letters	No	Yes	No	Yes
Style	No	Yes		No
Audience analysis	No			
Graphics	No	Yes	No	Yes

In this case, blocking responses produces a less cluttered, easier-to-read table. However, it can be improved further by switching the positions of the column headings (books) and line headings (topics covered). The restructured table assumes the following form, which better enables the reader to compare the contents of the four books and achieves the purpose of the table. This new arrangement. Table 4-12, allows the comparison to be made from left to right, following normal reading order.

Table 4-12

Books Surveyed	Topics Covered							
	Formal Reports	Technical Description	Process Analysis	Instruc-tions	Memos, Letters	Style	Audience Analysis	Graphics
A	Yes			No				
B	Yes	No	Yes	No	Yes		No	Yes
C	Yes		No	Yes	No	Yes	No	
D	Yes	No	Yes			No		Yes

WORK PROJECT 9

Graphics

1. The Howard Company, which manufactures fans, revealed in its annual report the following results of fan sales during the past ten years. During 1968, 2,300 floor fans and 1,400 ceiling fans were sold. In 1969, 2,250 floor fans and 1,350 ceiling fans were sold. The 1970 figures showed 2,200 floor fans sold and 1,300 ceiling fans sold. Sales figures for 1971–1979 were as follows: floor fans 2,300, ceiling fans 1,550 (1971); floor fans 2,400, ceiling fans 1,600 (1972); floor fans 2,450, ceiling fans, 2,000 (1973); floor fans 2,600, ceiling fans 2,300 (1974); floor fans 2,700, ceiling fans 2,550 (1975); floor fans 2,750, ceiling fans 2,600 (1976); floor fans 3,100, ceiling fans 2,700 (1977); floor fans 3,400, ceiling fans 2,900 (1978); floor fans 3,800, ceiling fans 3,500 (1979).

Express this data in a table, a bar graph, and a line graph, properly identifying all parts of each graphic. Use a separate sheet of paper for each of the three graphics.

2. A survey of students interested in a local junior college showed that 27 percent of the students were planning careers in business. Half of that number indicated a preference for management, while the other half indicated a desire to study marketing, personnel, and distribution. Thirty percent indicated a preference for teaching. Forty-three percent indicated a desire to enter technological fields. An overwhelming number of technology students (75 percent) indicated an interest in electronic technology, while the remaining respondents stated a preference for civil and mechanical technology.

Choose a graphic to express this data. Assume in preparing it that it will be part of a report to the board of regents.

3. In a recent laboratory test, five caulking compounds, either oil or acrylic latex type, were tested for four desirable qualities: (1) ease of application; (2) shrinkage; (3) resistance to mildew; and (4) resistance to dirt pickup. The results were as follows: Caulk A (oil) in quality (1) good; in quality (2) good; in quality (3) good; in quality (4) good. Caulk B (acrylic latex) in quality (1) good; in quality (2) good; in quality (3) poor; in quality (4) fair. Caulk C (oil) in (1) good; in (2) good; in (3) poor; in (4) fair. Caulk D (oil) in (1) fair; in (2) fair; in (3) good; in (4) fair. Caulk E (acrylic latex) in (1) good; in (2) good; in (3) good; in (4) fair.

Choose a graphic to express this data. Assume the report will be published in a consumer magazine.

4. As part of a proposal, Smith Technology Institute prepared a study showing the ratio of men to women in technology programs. In 1970, eight hundred students were enrolled in technology, which included mechanical and civil technology only. Of that number, seven hundred were men, and one hundred were women. By 1972, 850 students were enrolled in technology programs, which by then had added a third option in drafting. Of that number, only ninety were women. In 1974, a fourth technology option, electronics, had been added. Eleven hundred students were enrolled, of which 180 were women. By 1976, twelve hundred men and three hundred women were enrolled in technology, and by 1978, when automotive technology was added as a fifth option, fifteen hundred men and six hundred women were enrolled.

Express this data in a suitable graphic to be included in a promotional brochure for high school counselors.

5. At XYZ University, a survey was made of students taking technical writing during the 1977 spring semester. The purpose of the questionnaire was to draw a profile of the freshman composition background of these students.

The questionnaire asked three questions: Did you write a research paper in Composition I? Did you receive instruction in how to do research? Did you receive basic library instruction? In response to the first question, seventy-two students said "yes," and three said "no." In answering the second question, fifty-nine students said "yes," and sixteen said "no." In response to the third question, fifty-five students said "yes," and sixteen said "no." Some students, however, had not taken Composition I at XYZ University, as they had transferred from other colleges where they took the course. These students responded to the three questions as follows: 8—yes, 7—no (question 1); 2—yes, 13—no (question 2); 7—yes, 8—no (question 3). Students who took Composition I at a junior college stated the following: 17—yes, 10—no (question 1); 13—yes, 20—no (question 2); 13—yes, 14—no (question 3).

Prepare a graphic to show the results of the questionnaire. Assume the graphic will be used by the curriculum committee for course analysis purposes.

6. A national marketing society with affiliate chapters in high schools, colleges, and junior colleges across the United States decided to attempt an analysis of membership patterns. The society's national officers became interested in determining two points: (1) in what geographic areas are changes in membership taking place; and (2) in what membership categories are changes in membership taking place? The national president of Beta Marketing Society decided to analyze 1976, 1977, 1978, and 1979 membership figures to answer these two questions. The following data were compiled by computer to record the membership profiles desired by the society. See pages 158 to 161. Use these four printouts to approach the membership analysis problems in Category I, Category II, and Category III.

The geographic regions of the society are as follows:

NE (Northeast)	E (East)	SE (Southeast)
Connecticut	Delaware	District of Columbia
Maine	Maryland	Kentucky
Massachusetts	New Jersey	North Carolina
New Hampshire	New York	Tennessee
Rhode Island	Pennsylvania	Virginia
Vermont		West Virginia

S (South)	NC (North Central)	C (Central)
Alabama	Illinois	Colorado
Florida	Michigan	Indiana
Georgia	Minnesota	Iowa
South Carolina	North Dakota	Missouri
	Ohio	Nebraska
	South Dakota	
	Wisconsin	

SC (South Central)	NW (Northwest)	SW (Southwest)
Arkansas	Idaho	Arizona
Kansas	Montana	California
Louisiana	Oregon	Nevada
Mississippi	Utah	New Mexico
Oklahoma	Washington	Texas
	Wyoming	

PROBLEMS—CATEGORY I

1.0   Develop nine tables displaying membership information for junior colleges in all nine regions for 1976–1979.

1.1   Develop one table displaying total junior college membership (using totals for nine regions) for 1976–1979.

1.2   Write a paragraph analyzing junior college membership patterns for 1976–1979.

1.3   Write a report to the membership vice president for junior college recruitment, Ms. Susan Snell, explaining your findings.

154

2.0 Develop nine tables each displaying membership information for four-year colleges in one of the nine regions for 1976–1979.

2.1 Develop one table displaying total four-year college membership (using totals for nine regions) for 1976–1979.

2.2 Write a paragraph about four-year college membership in all nine regions for 1976–1979.

2.3 Write a report to the membership vice president for college recruitment, Mr. Dan Bunker, explaining your findings.

3.0 Develop nine tables each displaying membership information for high schools in one of the nine regions for 1976–1979.

3.1 Develop one table displaying total high school membership (using totals for nine regions) for 1976–1979.

3.2 Write a paragraph analyzing high school membership patterns, 1976–1979.

3.3 Write a report to the membership vice president for high school recruitment, Ms. Sally Hicks, explaining your findings.

4.0 Write a report to the membership vice president for recruitment, Mr. Lawrence Kelley, describing changes in high school, junior college, and college membership patterns for 1976–1979. The distribution list should include Ms. Susan Snell, Ms. Sally Hicks, and Mr. Dan Bunker (see 1.3, 2.3, 3.3).

PROBLEMS—CATEGORY II

1.0 Examine total enrollment figures for 1976, 1977, 1978, and 1979.

Draw 4 circle graphs, one for each year, showing what percentages of the total membership were attributed to high schools, junior colleges, and colleges.

1.1 Examine enrollment figures of the SW region for 1976–1979. Draw four circle graphs showing what percentage of each year's total was attributed to high schools, junior colleges, and colleges.

(Before developing the circle graphs, present the data in a table.)

1.2 Repeat 1.1 for NW.

1.3 Repeat 1.1 for NC.

1.4 Repeat 1.1 for C.

1.5 Repeat 1.1 for SC.

1.6　Repeat 1.1 for NE.

1.7　Repeat 1.1 for E.

1.8　Repeat 1.1 for S.

1.9　Repeat 1.1 for SE.

2.0　Draw a comparative bar graph showing comparative figures for colleges, junior colleges, and high schools for 1976–1979 for the SC region.

2.1　Repeat 2.0 for the NC region.

2.2　Repeat 2.0 for the C region.

2.3　Repeat 2.0 for the NE region.

2.4　Repeat 2.0 for the E region.

2.5　Repeat 2.0 for the SE region.

2.6　Repeat 2.0 for the S region.

2.7　Repeat 2.0 for the NW region.

2.8　Repeat 2.0 for the SW region.

PROBLEMS—CATEGORY III

1.0　Develop a table displaying all membership information for the S region, 1976–1979.

1.1　Based on this table, write a paragraph analyzing membership changes in the S region, 1976–1979.

1.2　Draw a line graph (placing data for all four states on one graph) showing total membership for each S region state for 1976–1979.

2.0　Develop a table displaying membership information for the NE states, 1976–1979.

2.1　Based on this table, write a paragraph analyzing membership changes in the NE region, 1976–1979.

2.2　Draw a line graph (placing data for all six states on one graph) showing total membership for each state in the NE region, 1976–1979.

3.0　Write a paragraph comparing membership in the NE region and the S region for 1976–1979.

3.1　Develop a suitable graph to accompany this analysis.

156

4.0 Repeat problems 1 and 2 for the SW states and the E states.

4.1 Compare the membership patterns for the SW region and the E region.

4.2 Develop a suitable graphic to accompany the analysis in 4.1.

5.0 Based on the analysis of these four regions, what membership pattern seems to be developing?

5.1 Analyze the membership pattern for the C region, then for the SC region. Develop a table for each region. Then write a paragraph analyzing the data.

5.2 Does this table support or refute the pattern established by comparing the NE region with the S region and comparing the SW region with the E region?

6.0 Analyze membership patterns for each remaining geographic region. Write a report to the national membership president, Mr. Joe Kyle Morgan, showing the pattern of membership for the society for the last four years, 1976–1979. The distribution list for the report is as follows:

Mary Lynn Howard	NE	Hartford, Connecticut
Gerald Hawkins	E	Albany, New York
John Hayer	S	Tallahassee, Florida
Annette Nuchols	SE	Chattanooga, Tennessee
Melinda Drake	NC	Chicago, Illinois
Paula Francis	C	Denver, Colorado
Richard Gonzales	SC	Kansas City, Kansas
Ronnie Simpson	NW	Tacoma, Washington
Dorris Langley	SW	Tucson, Arizona

State	High School CHAP	MEM	Jr. College CHAP	MEM	College CHAP	MEM	TOTAL
Alabama	8	98	0	0	0	0	98
Alaska	0	0	0	0	0	0	0
Arizona	53	2430	0	0	0	0	2430
Arkansas	34	1670	0	0	0	0	1670
California	37	812	0	0	0	0	812
Colorado	74	3490	5	46	1	17	3553
Connecticut	83	3735	7	210	3	85	4030
D.C.	14	394	0	0	0	0	394
Delaware	23	618	3	35	0	0	653
Florida	160	6423	15	575	2	35	7033
Georgia	101	4200	5	75	1	13	4288
Hawaii	5	129	0	0	0	0	129
Idaho	22	965	4	50	0	0	1015
Illinois	145	2855	1	10	0	0	2865
Indiana	102	4100	2	32	3	45	4177
Iowa	56	1499	10	270	1	15	1784
Kansas	69	1390	10	204	0	0	1594
Kentucky	109	5100	8	95	0	0	5195
Louisiana	83	2804	0	0	0	0	2804
Maine	16	242	0	0	2	48	290
Maryland	48	1560	4	110	0	0	1670
Massachusetts	165	2541	2	48	2	26	2515
Michigan	145	2965	13	279	0	0	3244
Minnesota	97	2910	24	670	4	50	3630
Mississippi	68	2230	11	388	1	16	2634
Missouri	118	5932	5	120	0	0	6052
Montana	15	500	0	0	0	0	500
Nebraska	41	1898	2	23	0	0	1921
Nevada	5	165	0	0	0	0	165
New Hampshire	24	620	2	45	0	0	665
New Jersey	220	6004	5	138	1	46	6188
New Mexico	28	1764	0	0	1	13	1777
New York	143	4240	18	470	2	88	4798
No. Carolina	206	8228	0	0	1	16	8244
No. Dakota	23	841	6	119	3	78	1038
Ohio	375	8186	0	0	2	26	8212
Oklahoma	63	3004	0	0	2	19	3023
Oregon	39	1063	3	35	0	0	1098
Pennsylvania	144	6630	4	162	3	121	6913
Rhode Island	21	850	4	138	0	0	988
So. Carolina	130	2584	0	0	0	0	2584
So. Dakota	25	790	0	0	1	29	819
Tennessee	149	7555	0	0	2	40	7595
Texas	662	18,141	14	488	2	18	18,647
Utah	40	1810	6	180	0	0	1990
Vermont	14	350	0	0	0	0	350
Virginia	320	9773	0	0	4	135	9908
Washington	223	4994	11	300	2	30	5324
West Virginia	56	1842	0	0	0	0	1842
Wisconsin	97	5300	17	750	2	20	6070
Wyoming	22	940	6	170	4	78	1188
TOTALS	4898	159,161	221	6235	48	1107	166,403

From: National President of Beta Marketing Society.

State	High School CHAP	High School MEM	Jr. College CHAP	Jr. College MEM	College CHAP	College MEM	TOTAL
Alabama	9	110	0	0	0	0	110
Alaska	0	0	0	0	0	0	0
Arizona	55	2500	0	0	0	0	2500
Arkansas	34	1695	0	0	0	0	1695
California	40	920	6	300	0	0	1220
Colorado	74	3488	5	40	1	18	3546
Connecticut	80	3600	6	180	3	55	3835
D.C.	12	360	0	0	0	0	360
Delaware	20	604	3	38	0	0	642
Florida	164	6680	17	600	2	23	7303
Georgia	112	4655	6	85	2	23	4763
Hawaii	8	178	0	0	0	0	178
Idaho	23	980	4	62	0	0	1042
Illinois	145	2840	0	0	0	0	2840
Indiana	103	4120	2	41	3	49	4210
Iowa	56	1521	13	330	1	18	1869
Kansas	68	1380	7	210	0	0	1590
Kentucky	109	5125	8	100	2	45	5270
Louisiana	90	3005	0	0	0	0	3005
Maine	15	212	0	0	2	37	249
Maryland	50	1620	4	115	0	0	1735
Massachusetts	160	2440	2	38	1	19	2497
Michigan	146	2944	13	275	0	0	3219
Minnesota	97	3303	26	700	4	54	4057
Mississippi	72	2577	12	404	1	20	3001
Missouri	119	5980	5	135	1	16	6131
Montana	16	509	0	0	0	0	509
Nebraska	40	1871	2	16	0	0	1887
Nevada	4	160	0	0	0	0	160
New Hampshire	22	590	2	21	0	0	611
New Jersey	212	5810	5	120	1	49	5979
New Mexico	30	1820	1	10	1	9	1839
New York	139	3936	17	422	2	74	4432
No. Carolina	210	8433	0	0	2	20	8453
No. Dakota	23	812	6	101	2	38	951
Ohio	376	8190	0	0	2	24	8214
Oklahoma	64	3005	0	0	2	22	3027
Oregon	39	1006	3	40	0	0	1046
Pennsylvania	140	6480	4	150	3	100	6730
Rhode Island	18	742	4	115	0	0	857
So. Carolina	133	2739	0	0	0	0	2739
So. Dakota	24	790	0	0	1	20	810
Tennessee	149	7510	0	0	2	35	7545
Texas	671	18550	15	521	2	22	19,093
Utah	40	1800	6	175	1	19	1994
Vermont	12	294	0	0	0	0	294
Virginia	323	9856	0	0	4	105	9961
Washington	223	4988	11	290	2	28	5306
West Virginia	57	1877	0	0	0	0	1877
Wisconsin	98	5325	17	768	2	33	6126
Wyoming	23	1000	6	199	4	96	1295
TOTALS	4924	160,930	232	6596	52	1071	168,597

State	High School		Jr. College		College		TOTAL
	CHAP	MEM	CHAP	MEM	CHAP	MEM	
Alabama	10	120	0	0	1	9	129
Alaska	0	0	0	0	0	0	0
Arizona	57	2560	0	0	1	8	2568
Arkansas	36	1740	0	0	0	0	1740
California	44	1130	7	328	1	8	1466
Colorado	74	3498	5	50	1	20	3568
Connecticut	78	3462	6	150	3	38	3650
D.C.	11	332	0	0	0	0	332
Delaware	19	552	4	50	0	0	602
Florida	168	6970	19	650	2	20	7640
Georgia	114	4728	6	94	2	22	4844
Hawaii	11	230	0	0	0	0	230
Idaho	23	990	4	65	0	0	1055
Illinois	145	2880	0	0	0	0	2880
Indiana	103	4130	2	50	3	51	4231
Iowa	57	1524	13	333	1	18	1875
Kansas	69	1400	12	250	0	0	1650
Kentucky	114	5550	9	114	2	40	5704
Louisiana	95	3420	1	15	0	0	3435
Maine	12	185	0	0	2	19	204
Maryland	52	1650	4	125	0	0	1775
Massachusetts	157	2270	2	30	1	12	2312
Michigan	146	2980	15	311	1	10	3301
Minnesota	98	3329	29	740	4	55	4124
Mississippi	77	2824	14	460	1	25	3309
Missouri	120	6140	5	137	2	30	6307
Montana	17	541	0	0	0	0	541
Nebraska	39	1810	1	19	0	0	1829
Nevada	4	148	0	0	1	14	162
New Hampshire	20	550	1	13	0	0	563
New Jersey	209	5772	4	90	1	50	5912
New Mexico	31	1840	1	10	1	8	1858
New York	138	3875	16	365	2	55	4295
No. Carolina	217	8766	0	0	2	21	8787
No. Dakota	22	780	5	100	1	31	911
Ohio	376	8216	1	19	3	30	8265
Oklahoma	64	3040	0	0	2	28	3068
Oregon	39	1055	3	40	0	0	1095
Pennsylvania	138	6290	3	128	3	80	6498
Rhode Island	16	580	3	95	1	27	702
So. Carolina	135	2942	0	0	0	0	2942
So. Dakota	23	770	0	0	1	13	783
Tennessee	149	7443	0	0	2	30	7473
Texas	676	19,300	16	560	3	25	19,885
Utah	40	1760	6	188	1	20	1968
Vermont	11	260	0	0	0	0	260
Virginia	325	9900	1	12	4	110	10,022
Washington	223	5009	11	280	2	27	5316
West Virginia	58	1930	0	0	1	29	1959
Wisconsin	98	5340	17	780	2	42	6162
Wyoming	25	1060	6	208	4	128	1396
TOTALS	4958	163,571	309	6859	61	1153	171,583

State	High School		Jr. College		College		
	CHAP	MEM	CHAP	MEM	CHAP	MEM	TOTAL
Alabama	16	380	0	0	2	23	403
Alaska	10	123	0	0	0	0	123
Arizona	58	2587	0	0	1	9	2596
Arkansas	36	1763	0	0	0	0	1763
California	48	1290	8	350	1	8	1648
Colorado	74	3496	5	49	1	21	3566
Connecticut	76	3306	5	123	2	27	3456
D.C.	9	295	0	0	0	0	295
Delaware	18	475	4	89	1	10	574
Florida	172	7143	20	670	2	39	7852
Georgia	122	5089	7	103	2	26	5218
Hawaii	12	273	0	0	0	0	273
Idaho	23	1084	4	68	1	15	1167
Illinois	145	2887	0	0	0	0	2887
Indiana	105	4138	3	54	3	57	4249
Iowa	57	1528	15	316	1	17	1861
Kansas	69	1404	15	287	1	12	1703
Kentucky	115	5563	9	123	3	65	5751
Louisiana	103	3748	1	27	0	0	3775
Maine	11	179	0	0	0	0	179
Maryland	54	1708	4	119	0	0	1827
Massachusetts	151	2231	2	16	0	0	2247
Michigan	148	2993	15	314	2	25	3332
Minnesota	98	3348	30	802	4	61	4211
Mississippi	80	3234	15	483	1	31	3748
Missouri	122	6298	5	142	2	38	6478
Montana	18	569	0	0	1	15	584
Nebraska	39	1736	1	13	0	0	1749
Nevada	4	143	0	0	0	0	143
New Hampshire	19	529	0	0	0	0	529
New Jersey	206	5392	4	76	3	96	5564
New Mexico	32	1858	0	0	1	9	1867
New York	138	3728	15	369	2	31	4128
No. Carolina	219	8917	0	0	3	32	8949
No. Dakota	20	746	5	104	1	20	870
Ohio	376	8203	1	24	3	26	8253
Oklahoma	64	3068	1	22	2	34	3124
Oregon	39	1065	3	35	1	12	1112
Pennsylvania	137	6242	3	105	3	64	6411
Rhode Island	14	460	3	86	0	0	546
So. Carolina	136	3067	1	16	0	0	3083
So. Dakota	23	766	0	0	0	0	766
Tennessee	149	7339	0	0	2	25	7364
Texas	680	19,494	18	610	3	43	20,147
Utah	40	1714	6	198	1	23	1935
Vermont	10	234	0	0	0	0	234
Virginia	327	9925	0	0	4	90	10,015
Washington	223	5004	11	279	2	24	5307
West Virginia	59	2023	0	0	1	31	2054
Wisconsin	98	5333	18	789	2	58	6180
Wyoming	30	1180	6	225	4	165	1570
TOTALS	5172	169,493	272	7086	66	1273	177,852

5

Reports: Informal and Formal

THE INTRODUCTION

As it is with letters, organization is also the most important characteristic of *technical* writing. Every document must be carefully organized to insure the clarity and accessibility of information. Therefore, technical reports are generally divided into three basic parts: introduction, discussion, and conclusion. What each of these main sections includes will vary, depending on the type of report, but a good introduction is the most important part of any report. After reading the introduction, the reader should know the following information:

1. subject of the report

2. pertinent background information

3. major points to be discussed

4. purpose of the report

The example introduction on the next page incorporates all four elements:

The petroleum industry uses two major types of machinery that require alignment—reciprocating compressors and centrifugal compressor trains.

A reciprocating compressor is similar to an automobile engine. The compressor has pistons and cylinders along with compressor cylinders on one side of the engine block. The compressors are approximately the size of a V8 engine with the engine measuring twenty to forty feet long. Reciprocating compressors must be aligned to prevent the crankcase from sagging and twisting. If the crankcase is sagging or twisted, pressure on the crankshaft will cause premature wear on the bearings and possibly break the crankshaft.

A reciprocating compressor can be aligned in two ways. The first means of alignment used was the wire method, which consisted of tightly stretching a wire from one end of the compressor to the other and measuring the distance from the bearing saddle to the wire. This procedure is repeated at each bearing saddle. The second method, optical alignment, consists of two targets fixed at each end of the compressor. A line of sight at the two targets is established by looking through a telescope. A third target is placed on a bearing saddle, and the distance off the line of sight is measured. This procedure is repeated at each bearing saddle. Once the amount of misalignment is determined, corrections can be made. Given two alignment methods, which one is better?

A centrifugal compressor train consists of a motor, gearcase, and one or more compressors. Each machine is linked to the next by coupling shafts. Couplings are connected to the main shaft between two machines. Centrifugal compressor trains need to be aligned to reduce vibration between components in the train. If misalignment exceeds the allowable tolerances, coupling failure will result, with possible damage to the bearings. Each machine in a compressor train operates at a different temperature, causing thermal growth to vary between machines. The variation in thermal growth causes misalignment because each machine rises a different distance with relationship to the temperature. Misalignment must be corrected to eliminate vibration which damages the bearings in the machine and eventually breaks the couplings.

Alignment of centrifugal compressor trains is done by establishing where a machine is located in relationship to other machines in the train. Before startup, this is called a cold check. After the machine is hot, the locations are rechecked. By comparing the cold check to the hot check, the amount of misalignment can be determined. Two methods can be used to align compressor trains, mechanical and optical. The mechanical method uses reverse indicator readings for both the cold and hot checks. The optical method reverses indicator readings for only the cold. The problem is to determine which method is better, mechanical or optical.

The purpose of this report is (1) to describe alignment procedures and (2) to show how optical alignment has changed the original methods and reduced the cost of alignment.

Subject
Topics 1, 2

Technical
Background
(Topic 1)

Major Point
(Topic 1)

Technical
Background
(Topic 2)

Major Point
(Topic 2)
Purpose
of the
Report

163

In long introductions, to further aid your reader, you may wish to provide a heading for each part, as in the following example:

Definition

Few management concepts have received more attention and caused as much confusion as Management by Objectives. MBO is a system involving a cycle that begins with a study of the organization's goals. One of the fundamental assumptions of MBO is that an organization can be understood as a hierarchy of goals. The management task is essentially one of collectively formulating specific objectives and organizing activities to accomplish these objectives. Therefore, MBO is closely associated with many organizational processes such as planning, motivation, control, and change. MBO is an umbrella concept which attempts to relate a set of formal organizational goals to a set of performance standards, whether at the individual or organizational level.

MBO is thought of as a series of phases or stages in the annual cycle of a planning-result environment. As the process is renewed annually, it builds on the prior year's planning and results. Understanding MBO requires analysis and understanding of its four major management stages: (1) goal setting, (2) action planning, (3) implementation of goals, and (4) periodic appraisals.

Background

Peter Drucker is usually credited with the MBO concept, which is now about twenty-five years old. It has been applied to all kinds of organizations, large and small, public and private, domestic and foreign, profit and nonprofit. This diversity of application allows researchers to study MBO in a variety of settings. The author of a study done about ten years ago expected a widespread change in managerial behavior because of MBO. He observed that MBO was in such general use that no company could claim to be "modern" if it did not profess to practice MBO. The early application of MBO was rather limited and focused primarily on appraisal of individuals. Later, the motivational aspects were also recognized. MBO was seen as a way to integrate personal needs with organizational demands.

Purpose

Some people believe that MBO is the answer to all of a manager's problems. Others see it as a useful tool, but one with shortcomings and problems of its own. The purpose of this report is to describe MBO and analyze the effectiveness of the system, its process and philosophy, by noting its advantages and disadvantages as revealed by current research.

VALUE OF HEADINGS

The use of headings and subheadings throughout the report is a major characteristic of technical writing. Headings in reports achieve the following goals:

1. As in the example introduction above, headings enable the reader to locate information quickly. Because most kinds of technical writing are not read from beginning to end, headings help the reader find needed information without groping through paragraphs of unbroken print.

2. Headings also help the reader see the total structure and layout of the report.

3. Headings help the writer organize the material logically.

KINDS OF REPORTS

The basic organizational pattern of reports—introduction, discussion, and conclusion—can be seen by examining three different kinds of reports: (1) reports that explain, analyze, or describe processes, problems, or procedures; (2) reports that describe mechanisms; and (3) sets of instructions which may occur as part of a longer report or be written specifically to enable a reader to perform a certain process or procedure or to operate a mechanism. Many times these basic types are combined, as in operation manuals for mechanisms. In this report type, the parts of the mechanism are described, and a set of operating instructions follows. The recommendation report and the feasibility report are both types of analytical reports. (The instructions report in this chapter is basically a recommendation for improving an office's filing system. The report gives instructions for carrying out the recommendation.)

All the plans given for the basic report types are only suggested approaches. Whenever you develop any report, consider audience, purpose, and content; then develop a plan to meet these needs. However, no matter what plan you develop, your report should generally have three basic divisions: introduction, discussion, and conclusion. To be sure that your report is off to a good start, develop a well-organized plan and write your introduction carefully so that your reader is prepared for the main discussion and fully understands the subject, background, procedure, and report purpose.

ANALYZING THE AUDIENCE

As stated in Chapter 1, the writer should always clearly define the following factors before beginning any report, even the plan for the report:

1. the purpose in writing the report;

2. the primary reader—the person to whom the report is addressed;

3. the primary reader's characteristics—educational background, job responsibilities, attitude toward the report topic;

4. the actions or responses required of the primary reader after reading the report;

5. the secondary readers—individuals who are affected by the report, in some cases even more so than the primary reader;

6. the secondary readers' background, attitudes, and responsibilities;

7. the life of the report—how long it will be useful and available to readers both known and unknown.

Before beginning any report, always complete the report analysis page shown in Chapter 1. Analyzing your audience according to the criteria above helps insure that your report is effective, that it achieves its goal, and that you have developed the information with your readers' interests and attitudes in mind. Never begin to write any business communication without having your purpose and your audience clearly determined. While audience and purpose determine the content of your message, they will also direct the style you use: the level of diction or technical jargon, the length of the sentences, the kind of visual aids needed, and even the length of the paragraphs in the report.

As mentioned in Chapter 2 in the discussion of active and passive voice, passive voice is often used in technical reports, such as process analysis. Basically, process analysis uses passive voice because the action rather than the actor is the focal point of the report. However, active voice is clearly effective in descriptions of many processes, procedures, or actions in series, particularly when the specific agent performing the action is vital to the success of the operation. Active voice descriptions are more concise and easier for the reader to visualize, as active sentences portray an agent performing an action. Generally, you should try to use active voice in process analysis and all reports whenever possible, but always try to avoid continued use of passive voice only. The following excerpt from a process description entitled "Pollarding in Pecan Wood" shows effective use of active voice. The writer emphasizes the role of the horticulturist because his expertise is essential to the success of the pollarding process.

> . . . The horticulturist binds these lengths of graftwood into bundles of ten tied with string. This number allows him easy inventory of the stocks he takes. He then dips each end of the bundle into warm melted paraffin or wax to prevent excessive drying. If the graftwood loses too much moisture it will not take when it is grafted. He places the graftwood in a polyethylene bag and packs a moist medium, such as sphagnum moss or sawdust, around the graftwood to prevent further drying.
>
> The horticulturist then places the bags of graftwood in cold storage to keep the wood in a dormant state. He must keep the temperature between thirty and forty-five degrees. If the temperature goes below thirty degrees F., the cold will damage the cell structure of the graftwood. If the temperature exceeds forty-five degrees F., the graftwood will grow until it uses all available food reserves.

Frequently, however, passive is more appropriate and more natural than active voice. The following sections are taken from a process description entitled "How to Prepare a Compost Pile." Since this procedure can be done by almost anyone, the emphasis is placed on the action. Therefore, the sentences are structured in passive voice:

Preparing an Area for the Compost Pile

. . . In selecting a spot for the compost pile, an area of relatively high ground, ranging from four to eight feet square, is chosen. High ground is chosen to allow better drainage of the pile. If water is allowed to stand for too long, the pile may give off an undesirable odor. After an area has been selected, it is cleared of any grass, roots, or debris that may hinder the quality of the compost mixture. No weed killers or poisons of any kind should be used to clear the area because the poison may be absorbed into the mixture and harm other plants.

Assembling the Pit

The pit is made by arranging four railroad cross-ties in a square over the cleared area. For added depth and more compost, four additional cross-ties may be stacked on the first four ties. These railroad cross-ties can be held in place by hammering three small stakes along the outside of each cross-tie. To keep the compost pile more attractive and neat, continuous weeding is required. . . .

Process analysis is a type of report which may be used to describe a procedure or analyze cause-effect relationships within procedures or processes. It is sometimes used to analyze situations. Like any report, the process report should have three main divisions: introduction, discussion, and conclusion. The following outline is a suggested plan for organizing a process analysis report:

I. Introduction
   A. Definition and/or purpose of the process
   B. Background information (where, when, why, by whom performed; principles of operation)
   C. Materials and working conditions required
   D. Precautions concerning safety and/or quality control
   E. Main steps in the process (list)
   F. Purpose of the report
II. Description of the Process
   A. Description of step 1
      1. purpose and/or definition
      2. materials needed to perform step 1
      3. description or analysis of step 1
   B., C., D., etc. Description of steps 2, 3, 4, etc.
III. Summary — Description of the Entire Process
IV. Conclusion — Value or Significance of the Process

The following examples show how the process analysis plan can be used to develop different kinds of process reports. The first example by a technology lab assistant, supplements a metallurgy laboratory manual which is periodically checked and revised by technology faculty. They are interested in all laboratory manuals and supplements being as clear and effective as possible, to reduce laboratory procedure errors and safety hazards. The writer's purpose was to familiarize students (sophomore technology students) in the metals lab with the process of preparing samples. The writer wants to do so before giving students specific oral and written instructions on how to perform the process by using all equipment. After reading the process analysis, the student should understand the steps in the process and be ready for specific instructions given by the lab assistant during class. Most students enrolled in the metals lab are interested in metallurgy as an option.

METALLOGRAPHIC SAMPLE PREPARATION

Introduction

Metallography is the study of metals by examining them under a microscope. The microscopic examination of metals reveals many useful facts about their content and structure. For example, the metallographic examination of a metal can establish its identity, give an approximation of its carbon content, show its grain size and structure, reveal defects and inclusions, and provide an indication of the metal's heat treatment history. The list of materials necessary to prepare a metallographic sample is as follows:

1. Abrasive cutoff machine

2. Specimen mounting press

3. Abrasive wheels with 60-, 120-, 180-, 240-grit sizes

4. Waterproof silicon carbide paper with 240-, 320-, 400-, and 600-grit sizes

5. Aluminum oxide

6. Low-Nap nylon cloth

7. Ethyl alcohol

8. Nitric acid

One must first prepare the sample by carefully polishing and etching it with the correct acid solution to examine the sample of metal and gain useful information. A poorly prepared metal sample would be of little value for examination; therefore, a quality specimen is necessary. The preparation process involves the following steps:

1. sectioning
2. mounting
3. coarse grinding

4. fine grinding
5. polishing
6. etching

The purpose of this process description is to familiarize you with the process of preparing metallographic samples. At our next class meeting we will actually prepare a sample. You will receive specific instructions for doing so at that time.

Sectioning

The purpose of sectioning is to cut off a suitable-size sample of metal. The sample must be cut so that the surface is flat, free of inclusions, and unburned. In this process, the metal specimen is cut by using an abrasive cutoff machine. The cutting device is a rotating disc consisting of abrasive particles bonded in a synthetic compound. The disc is very thin and rotates at a rapid speed. The heat of friction causes the bond to break down at a controlled rate, which provides the sharp abrasive grains to cut the metal. The preparation of a flat, inclusion-free, unburned surface involves selecting the correct wheel, uniform specimen cooling, and a constant uniform cutting pressure. Several varieties of wheels are available, ranging from those designed to cut very hard metals to those that will cut softer materials. The manufacturer's recommendations should be followed to insure that the correct wheel for the metal to be cut is used. Cooling is provided by a water-soluble coolant which flows over the wheel and cutting surface. Proper adjustment of the coolant flow is critical to prevent overheating the specimen. Although some sectioning machines have automatic cutting pressure, most are designed so that the cutting pressure is applied by hand. In this case, a firm, steady, even amount of pressure throughout the cut is required. Too much pressure will ruin the specimen.

Mounting

Most of the time, metal samples are too small to be held in the hand as they are ground and polished. Even if they were too large, the heat from the grinding process would make them too hot to hold. Therefore, metallographic samples are mounted to make them easy to hold. This mounting also protects the edges of the sample in case further examination is necessary. Compression molding is the most often used technique for mounting specimens. This process involves placing the specimen into a mold chamber of a specimen mounting press, along with a suitable quantity of mounting resin called Bakelite powder. The specimen and powder are then subjected to heat and pressure, causing the powder to form a hard synthetic base around the specimen.

Coarse Grinding

Coarse grinding involves a series of operations in which the specimen is exposed to several different sizes of abrasives. The purpose of coarse grinding is to remove the deformations caused by sectioning. A typical coarse grinding procedure would be to grind successively the sample on abrasive wheels starting with 60-grit, and continuing with 120-, 180-, and finally 240-grit paper. Each successive step is designed to remove deformations caused by the preceding step. The techniques involved are keeping the specimen flat on the wheel; applying steady, even pressure; moving the specimen steadily back and forth across the abrasive surface; and knowing when to go on to the next step. The best way to learn these techniques is to practice.

Fine Grinding

The purpose of fine grinding is to remove the large deformations caused by sectioning and rough grinding. As the larger layer is removed, a smaller, shallower deformation area is formed. This deformation is not as bad or as deep as the one caused by rough grinding. As successive applications of a finer abrasive are applied, the depth of the deformation will gradually lessen to the point that the remaining deformation can be removed by polishing. Therefore, waterproof silicon carbide papers in grit sizes 240, 320, 400, and 600 are used consecutively. Water is used for lubrication and for washing abrasive particles from the paper. Each step of the process must be carried out long enough to insure that all scratches from the previous step have been removed and replaced by finer scratches. A good technique is to rotate the specimen ninety degrees after each step.

Polishing

The last two steps in removing the deformations and exposing the microstructure are rough polishing and final polishing. Both steps are performed on rotating wheels, using low-nap nylon cloth surfaces covered with abrasive powders or liquids. Different types of abrasives are used for each step. Aluminum oxide is a typical abrasive for ferrous metals. Other abrasives often used are diamond paste, chromium oxide, and magnesium oxide.

Rough polishing must be sufficient to remove all the abrasive deformations so that the final polishing step will bring out the true microstructure. If a sufficient amount of the deformed surface layer has not been removed by rough polishing, fine polishing will not uncover the microstructure, or the microstructure will have scratches on the surface.

Final polishing exposes the true microstructure of the metal. Final polishing consists of a short polishing operation using micron sizes of synthetic liquids or powders. If the rough polishing step has been done properly, final polishing will produce a specimen free of scratches, with the true microstructure ready for etching and viewing under the microscope.

Etching

A metal specimen consists of different microconstituents, each having separate characteristics and degrees of impurities. If the specimen is exposed to a corrodant, the different microstructures will erode at different rates. The more impure the microstructure, the more the etchant will corrode. Since the grain boundaries are the most impure part of the specimen, they are etched more than the other parts. Therefore, separate grains are exposed, and the different microconstituents show a different shade of black, white, and gray. The etching process involves selecting the correct etchant for the material and soaking the metal in the etchant for the proper time. The ASTM Manual, Volume III, contains a list of etchants and times for most metals. The most common etchant is Nital, which is a combination of nitric acid and ethyl alcohol. The common mixture is 95 percent alcohol and 5 percent nitric acid by volume. The metal specimen is soaked in this mixture until the sample begins to turn a graying color. The sample is then taken out of the etchant and allowed to dry. When dry, the sample is ready to be viewed under the microscope.

Conclusion

Metallography has been one of the most important ways by which man has studied metals and advanced the art of metallurgy. A carefully prepared metallographic sample can be very useful in establishing its identity, giving an approximation of its carbon content, showing its grain size and structure, revealing defects and inclusions, and providing an indication of the metal's heat treatment history.

Because so many company reports are written to analyze problems and make appropriate conclusions and recommendations, the process report can be adapted to fit a business problem analysis situation. The following example, which also includes a complete audience analysis, shows how the process plan can be used to analyze an actual office problem.

The report is written by the bookkeeper of Artex, an import-export company. The writer's purpose is to familiarize three new, trained executive secretaries with the process of completing shipment files used by Artex. All three secretaries have two or three years' experience in other import-export firms. The writer recognizes that while she is responsible for completing the files, new secretaries need to understand the process in case they become involved with it. The report will have an indefinite life; it can be filed and later distributed to any new person joining the company who needs to know how to complete orders. The secondary readers are the company president and vice president, who are naturally interested in an important task like this one being correctly understood and performed.

```
       TO:  Dorothy Fuqua              DATE:  April 14, 1980
            Pamela Carney
            Brenda Perry

     FROM:  Melinda Johnson, Bookkeeper

  SUBJECT:  COMPLETION OF EXPORT SHIPMENT FILES

     DIST:  Steve Patin, President
            Cliff Carrollton, Vice President
```

Completing shipments is the final phase of our export transaction. The process of completing a shipment must be known by the entire staff because many jobs branch from this task. These jobs include monthly reports, accounts receivable statements, account-240 statements, closing the books, income and expense statements, and the balance sheet. The task is performed primarily by the bookkeeper, but sometimes other office personnel take some of the load. I am defining the process of completing shipments so the task will be done uniformly and correctly. Specific steps are as follows:

1. receive documents for shipment

2. put materials in order

3. check invoices against factura

4. complete shipment worksheet

5. prepare 240-Reserve Account material

6. have shipment checked

All materials needed for this task are included in the shipment folder and in the documents we receive from one of the various forwarders such as Behring International, Schenkers, Eudmarco, Air Express, or Wilson Shipping. The purpose of the report, again, is to be certain the entire staff at Artex, Inc. understand the process of completing a shipment.

Receive Documents for Shipment

When documents are received from the forwarder, the "open" shipment folder is pulled to be completed. If we have a vendor's invoice for everything we have shipped, the shipment can be completed. In short, we are charging our customer for goods we have already paid for. From the documents, we take a copy of the AWB (Airway Bill) or Bill of Lading, along with a copy of the original factura signed by the forwarder, and set them aside to mail to our customer in Brazil or Venezuela. He will prepare a sight draft to Artex from the AWB and factura.

Put Materials in Order

The documents should now be separated and put in their proper place. One copy of the original factura, the original AWB or Bill of Lading, the Export Declaration, and a copy of the forwarding charges is placed in the shipment folder. The following documents should be set aside: one original factura, one copy of each vendor's invoice, and one copy of the forwarding charges for the 240-Reserve Account statement which will be discussed later. The order of the shipment folder should be as follows:

1. original factura

2. our copy of factura

3. original AWB or Bill of Lading

4. Export Declaration

5. any extra material (notes, material receipts, telexes)

6. vendor invoices

7. forwarding invoice

Now the shipment folder is in the proper order. If the order is correct, further reference to the shipment is easier.

Check Invoices Against Factura

All the vendor's invoices should be checked off against our copy of the factura. If everything is complete, the shipment can be worked. If not, the entire shipment (including 240-material) is put back in the file to await the invoices. All invoices must be included to charge our customer exactly what we paid for the goods.

Complete Shipment Worksheet

The shipment worksheet is very important. It contains all information on the entire export transaction. The worksheet is printed on half-sheet-size paper and consists of three copies: white—accounts receivable, pink—shipment folder, and yellow—240-Reserve Account statement. The worksheet looks like this:

```
                                                    S3000
DATE SHIPPED _____
CUSTOMER _____      P.O. NO. _____
REFERENCE NO. _____  RELEASED: _____
AWB NO. _____        ETA: _____
CARRIER _____        WEIGHT: _____
    FOB COST OF GOODS                      see (1)
    HANDLING FEE: % of (1)                  (2)
    SHIPPING EXPENSE                        (3)
                                                              A/C
    TOTAL COST OF SHIPMENT                   (4)              600
    ACCOUNTS RECEIVABLE                      (5)              129
    RESERVE ACCOUNT DR__CR__                 (6)              240
```

(1) Total of Vendor's Invoices. This is what we paid for the goods.

(2) The handling fee gives Artex its profit. Depending on the total FOB cost of goods, a percentage is charged our customer. The handling fee table is as follows:

FOB Cost of Goods	Percentage
$0-$999	12 %
$1000-4999	10
$5000-9999	8
$10,000-24,999	7
$25,000-49,999	5
$50,000-74,999	3.5
$75,000-100,000+	2.5

(3) Shipping Expense. This is the amount our forwarders pay to ship the goods.

(4) Total Cost of Shipment. This is the total of lines 1, 2, and 3. Line 4 is the amount Artex paid to ship the goods to our customer in South America.

(5) Accounts Receivable. This is the amount charged our customer on the factura. The copy was sent in the mail for draft preparation.

(6) Reserve Account DR__ CR__. The difference of the amount Artex paid and the amount our customer paid is either debited or credited from the customer's reserve account.

Prepare 240-Reserve Account Material

After the worksheet is completed, the copies are separated. The pink copy is stapled to the material in the completed shipment folder. The yellow copy is stapled with the 240 material that was previously set aside. The white copy is given to the bookkeeper as a record of Accounts Receivable. Line six of the worksheet contains a debit or credit to our customer's account. We keep this 240 material from all shipments and compile a monthly statement from them for our customers so they will know how much is in their reserve account here in the United States.

Have Shipment Checked

Now the shipment is complete. It is checked by Mr. Patin or Mr. Carrollton to make sure everything is correct. Whoever checks the shipment initials it, and we type a red label for it. Now the folder is placed in the completed shipment file.

Conclusion

Although the process of completing a shipment may seem complicated, it becomes easier after one is familiar with the complete process. However, it is very important to our operation here at Artex. I hope this report will help our entire staff complete this process uniformly, correctly, and confidently. We cannot afford errors in a process that is at the heart of our company.

DESCRIPTION OF MECHANISMS

Like the process report, a description of a mechanism can be found in many contexts. Typically, descriptions appear in reports designed to describe, evaluate, and recommend the purchase of a piece of equipment or in overhaul, repair, and industrial design manuals.

Whatever your purpose in describing a mechanism, you must have an organized plan. Furthermore, you must have a thorough knowledge of the mechanism, the correct name of each part, the size and shape of the mechanism and of each part, the material from which each part is made, the relationship among parts, and the function of each part within the mechanism as a whole. Like the process report, the mechanism description needs three main parts—an introduction, a discussion section for the actual description, and a conclusion. Depending on the purpose of the description, it may be either detailed or general.

PLAN FOR A DETAILED DESCRIPTION OF A MECHANISM

I. Introduction
  A. Definition of the mechanism
  B. Purpose of the mechanism; background information
  C. General description, including a pictorial view
  D. Major parts of the mechanism—list
  E. Purpose of the report

II. Description of the Parts
  A. Description of Part 1
    1. Definition and/or purpose of the part
    2. General description—size, shape, material; graphic of Part 1
    3. Theory of operation (if needed)
    4. Relation of Part 1 to other parts

5. List of subparts (if applicable)
    a. Piece 1
       (1) definition or purpose
       (2) general description—size, shape, material; graphic of Piece 1
       (3) relationship of Piece 1 to other pieces.
    b. Piece 2
       etc.
  B. Description of Part 2
     etc.

III. Description of the Mechanism in Operation.

IV. Conclusion (content will vary, but could include items like the following):
  A. Importance of the mechanism
  B. Maintenance or care of the mechanism
  C. Cost—initial or maintenance

The following detailed description of a compression faucet was written by a mechanical technology major for a high school student taking a shop course. The purpose of the description is to familiarize the student with the complete structure of a compression faucet. Knowing this information, the student would then proceed to learn how to repair compression faucets. As instructional material, the life of this particular description is indefinite.

DESCRIPTION OF A COMPRESSION FAUCET

Introduction

A compression faucet is a valve used to regulate the flow of a liquid from a pipe or reservoir. The faucet (see Figure 5-1) is a tubular "J"-shaped object with a knoblike handle. The faucet is made of two parts: (1) the body and (2) the handle assembly. The purpose of this description is to familiarize students taking Shop I with the structure of the compression faucet before they proceed to methods of maintenance and repair.

Figure 5-1. Compression Faucet

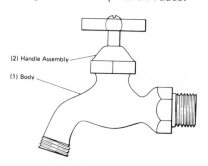

(2) Handle Assembly

(1) Body

Description of Parts

The Body

The body (see Figure 5-2) is the part of the faucet that fluid flows through. The handle assembly screws into it and controls the rate of the fluid flow. The body is made of unfinished brass and has a height of 2.687 in. and a length of 4.625 in. The faucet has a 1.0-in. diameter base (A). The base has external threads (B) for .50 in. Near the base is a six-sided, 1.250-in. wrench grip (C). The spout end (D) of the faucet curves 105 degrees downward from the faucet's center line. The 1.0-in. diameter spout has 0.375 in. of external threads (E). The top of the faucet (F) has .3125 in. of external threads (G) on a 1.1875-in. diameter opening (H) on the top of the faucet. The inside of this opening is threaded for .875 in. to receive the handle assembly. Inside this opening is a chamber (I) 1.250 in. deep. This chamber is connected to the spout. At the bottom of this chamber is an opening .6250 in. in diameter. This opening is the valve seat (J), which is created when the handle assembly is in place. This valve, formed by the handle assembly, regulates the flow of fluid through the faucet.

Figure 5-2. Body

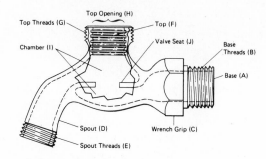

Handle Assembly

The handle assembly (see Figure 5-3) is the part of the faucet that is turned to control the flow of fluid through the faucet. It is a T-shaped object made of rubber and unfinished brass and is 3.0 in. long. The handle assembly has eight pieces: (A) valve washer, (B) valve screw, (C) spindle, (D) brass washer, (E) cap washer, (F) cap, (G) handle, (H) handle screw.

Figure 5-3. Handle Assembly

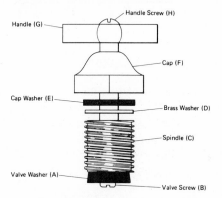

Valve Washer (A). The valve washer (see Figure 5-4) is the piece of the handle assembly that seals the valve joint of the faucet. The valve washer is a disc-shaped piece of hard rubber 0.1875 in. thick and 0.750 in. in diameter. It has a 0.125-in. diameter hole in its center. This hole allows the valve washer to be screwed to the spindle of the handle assembly.

Figure 5-4. Valve Washer

Washer Screw (B). The washer screw (see Figure 5-5), which attaches the valve washer to the spindle, is a 0.375-in. long threaded rod of unfinished brass with a button-shaped slotted head. The threaded portion of the screw is 0.250 in. long and has a 0.125-in. diameter. The head of the screw has a diameter of 0.3125 in. and is 0.125 in. thick.

Figure 5.5. Washer Screw

Spindle (C). The spindle (see Figure 5-6) is the central piece of the handle assembly, and all other pieces are attached to it. The spindle is a 2.375-in. unfinished brass rod. The top 1.4375 in. of the spindle has a diameter of 0.375 in. The bottom 0.9375-in. section of the spindle is threaded to fit into the top of the body of the faucet. Both ends of the spindle have threaded screw holes 0.125 in. in diameter. These holes are used to attach the handle and the valve washer.

Figure 5-6. Spindle

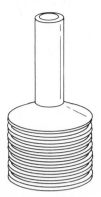

Brass Washer (D). The brass washer (see Figure 5-7) is a piece of the handle assembly that keeps fluid from leaking through the top of the faucet. It adds stiffness to the cap washer to seal the faucet. The brass washer is a flat, round piece of unfinished brass. It is 0.0625 in. thick, has a diameter of 1.0 in., and has a 0.4375-in. diameter hole in its center.

Figure 5-7. Brass Washer

Cap Washer (E). The cap washer (see Figure 5-8) is a piece of the handle assembly that seals the top of the faucet. It fits around the spindle and under the cap of the faucet. It is a disc-shaped piece of rubber 0.0625 in. thick with a diameter of 1.1250 in. The cap washer has a 0.40-in. diameter hole in its center.

Figure 5-8. Cap Washer

Cap (F). The cap (see Figure 5-9) is the piece of the handle assembly that closes the top of the faucet. It is a bell-shaped piece of unfinished brass. The cap is 0.750 in. tall with a 0.375-in. tall, six-sided wrench grip at its base. The top of the spindle passes through a 0.4375-in. hole in the top of the cap. The lower inside of the cap is threaded so that the cap may be screwed onto the body of the faucet.

Figure 5-9. Cap

Handle (G). The handle (see Figure 5-10) is the part of the handle assembly that is turned to operate the faucet. It is a rod made of unfinished brass with a bulge in its middle. The handle is 2.0 in. long with a diameter of 0.375 in. and a 0.1875-in. diameter hole through the middle of the bulge. A screw passes through this hole to attach the handle to the spindle.

Figure 5-10. Handle

Handle Screw (H). The handle screw (see Figure 5-11) is the piece of the handle assembly that attaches the handle to the spindle. The handle screw is a 0.375-in.-long threaded rod of unfinished brass with a button-shaped slotted head. The threaded portion of the screw is 0.250 in. long and has a 0.125-in. diameter. The head of the screw has a diameter of 0.3125 in. and is 0.1250 in. thick.

Figure 5-11. Handle Screw

Mechanism in Use

A compression faucet operates by a simple principle. A counterclockwise turn of the handle will open the valve in the faucet and start a flow of fluid from the spout. Turning the handle further will increase the flow. Turning the handle of the faucet moves the valve washer away from the valve seat. This upward movement of the washer allows fluid to move from the base chamber of the faucet through the hole in the valve seat and out the spout. A clockwise turn of the handle will decrease the flow of fluid from the spout. Turning the handle until it will turn no further will stop the flow. The flow is stopped because the valve washer has made contact with the valve seat.

Conclusion

The compression faucet is a versatile device whose most common use is as a household water faucet. It is usually found outdoors with garden hoses, but it can also be used to tap drums and vats of fluids. The compression faucet is durable and maintenance-free except for periodic replacement of the valve washer and valve seat. If a faucet is turned off and on frequently, the valve washer will not seal properly and will produce leakage. Frequently, older compressions will develop valve seat wear. When either of these conditions develops, the washer can be replaced by removing the handle assembly. Valve seat repair devices are available. See Section 2.4 for valve seat repair instructions.

When a more general description of a mechanism is required, the following plan can be used. Note that both plans for mechanism descriptions can and should be modified in actual practice to fit the particular topic and purpose.

PLAN FOR A GENERAL DESCRIPTION OF A MECHANISM

I. Introduction
   A. Definition of the mechanism
   B. Purpose of the mechanism; background information
   C. General description; pictorial view
   D. Major parts—list
   E. Purpose of the report

II. Description of the parts
   A. Description of Part A.
      1. Definition or purposes of Part A
      2. General description
   B. Description of Part B,
      etc.

III. Theory of Operation of the Mechanism

IV. The Mechanism in Use

V. Conclusion

The following general description of a tube cutter was written by a mechanical technology major for a high school student taking a shop course. The purpose of the description is to familiarize the student with the tube cutter before he begins to cut tubing with the device. The life of this instructional report is indefinite.

A tube cutter is a hand-held tool used to cut copper, aluminum, or steel tubing. It is an adjustable clamp with a steel blade that cuts tubing as large as ¾" in diameter.

Figure 5-12. Tube Cutter

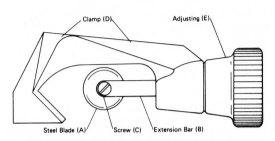

List of Parts

The tube cutter consists of five parts: (A) a steel blade, (B) a screw, (C) an extension bar, (D) a clamp, and (E) an adjusting knob.

A. *The Steel Blade.* The steel blade does the actual cutting. For the blade to cut properly, continuous pressure must be applied by the adjusting knob.

B. *The Extension Bar.* The extension bar holds the steel blade in a cutting position. It extends and retracts to the desired positions required for different sizes of tubing. It is controlled by the adjusting knob.

C. *The Screw.* The screw acts as a pin on which the blade rotates. The pin also holds the blade in position on the extension bar.

D. *The Clamp.* The clamp has two purposes. It holds the material to be cut in a position that allows the blade to make a perpendicular cut. It also houses the extension bar.

E. *The Adjusting Knob.* The adjusting knob controls the extension bar and the amount of pressure that is applied on the material to be cut. It is mounted on the end of the clamp.

Tube Cutter in Use

To cut tubing, the device is placed around the tubing at the point it is to be cut. The steel blade is adjusted to the surface of the tube and slightly tightened. Then the device is turned around the tube at least three turns. When the adjusting knob is tightened, the tubing is securely positioned between the clamp and the steel blade. The pressure prevents the tubing from slipping during the cutting process.

After the first three turns, the adjusting knob should be tightened and the turning process repeated until the tubing walls are severed.

Conclusion

The tube cutter is a handy shop or hobby tool. It enables the user to make perfect cuts every time and is much faster to use than a saw. The cut produced by the blade prevents the ragged edges caused by a saw. The tube cutter has no maintenance requirements.

HEADINGS AND VISUAL AIDS

Like the process report, the mechanism report should use appropriate headings. Detailed descriptions of mechanisms may require extensive headings and subheadings to control the organization of the report properly. Visual aids must also be included. However, how detailed these visuals are depends on (1) the purpose of the description and (2) the needs of the readers. Clearly, a general description will require less detailed visuals (drawings or pictures) than a detailed description. Whatever kind of visual you choose, remember to adhere to the conventions regarding illustrations (see chapter 4, Graphics). In addition, keep in mind the following guidelines:

1. Integrate each visual with the accompanying verbal description. Precise correlation between the visual and its verbal counterpart should be evident.

2. Label only the parts that you will discuss in the verbal description. Never label (or letter) any part that you will not refer to in the description.

3. Do not include dimensions on the drawings that are not needed or not referred to in the verbal description.

4. Place all visuals as close to the description as possible to allow the reader to move easily between the verbal and the visual.

SETS OF DIRECTIONS

The third basic type of report is the set of directions. While instructions may be given within a regular business report context, the following plan for a set of directions is designed to create an organized, clear, and complete set of instructions to operate a machine or to explain how to perform a process. Like all reports, the instructions report should have an introduction, a discussion section where instructions are given, and a conclusion.

PLAN FOR A SET OF DIRECTIONS
I. Introduction
   A. Definition of the process or purpose of the process
   B. Audience—skills and knowledge necessary to perform the process (where, when, why, by whom performed)
   C. Theory of operation (machine operation instructions)
   D. Preparations
     1. Place, time required, particular conditions
     2. Material and equipment needed (tabulate)
   E. Cautions—safety or quality control
   F. List of steps (tabulate)
   G. Purpose of the report
II. Instructions for Performing Each Step
   A. Step 1
     1. Definition or purpose
     2. Description of entire step
     3. Materials required for this step
     4. Directions for Step 1 (number and tabulate each step)
     5. Cautions for this step
   B. Step 2
     etc.
III. Conclusion—Synthesis, Interrelation of All Steps

Many items on this plan may not be relevant in every set of directions, but adhering to the plan as closely as is feasible will insure a complete set of instructions. In addition, keep the following considerations in mind when you plan and write instructions:

178

1. Aim your instructions at the reader who will really need them. The reader who doesn't need instructions can always throw them away.

2. Avoid assuming your reader knows more than he does. Explain technical terms he may not understand. Do not omit "obvious" steps unless you are sure your reader will clearly apprehend the "obvious."

3. Carefully explain general theory preceding actual directions. People make fewer errors when they know the logic behind the process to be performed. Frequently, directions for operating a machine are preceded by a general description of the machine to help the reader understand the machine's operation before attempting to operate it.

4. Explain the reason for doing each important step, especially if you think the reader might omit the step or take a short cut that could be dangerous or affect the success of the operation. Mark crucial explanations with "NOTE" or "WARNING" to be sure the reader understands the importance of following specific steps.

5. Carefully number and tabulate each step to help the reader proceed without losing track of the steps. Make each step easy to see.

6. Use pictures, sketches, and diagrams if they will help the reader. Like all other graphics, they should be placed as close as possible to the specific direction they refer to. All graphic aids should be numbered, and these numbers should be referred to in the appropriate step.

7. State all instructions in imperative mood. Use passive or active voice to explain instructions.

The following set of instructions was written for service personnel at a radio-TV sales and service store, where the writer works. The purpose of the instructions is to give service personnel directions in testing and adjusting AM transmitters. The writer assumes that the service personnel are familiar with the equipment necessary for the testing procedure.

**Procedure for Checking Amplitude Modulation
Using the Sinewave Method**

**NOTICE: THIS PROCEDURE SHOULD BE DONE BY
QUALIFIED SERVICE PERSONNEL ONLY**

Part I

This procedure is used during the testing and adjustment of AM transmitters. The output of the transmitter's modulated R.F. amplifier stage is tested to determine the percentage of modulation and to observe whether the output waveform is being undermodulated or overmodulated. Overmodulation causes distortion of the transmitted signal. Undermodulation causes loss of power to the sidebands which contain the signal intelligence. The ideal amount of modulation is 100 percent, which supplies maximum power to the sidebands.

The following procedure is usually done at a test bench; however, it can be done in the field if a portable oscilloscope is used and if a source of A.C. voltage is available.

The time required to perform this procedure should be approximately thirty minutes.
Equipment required:

---

1. Oscilloscope

2. Low capacitance probe

3. Pickup coil

4. Audio frequency signal generator

Two steps are required to perform this procedure:

A. Oscilloscope Setup

B. Test Procedure

Part II

Step A is the setup of the oscilloscope so that it will be ready for use in the test procedure. This setup is necessary for accurate measurement during the test process.

Step A—Oscilloscope Setup

1. Turn INTENSITY, FOCUS, GAIN, and SYNC CONTROLS to lowest setting.

2. Switch off INTERNAL SWEEP.

3. Set SWEEP selector to EXTERNAL.

4. Set HORIZONTAL and VERTICAL POSITION controls to their middle range.

5. Turn POWER switch to ON.

6. Wait for warmup and turn INTENSITY control until a spot just appears on the screen. If a spot does not appear, use HORIZONTAL and VERTICAL POSITION controls to move the spot into view.

7. Adjust FOCUS to sharpen spot image.

8. Center spot with POSITION controls.

9. Set SWEEP SELECTOR to INTERNAL.

10. Adjust SWEEP FREQUENCY to over 100 cps.

11. Turn HORIZONTAL GAIN until the spot is deflected as a horizontal line across the face of the screen.

12. Adjust VERTICAL GAIN until the horizontal trace is centered across the face of the screen.

13. Connect the probe to the VERTICAL INPUT connection. The oscilloscope is now ready to use.

Step B—Test Procedure

Step B involves the actual process for measuring the AM modulation of a transmitter. During the test procedure, the degree of modulation of the carrier frequency is observed.

1. Set up oscilloscope.

2. Switch SYNC SELECTOR to INTERNAL.

3. Set up equipment as shown in Figure 5-13 or 5-14 according to the following conditions:
   a. If the vertical amplifier frequency response of the oscilloscope does not reach the carrier frequency of the transmitter, use a small pickup coil inductively

180

Figure 5-13. Inductive Coupling Using Pickup Coil

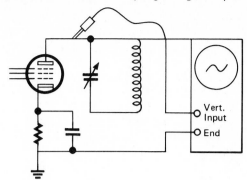

Vert.
Input

End

Figure 5-14. Inductive Coupling Using Capacitance Probe

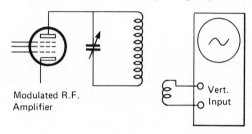

Modulated R.F.
Amplifier

Vert.
Input

coupled to the tank circuit of the modulated R.F. amplifier, as shown in Figure 5-13.

  b. If the carrier frequency is within the range of the oscilloscope, use either inductive coupling (Figure 5-13) or the low-capacitance probe (Figure 5-14).

CAUTION: BE SURE VOLTAGES IN THIS STAGE DO NOT EXCEED PROBE OR OSCIL-LOSCOPE RATINGS. DAMAGE MAY RESULT TO OSCILLOSCOPE. CONNECT GROUND TERMINAL OF OSCILLOSCOPE TO GROUND POINT OF TRANSMITTER BEFORE CONNECTING PROBE.
IF BOTH CONNECTION POINTS TO TRANSMITTER ARE ABOVE GROUND, CHASSIS OR OSCILLOSCOPE WILL BE CONNECTED TO HIGH VOLTAGE AND CAUSE ELECTRIC SHOCK.

  4. Connect probe or coil to location indicated in Figure 5-13 or 5-14.

  5. Turn transmitter on and switch to UNMODULATED CARRIER. The pattern visible should be Figure 5-15. Figure 5-16 would indicate a lack of carrier frequency.

Figure 5-15. Unmodulated Carrier

Figure 5-16. No Signal

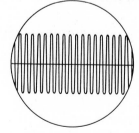

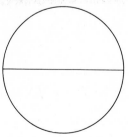

  6. MODULATE transmitter with a sinewave audio frequency generator connected to the input stage of the transmitter.

181

7. Adjust HORIZONTAL and VERTICAL GAIN controls for desired width and height of the resulting pattern.

8. Adjust SWEEP FREQUENCY and SYNC controls for number of patterns desired to be displayed on the screen. Compare patterns to Figures 5-17 through 5-20.

Figure 5-17. 50% Modulation

Figure 5-18. 100% Modulation

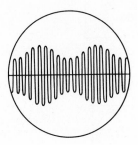

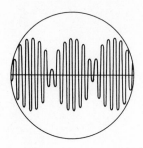

Figure 5-19. Undermodulation

Figure 5-20. Overmodulation

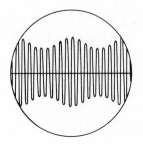

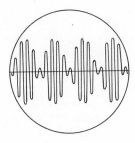

9. Measure amplitudes at points A and B (as shown in Figure 5-21) of pattern.

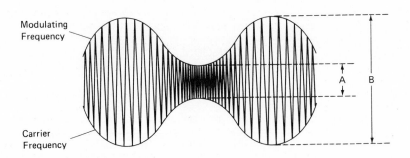

Modulating Frequency

Carrier Frequency

10. Calculate percent of modulation.

$$\%M = \frac{B-A}{B+A} \times 100\%$$

Frequently, sets of instructions can be found in actual business reports. The following report, written by a records' management consultant, informs an accountant about specific actions he should take to improve his office's filing system. Secondary readers are the accountant's secretary and his administrative assistant, who will most likely be responsible for implementing the recommendations made by the consultant.

182

TO: James H. Mixon, CPA

FROM: Ann Covington, Associate
           APS Records Management Service

SUBJECT: RECOMMENDATIONS FOR FILING SYSTEM IMPROVEMENT

DIST: Rachael Moore, Administrative Assistant
           Lynda Hyatt, Secretary

BACKGROUND

On October 10, I visited your accounting firm to review the filing system. On the basis of my findings, I have prepared a report describing and evaluating your present filing system. In retaining APS to analyze your system, you stated that your staff is having problems obtaining adequate service from the files because needed records were difficult to locate and had often been reported missing.

PROBLEM

After initially inspecting the files, I noticed that they were crowded enough to prevent a filing clerk from doing a good job in filing or retrieving documents. A closer examination revealed that active and inactive records were being kept in the same drawers and that some of the inactive records are several years old. Some records of clients no longer being served by the firm were still kept.

RECOMMENDATIONS FOR FILING SYSTEM IMPROVEMENT

To correct these specific problems in your filing system, I am writing this report to make the following recommendations:

1. Establish standards for classifying records as active, inactive, or no longer needed.

2. Analyze the content of the files to classify them according to criteria developed in the previous step.

3. Establish separate files for active and inactive records and destroy records no longer needed.

I. ESTABLISH STANDARDS FOR CLASSIFYING RECORDS AS ACTIVE, INACTIVE, OR NO LONGER NEEDED.
   A. Determine which documents are used often in performing accounting work for clients.
   B. Establish criteria for classifying records as active or inactive. Active records are those used frequently in performing accounting work for clients. Because of frequent reference to the previous accounting period in compiling financial reports with results of operations given in year-to-date figures, current and previous fiscal or calendar years should be kept in active files. All other records should be removed to another area and classified as inactive records.
   C. Communicate these classification criteria to your staff in written guidelines.
   D. Strictly adhere to these criteria in the future.

NOTE: Be aware of the legal requirements for keeping records. Useful publications are available which can assist in setting criteria for disposition of records. The Code of Federal Regulations is a codification of rules and regulations issued by the administrative agencies of the federal government. The National Records Management Council publishes the Index to the Federal Record-Keeping Requirements. Other publications are Retention and Preservation of Records with Destruction Schedules by Records Control, Inc., and the records retention timetable developed by Modern Office Procedures.

II. ANALYZE THE CONTENT OF THE FILES TO CLASSIFY THEM AS ACTIVE, INACTIVE, OR NO LONGER NEEDED.
   In analyzing the content of files, your staff must make decisions as to the type of information to be collected for analysis and the methods needed to collect and analyze the information.

A. Information to be collected. The information must identify the records by name and location.

   1. Specify what kind of documents they are--contracts, deeds, correspondence, working papers, journals, ledgers.

   2. Give dates covered by the records.

B. Method to collect the information.
   1. Determine the means for collecting the information.

      a. Use a form similar to the one below to obtain uniform information. The form describes a folder by location, name folder, kind of documents in the folder, and date of the document. The area in the upper right-hand corner is used at the time of analysis to check the status of the records. (See Figure 5-22)

   2. Determine the identification and location of data. Accurate description of the physical location of folders will prevent mistakes when carrying out the recommendations made by the staff performing the file analysis.

      a. Use a decimal number system to identify cabinets, drawers, and folders. This system is easier than long captions and dates.

      b. Use the first number for drawers, and the third number for folders. For example, the fifth folder in the second drawer of the third cabinet will be numbered 3.2.5.

      c. Number cabinets from right to left, as one enters the filing room; drawers, vertically, from top to bottom; and folders, from front to back of the drawers.

      d. Put a label on each drawer showing cabinet number, drawer number, and number of folders contained in the drawer.

      e. Mark or label each folder with the appropriate code for cabinet, drawer, and folder.

   3. Determine the time and personnel necessary to do the work. The best time to do the work is during a slow period of office activity or on a Saturday.

      a. Prepare hand-outs explaining very clearly the decimal identification system, the data to be collected, and the procedures that will be used to collect the data.

      b. Call a meeting of the staff to inform them of the project.

      c. Distribute the hand-outs and discuss the system and procedures to be used in collecting data.

      d. Set a time limit on the time required to do the work.

      e. Agree on a definite time to begin the project.

C. Methods to analyze the data.
   1. After the needed information has been collected, arrange the forms in sequence of cabinet, drawer, and folder number.

   2. Using the criteria developed by classifying records as active, inactive, or no longer needed, put a checkmark in the appropriate space of the form to identify the proper classification of the records.

NOTE: The staff doing the analysis and classification should be thoroughly familiar with the standards and with the records being analyzed. A member of the accounting staff, someone familiar with the clients and their work, should be on hand to answer questions and to check the work of the clerical staff.

III. ESTABLISH SEPARATE FILES FOR ACTIVE AND INACTIVE RECORDS AND DESTROY RECORDS NO LONGER NEEDED.
   A. Arrange the forms in numerical order and use them to go through the files.
   B. Pull the records marked on the form as inactive or no longer needed and place them in separate piles.
   C. Concentrate the active records in the cabinets more conveniently located for easy access.
   D. Relabel the cabinets housing the active records to reflect the content of the drawers.
   E. In the cabinets that remain empty, file the inactive records following the classification of active records.
   F. Set up inside guides and label the drawers.
   G. Randomly check the records no longer needed to prevent mistakes.
   H. Properly dispose of files no longer needed.

184

Conclusion

By completing the process described here, the objectives of the file reorganization should be accomplished. The active records will be easy to locate because they will be free of inactive records, and the inactive records will be decongested because useless records will have been eliminated. Additionally, the record analysis will give the staff a good opportunity to become familiar with the information contained in the files.

To insure organization of the files, the clerical staff should transfer out of active files the records that become inactive and destroy those documents that are obsolete or no longer needed. These goals can be accomplished if every staff member will keep in mind the standards for classifying records discussed in Recommendation 1.

RECORDS ANALYSIS FORM

Location of Record:

Cabinet   Drawer   Folder

Classification of Record:

(check)
Active _____
Inactive _____
No Longer Needed _____

Date: _____ through _____

Name: _____

Remarks: _____

_____

PROGRESS REPORTS

Progress reports do exactly what their name implies—describe and evaluate progress on a project. Generally, the progress report is addressed to and written for the person who authorized the project. The format for the progress report varies, but it is generally divided into three parts: work done, work remaining, evaluation of work completed to date. To aid the reader, the progress report should include an introduction, which states subject, background, and purpose of the report before describing what has been done. The progress report outline, therefore, will assume the following general form:

    I.   Introduction
          Subject and purpose of the report
   II.   Background
          Description of the project
  III.   Work Completed
          A. Task 1
          B. Task 2
          C. Task 3
          etc.
  IV.   Evaluation of Progress to Date
   V.   Work Remaining
  VI.   Work Schedule

```
Chicago, April 10, 19__


Vice President--Kansas--Kansas City
Vice President--Texas--Houston
Vice President--Oklahoma--Oklahoma City
Vice President--New Mexico--Albuquerque
Vice President--Arizona--Tucson
Vice President--Colorado--Denver

Through the first quarter, in relation to budget, we have the following
deviations:

1.  Net Income           21.8M under
2.  Operating Revenue    36.6M under
3.  Operating Expenses   10.6M over
4.  Total Company Gain   24.6% under

Therefore, to adjust operations more nearly in line with current economic
realities, you should implement the following immediately:

1.  Reduce all expense factors in all departments to an absolute minimum. Avoid
    current adverse effects on service whenever possible.

2.  Stop all hiring, including replacements. All exceptions must be approved by a
    corporate officer.

3.  Limit overtime to areas which immediately affect services.

4.  Reduce capital program using guidelines which will be outlined by April 20.

5.  Stop all building rearrangements that do not immediately affect service.

6.  Reexamine all optional programs. Stop those where a positive payback is not
    likely to occur in a short term.

7.  Implement frequent reports about cost cuts enacted.

8.  Reduce travel to an absolute minimum.

Today we will present the board our revised view of the current year. Our forecasts
are not final. However, the 24.6% underrun is unacceptable. To reduce costs, we
need immediate help from all states in the region.


Howard C. Morgan
Financial Vice President
```

Figure 5-23. Teletype Instructions Report

This form is suitable for the first progress report on a project. Later project reports, usually submitted at previously agreed-upon intervals, can be submitted in the following form. This form summarizes what has been accomplished during each previous reporting period before carefully describing the work accomplished during the most recent period:

    I. Introduction
        Subject and purpose of the report
   II. Description of the Project
  III. Work Completed
        A. Period 1 (dates)—summary of work completed

    B. Period 2 (dates)—summary of work completed
    etc.
IV. Work Done in Most Recent Period
    A. Task 1
    B. Task 2
    C. Task 3
 V. Evaluation of Progress to Date
VI. Work Remaining
VII. Work Schedule

The complete student research report at the end of the section on formal reports includes the student's progress report. Because this formal report is a research report, the "work completed" section gives an annotated list of important works consulted to date and a second list of works yet to consult.

RECOMMENDATION REPORTS

Another important kind of business report is the recommendation report. The recommendation is a type of analytical report concerned primarily with providing a specific recommendation about a problem. Usually the recommendation is placed near the beginning of the report, as the recommendation itself is the main concern to the reader. A good plan for a recommendation report is as follows:

  I. Introduction
      Subject and purpose of the report
 II. Recommendations
      1.
      2.
      etc.
III. Background
 IV. Tables (include in report or add as attachments)
  V. Conclusions

TO: Andrew Keller

FROM: Howard M. Damon

DATE: August 19, 1979

SUBJECT: BAKERTON PRODUCED SALT WATER DISPOSAL SYSTEM (SWD)

Introduction

This report documents a study of past, present, and anticipated produced water from the S.S. 66 Field for disposal at the Bakerton Separation Station. It also evaluates the adequacy of the present system and forecasts future needs.

Conclusion

1. The produced water disposal system at the Bakerton Separation Station periodically receives surges from liquid dumps on F.W.K.O. and treaters above the rated 1700 BWPD capacity of the S.W.D. system.

2. The D.V. tank and Jebco (Model 66-1700 BWPD skim capacity) arrangement, as designed, limits the surge capacity to only what the Jebco can accommodate.

---

3.   With workover operations still under way on S.D. 64C platform, only a fraction of the expected yield of produced salt water is arriving at Bakerton; therefore, at present there are no surge problems. Workover rig is expected to move off S.D. 64C by 11/11/80. Thereafter, peak rates are again expected.

4.   Installation of water polishing equipment on S.S. 66 Field platforms will allow treatment and disposal of produced water.

5.   Upon upset of polishing equipment on the S.S. 66 platforms, produced water will be diverted into Bakerton P/L for treatment and disposal.

6.   Modifications are required for the existing S.W.D. system to accommodate the surges (that create operating problems) that will continue during the interim period until water treaters are placed offshore.

Recommendation

Engineering recommends that modification to the existing S.W.D. system include the following:
Installation of small centrifugal pump downstream of D.V. tank to pump into the Model 66 Jebco to provide a constant flow to the Jebco. By pumping from the skimmer tank, a lower operating level can be maintained in the tank to allow for as much as a 350 bbl. instantaneous surge situation before creating operating problems.

Discussion

At the Bakerton Separation Station, produced water is separated from the product stream in the A.K.B. converter. . . .
During adverse surge conditions spillover from the oil skim chamber of the Jebco flows into the oil holding tank and is pumped to the bad oil tank for recirculation to the treaters.
To prevent overflow, the operator may manually bypass the Jebco by throttling the block value on the 8-inch bypass line and diverting a portion of the flow directly into injection pump suction tank.
Since it is undesirable to allow BS&W to enter the bad oil tank from the S.W.D. system as well as to inject improperly treated salt water into the disposal wells, modification to the existing system is warranted. . . .
Several methods were investigated to remedy the periodic surges which occur. From this investigation three possible options may be available.

Option I

Modify the salt water disposal as shown in Figure 3 enabling the water clarification equipment to allow for surges. . . .

Option II

Modify existing S. W. D. as indicated in Figure 4 to allow for maximum yield to 4500 BWPD. . . .

Option III

Continue to operate with existing system. . . . See Figure 5.

Final Remarks

As noted in the discussion, the planned water treating equipment in S.S. 66 Field will decrease the amounts of produced water arriving at Bakerton. However, this modification, discussed in Option I, would allow for handling surges whenever such situations arose and would solve long-term operating problems.

Prepared by: _____

                          Approved: _____

                          Approved: _____

FEASIBILITY REPORTS

Feasibility reports analyze a situation or problem and show why a particular solution will succeed. Frequently they will analyze various solutions, determine which is best, and suggest how the solution can be implemented. Thus, feasibility reports are similar to recommendation reports, but they usually proceed inductively, with intense analysis of each solution. The report ends with a conclusion to the problem, but the conclusion must evolve from the analysis. A general outline for a feasibility report is as follows:

I. Introduction
   Subject (Problem)
   Background
   Possible Solutions
   Purpose of the Report
II. Discussion
   Solution A—analysis
   Solution B—analysis
   Solution C—analysis
III. Evaluation of A, B, and C.
IV. Conclusion—best solution
V. Recommendation—implementation of best solution

Here is an example of a short feasibility study:

TO: George Farrell, Director of Distribution

FROM: Randy Johnson

SUBJECT: REDUCTION OF IN TRANSIT FREIGHT DAMAGE TO VASELINE INTENSIVE CARE
         BATH BEADS

Problem

As you are well aware from past product cost reports, we have been having severe product losses in our Vaseline Intensive Care Bath Bead product line. We have in the past been shipping trailer load quantities via railroad freight plan $II\frac{1}{4}$ to our distribution centers throughout the country. The results of this system have been disastrous. We have had product losses in in transit damage that amount to 20 percent of the contents of each trailer load. We have, however, from early test results, found a solution to this problem. Extensive research by our traffic department dictates a change in shipping is necessary to solve this problem. The purpose of this report is to recommend a new shipping method.

Background

Past shipping history in all product lines has shown us that the use of the railroad generates a significantly higher percentage of in transit damage than the use of common motor carriers. Under normal business conditions, considering the significant savings in freight rates and our right to file damage claims with the railroad, the system has been advantageous for us. We find ourselves in a different situation, however, with our Bath Beads product. Because of the fragile nature of our product, the railroads refuse to take responsibility for in transit freight damage, and we ship the product at our own risk. At this time there is virtually no possible way, considering cost and profit limitations, to protect the palletized product at the nose and the rear of the trailers from extensive handling damage.

Reduction of this damage is of paramount importance to us for a number of reasons other than cost. Our packaging lines are already in a situation of continuous overtime, and each carton lost due to damage magnifies a serious

---

problem. Labor in the distribution centers is at a premium. Each facility is operating at full capacity, and time lost for processing and disposing of this damage is generating serious overtime costs in the warehouse. The damaged material, due to packaging problems, cannot be reworked. It is, therefore, a total loss. We are presently showing a profit on this product line, but due to heavy competition and rising packaging expenses, it is a very narrow one.

Conclusion

Our Product Design and Traffic departments have spent extensive time and research on solving this problem, and we believe that they have arrived at a solution that is advantageous to us. The Sealand Corporation services all the cities where our network of warehouses is located. Freight rates and a ten-day delivery time are comparable to railroad service. The advantage here is that the trailer loads of product are moved by sea, thus eliminating the handling problems associated with rail. Unlike the railroads, they will assume responsibility for in transit damage. The advantage in that respect is obvious.

Last month, we shipped four trailers of bath beads to our Houston facility using Sealand's service. The results of the trial were, to say the least, beyond all expectations. The Houston warehouse reported no product losses in any of the four containers. The significant savings associated with these results cannot be stated in terms of cost and expense. Potentially, this savings will place us in an equal range of profit with our competitors and will be a major step in alleviating the overtime situation in the production department and in the distribution warehouses. This overtime situation has been of major concern to all of us.

Recommendation

Contingent upon your approval, we have instructed the Sealand Corporation to provide a supply of tractor trailers in sufficient quantities to service 20 percent of our total production in all product lines as of April 15. As manager of distribution, we realize the responsibility for this move is yours. If for any reason you believe that this change will not be to our advantage, please let me know before this date.

For an extensive example of a feasibility study, see the complete formal report toward the end of this chapter.

INFORMATION REPORTS

Both the recommendation report and the feasibility report differ from the information report, which provides information and supporting details without any analysis or recommendations. Here is an example of a short informational report:

TO: Mr. R. C. Thompson, President   DATE: July 11, 19__

FROM: B. G. Weston

SUBJECT: Survey of Current Status of Company Publication of 22 Comparable Companies in the Pasadena Area

I have completed the survey concerning the publishing and distribution of employee publications in this area and am gratified that the facts are clear and conclusive. A 65 percent increase in the number of persons receiving the various company publications during the last six years shows that people are more and more interested in reading such materials. A list of the twenty-two responding companies is attached.

The company newspaper, newsletter, and bulletin board poster sheets were the most popular types of house organs, with the policy manual and magazine least favored. Spokesmen for the twenty-two companies said they had increased their circulation of the company newspaper this year, the growth ranging from seventeen percent for the least increase to 133 percent for the greatest.

Questionnaires sent to the companies about their publications also revealed that most of them believed company newspapers, newsletters, and bulletin board placards are excellent ways to communicate with the personnel. Members of management in eight of the firms volunteered opinions that such house organs help maintain good morale. They also cautioned against having more publications than are needed, because content overlap can create an expense not justified by the little extra interest one other publication might cause.

I shall be interested to learn what decision is made as to reviving our company newspaper. Please let me know if you would like to study costs, persons, and activities involved in such an undertaking. I believe that the twenty-two companies who so enthusiastically furnished these facts and opinions would be glad to advise us further.

BGW: tja

Enclosure

THE FORMAL REPORT

Your written communication responsibilities may from time to time require you to present reports in a formal format. Usually, a long, complex report should be written in formal format. Doing so makes the report material more organized and accessible to the reader. Generally, reports that are expected to have an extended period of use should be formally presented, as the formal report, with its many elements, is designed to provide information for readers with different interests in the report itself. The formal report structure presents information so that a reader can quickly find precisely what he needs from the report.

The actual content arrangement of the formal report is the same as that of the short, informal reports, but the formal report adds all or part of the following items to help organize the report more effectively—cover, title page, letter of transmittal, table of contents, list of illustrations, glossary, descriptive abstract, informative abstract (summary), and appendix. Nearly every company will have its own preferred format specifications, designed to meet the particular needs of the company. Therefore, the discussion of each formal report element is meant to be a general description to familiarize you with the general conventions regarding the content and arrangement of each element.

Cover

Formal reports have covers to protect them during handling over an extended period of time. Covers frequently use labels which identify the report title, author, report purpose, and date—information sufficient to identify the report to the prospective reader. Many companies have designed covers to be used for all company reports. In addition, company covers may feature artwork or photographs which visualize specific concepts discussed in the report. Figure 5-23 exemplifies a typical label from a formal report:

Figure 5-23

```
┌─────────────────────────────────────┐
│          AN ANALYSIS OF CPA         │
│         PROFESSIONAL ETHICS:        │
│        THE ADVERTISING DILEMMA      │
│                                     │
│                 by                  │
│                                     │
│            Janet M. Barnes          │
│                                     │
│  English 301          April 20, 19__│
└─────────────────────────────────────┘
```

Title Page

The title page of the report should be neat and effectively designed. It should contain information necessary to identify the report. Identification elements will vary, depending on the company and the kind of report, but every title page should contain the following items: title of the report; subtitle (if appropriate); name of the company, course, or individual for whom the report was prepared; date of submission; and author of the report. If the report needs a descriptive abstract, the lower portion of the title page is a convenient location for it. The descriptive abstract placed here will further help identify the report to the prospective reader.

Letter of Transmittal

The letter of transmittal should be addressed to the person for whom the report was prepared, the person who authorized the report. This is essentially a courtesy letter designed to introduce the report content to the reader. Generally, it contains two or three paragraphs and, like any other business letter, should state the purpose in the first paragraph:

> I submit the accompanying report "Computerized Hospital Purchasing,"
> as the final project for BST 362, Business and Technical Writing.

In paragraph two, you may wish to note specific points covered by the report, particularly points which will be of special interest to the reader:

> The report examines various ways that electronic data processing (EDP)
> can be applied to the purchasing functions of a large (1000-patient-bed) hospital.

192

I have explained the overall role and organization of the hospital purchasing department. Then, I have explored the current purchasing applications for electronic data processing.

The final paragraph may present significant conclusions or recommendations, or acknowledge individuals or departments who provided information which you used in the report:

> I am indebted to Mr. Dan M. Brock, Sr., for his assistance in advising me on this report. Mr. Brock is Director for St. Luke's Hospital System. Mr. Michael P. Figar, a computer programmer for St. Luke's, was also most helpful in sharing with me his expertise in data processing.

Table of Contents

Both informal and formal reports use headings and subheadings. In the formal report, the table of contents includes all headings and subheadings shown in the body of the report and indicates the page on which each heading is located, thus enabling the reader to find a specific section immediately. The table of contents also shows the reader the organization of the report, the topics covered, and the range and extent of coverage of each topic. A table of contents may be developed according to several systems, but the following two systems are the most common:

Standard Outline

. . . .

   II.   EXPLANATION OF TYPESETTING
      A. Definition
      B. Hot Type
      C. Cold Type
          1. Strike On-Direct Impression
          2. Transfer Lettering or Cutout Lettering
          3. Photocomposition
  III. MARKET RESEARCH SURVEY
      A. Purpose
      B. Results of the Survey
      C. Evaluation of the Survey

The standard outline system is most frequently used by omitting the numerals and letters. The level of the headings is maintained by indention. In the body of the report, the headings of the preceding example would coincide as follows:

Explanation of Typesetting

Definition

_____
_____

Hot Type

_____
_____

Cold Type

Strike On-Direct Impression. _____

_____

Transfer Lettering or Cutout Lettering. _____

_____

Photocomposition. _____

_____

Market Research Survey

Purpose

_____

Results of the Survey

_____

_____

Evaluation of the Survey

_____

Decimal System

The decimal system works like the standard outline, except that the decimal numbers are included in both the body of the report and the table of contents.

1. Introduction
2. History of Radar Development
3. Basic Radar System
   3.1 Transmitter
   3.2 Antenna
   3.3 Receiver
4. Radar Operating Parameters
   4.1 Frequency
   4.2 Pulse Characteristics
      4.2.1. PRT
      4.2.2. Pulse Power
      4.2.3. Receiver

In the body of the report, the headings would appear as follows:

. . . .
3. BASIC RADAR SYSTEM

3.1 TRANSMITTER
_____

3.2 ANTENNA
_____

3.3 RECEIVER
_____

4. RADAR OPERATING PARAMETERS

4.1 FREQUENCY
_____

4.2 PULSE CHARACTERISTICS
_____

   4.2.1. PRT. _____
   4.2.2. Pulse Power. _____
   4.2.3. Receiver. _____

In developing the table of contents, be sure to include all headings that occur in the body of the report. Wording and rank must also be preserved, as in the two preceding examples. Also, be sure to include any preliminary items in your report—such as a glossary, list of illustrations, list of symbols, summary, and your introduction. Also, list the appendix, if your report has one. List each appendix item separately. Examples follow shortly.

List of Illustrations

As you learned in Chapter 4, Graphics, every visual aid must be numbered and labeled. If you use any visual aids in the formal report, compile a list of illustrations like the one below. The list of illustrations follows the table of contents in the assembled report. Generally, in the list of illustrations, tables are separated from figures, as shown by the example.

Illustrations

Glossary

A glossary is an alphabetized list of defined terms or symbols. It is included solely to help the reader. Ideally, you should define terms in context; that is, as you use them in presenting your ideas. However, a large number of technical terms may be conveniently defined in a glossary placed in the introductory pages of the report. While the glossary may be placed in the appendix, at the end of the report, you risk the reader's not finding it.

Glossary

Attenuation	the reduction of the signal or pulse as it travels through the transmission medium
Bandwidth	range of frequencies at which the circuit will operate properly
Cladding	a metal coating bonded onto another object
Crosstalk	the noise or garbled sounds heard on an electric receiver caused by interference from another channel
Discontinuities	a shorted circuit or an open circuit
Noise	any disturbance that obscures the clarity of a signal
Parallax	an apparent change in the direction of an object caused by a change in observational position that provides a new line of sight
Photodiode	a solid state device which converts light pulses into electrical pulses

---

Abstracts

A formal report generally includes two kinds of abstracts—the descriptive abstract and the informative abstract, also called a summary.

The *descriptive abstract* tells what the report is about. Short abstracts are usually descriptive. Frequently, the descriptive abstract appears on the title page. The following are examples of descriptive abstracts:

This report describes new applications of computer graphics and includes explanations of some fundamental computer graphics concepts.

This report contains the following:

1. Brief description of radar development.

2. Description of the operation of a basic radar system.

3. Discussion of factors which affect radar operation.

4. Description of the PPI and Type A indicators.

5. Description of the main types of pulse systems.

6. Description of the major continuous wave radar system.

7. Brief overview of the major radar types and their applications.

The *informative abstract* (summary) gives the main ideas presented in the report. The informative abstract begins with a sentence that expresses the central idea of the report. Subsequent sentences state the main supporting ideas in the same order as they occur in the report. The final sentences state conclusions and recommendations of the report. The informative abstract should reflect and follow the table of contents, as the following example does:

Summary

Salmonellosis is a widespread infectious disease in the United States. It is caused by any of some 1,300 serotypes in the genus *Salmonella*. It may occur in either humans or animals with varying accompanying symptoms. The problem of controlling salmonellosis in humans is greatly complicated because of the widespread distribution of the organisms in the environment and the many ways they can reach the host. Salmonella cannot be totally eliminated at this time. A great deal of improvement can be realized, however, by minimizing infection among domestic animals; by improving food handling practices; by giving careful attention to processed foods to prevent growth of the disease organism; by requiring universal usage of clean water; by raising standards of cleanliness for food equipment and food handlers; and by practicing better overall sanitation in kitchens, hospitals, and restaurants. The current most realistic means of reducing salmonella are to work toward ridding domestic animals of the disease and to train all food handlers in the proper ways to treat contaminated raw foods. Control of salmonellosis is not simply a matter of interrupting a cycle in nature. It must be attacked at the farm, in the restaurant, and in the home.

Table of Contents

Introduction

Every report, formal or informal, should contain an introduction which includes the four points previously discussed: subject of the report, background information, list of steps or major topics that will be discussed, and purpose of the report. In the formal report, conclusions and recommendations are usually included in the introduction. The summary may then appear after the introduction. This arrangement allows the reader to find exactly what he wants and needs in the report, as few readers will read the report from beginning to end. For an example of this type of introduction, see the student report toward the end of Chapter 5.

The report must show an effective system of documentation to identify the sources of any ideas other than those of the writer. The communicator has the ethical responsibility of giving credit where credit is due. In addition, credit documentation allows the reader to follow up the writer's sources if further investigation is necessary.

A wide variety of documentation is available. Many fields have their own particular documentation systems, as do most journals. Should you ever decide to submit an article or report for publication in a journal, be sure to consult recent issues of the journal to determine the documentation style used, and then prepare your article by using the same system. There is no one "best" system of documentation. The important point is to use a system that clearly gives credit to outside sources you use in writing your report.

Today the trend is to compile all footnotes on separate sheets immediately after the body of the report, rather than placing the footnotes at the bottom of each page. Most journals require articles submitted to have documenting notes placed on separate pages at the end of the article. A typical "Notes" or "Reference" page is as follows. Corresponding notes or reference numbers within the article itself may appear as superscripts, in parentheses ( ), or in brackets [ ].

REFERENCES

1. R. L. Gallawa, "Telecommunication Alternatives with Emphasis on Optical Waveguide Systems," *O.T. Report* (November 17, 1975); 65–71.

2. Gallawa, p. 75.

3. "Fiber Optics Applications/Technology Barriers for Signal Transfer," *Proceedings of the Second European Electro-Optics Markets and Technology Conference* (IPC Science and Technology, 1973): 411.

4. John Fulenwider and George Killinger, "Optical T-Carrier Systems on Glass Fiber Cable: A Promising New Technology," *Telephony* (June 2, 1975): 34–35.

5. Bruce LeBoss, "Army Speeds Fiber Optics," *Electronics* (March 3, 1977): 69.

6. "The Beam That Lights the Future," *Telephony* (August 9, 1976): 40.

7. Fulenwider and Killinger, p. 45.*

8. "Airborne Light Optical Fiber Technology," *Naval Research Review* (January 1976): 31–33.

9. Mikhail P. Lisitsa, *Fiber Optics* (New York: Keter Inc., 1972): 195.

10. Lisitsa, p. 156.

*Do not use Ibid. Ref. 7—List short title *only* if author(s) have written more than one work that is given in the References.

A second system of documentation is exemplified below. Each source is alphabetized and numbered on the "References" page located at the end of the article. In the report itself, documentation is indicated in brackets. The first number refers to the number of the item on the reference page. The numbers following tell what page in the document the source was found:

. . . The military is confident that by the mid-1980s it will be replacing copper wire with optical fibers in its technical communication systems [4]. The question is whether or not fiber optics will improve the quality and efficiency of already existing systems [4, p. 82]. Currently the military is spending $35 million a year for research on optical communications [2, p. 418]. To date, all military applications are still in the research state. However, the principal military applications of fiber optics research are as follows: (1) data transmission system for the avionics of ships and aircrafts; (2) undersea tethers for various types of sonobuoy systems; and (3) portable land lines [5, p. 2]. Research on optical communications have proven successful on aircrafts, ships, and submarines [1]. In fact, the Navy has currently begun evaluating the A-7 ALOFT avionics interface system from the IBM Federal Systems Division [1, p. 42]. . . .

REFERENCES

1. "Airborne Light Optical Fiber Technology," *Naval Research Review* (January 1976), 31–33.
2. "Fiber Optics Applications/Technology Barriers for Signal Transfer," *Proceedings of the Second European Electro-Optics Markets and Technology Conference* (IPC Science and Technology, 1973), 411.
3. John Fulenwider and George Killinger, "Optical T-Carrier Systems on Glass Fiber Cable: A Promising New Technology," *Telephony* (June 2, 1975), 34–35.
4. R. L. Gallawa, "Telecommunication Alternatives with Emphasis on Optical Waveguide Systems," *O.T. Report* (November 17, 1975), 65–71.
5. Bruce LeBoss, "Army Speeds Fiber Optics," *Electronics* (March 3, 1977), 65.
6. . . .

A third type of documentation is shown in the following complete formal report. This system uses extensive internal documentation for subsequent references. The first time a source is used, its complete documentation is given on the "notes" or "references" page. Any subsequent references to this source are placed in the text itself. The value of internal documentation is that excessive note numbers for subsequent references are eliminated. This system also has the added advantage of helping the reader keep up with the sources the writer is referring to.

Appendix

The appendix is the final section of the report. The appendix includes any information which is not immediately essential to the reader's understanding of the main points and conclusions of the report. Highly technical calculations, tables, schematics, specifications, systems designs, and so on should not, as a general rule, be placed in the body of the report, since nontechnical readers will only be confused by such data. Placing items such as these in the appendix and then referring to each item at the appropriate time in the report itself will enable interested readers to turn to the appendix and locate substantiating technical documentation when they may need or wish to do so. But be sure to refer to appendix items in the text. Otherwise, readers will not know where or when to use the appendix items, which may be very important. The following excerpt from a report shows the correct use of allusions to the appendix.

> . . . Before the development of ICs, electronic circuits consisted of discrete (or separate) components wired together on a chassis or base. These circuits take up considerably more space than ICs, since ICs contain an entire circuit in a compact part, where the discrete circuits are composed of separate components which are larger. Appendix A provides a more detailed comparison of IC and discrete circuit capabilities. . . .

Many types of items can appear in an appendix—detailed descriptions of mechanisms or processes, illustrations, maps, drawings, diagrams, schematics, case histories, mathematical computations, reference letters, memos, a bibliography of suggested readings on the report topic, tables, and graphs.

TWO TYPICAL KINDS OF FORMAL REPORTS

The sample Research Report is presented with all essential parts except the cover.

The sample Proposal follows the outline and discussion of a typical proposal, and it is preceded by the transmittal letters that should accompany it.

2007 Langford
College Station, Texas 77840
April 20, 19__

Dr. Elizabeth Tebeaux
Department of English
Texas A&M University
College Station, Texas 77843

Dear Dr. Tebeaux:

I submit the accompanying report entitled "CPA Professional Ethics:
The Advertising Dilemma" as my research project for English 301,
Technical Writing.

The report includes an examination of the current controversy of advertising by the accounting profession. I have attempted to provide a base
for evaluating the advisability of changing the current professional
ethics rules of conduct to permit advertising. My conclusions are that
the interests of the public and the accounting profession would be best
served by permitting advertising, subject to certain restrictions.
Furthermore, the new rule of conduct on advertising and solicitation
proposed by the American Institute of Certified Public Accountants
(AICPA) would be a good example of such a rule.

I am indebted to Mr. Lorence L. Bravenec of the accounting department
since he helped locate resource information during the early part of my
research.

                                        Sincerely,

                                        Janet M. Barnes

Enclosure

CPA PROFESSIONAL ETHICS: THE ADVERTISING DILEMMA

A Research Report

Prepared

by

Janet M. Barnes

for

English 301

Technical Writing

Abstract

This report examines the current controversy about the
prohibitions by CPAs and against advertising by CPAs
and proposes that the public and CPAs would benefit if
advertising were allowed, subject to certain restrictions.

April 20, 19__

TABLE OF CONTENTS

INTRODUCTION

PURPOSE

The purpose of my research is to examine the current controversy of advertising by CPAs. To accomplish this examination, I attempt to determine the causes and significance of the pressures for permitting accountants to advertise. I describe the current status of advertising by CPAs and suggest different strategies that can be used. Finally, I evaluate the advisability of change and recommend the course of action to be taken.

BACKGROUND

In our complicated existence today, the corporation, sole proprietorship, and individual taxpayer would each probably benefit from the services of a Certified Public Accountant (CPA). These services may range from auditing a large corporation to filing an individual's income tax return. But how do these groups decide whether they will benefit from the services of a CPA and which CPA will best serve their needs? In the past, the accounting profession has had professional ethics prohibitions against advertising. However, there is a new mood abroad which emphasizes the consumer's right to know. Because of recent judicial decisions and consumer pressures, the accounting profession, along with other professions, is facing up to a reappraisal of its advertising prohibitions.[1]

CONCLUSIONS

The accounting profession is under significant dnager of legal action for its advertising prohibitions. If the profession does not act to reduce its restrictions on advertising, the government will probably intervene to force that action. Therefore, accountants could lose the opportunity to regulate themselves in this area.

The current prohibitions against advertising by CPAs are quite strict and allow little or no opportunity for informing the public about services and prices. However, accountants already engage in indirect publicity through such methods as giving speeches and public relations programs.

Accountants can react to the pressures for change in three ways: (1) by maintaining the current restrictions against advertising, (2) by eliminating all restrictions, and (3) by restricting only those advertising activities which are counter to the best interests of the public and the profession. Of these alternatives, the third is most reasonable since it would allow consumers greater access to information about services and prices but would still protect against such abuses as false, deceptive, or misleading advertising.

v

While there are a number of arguments against advertising by CPAs, these arguments generally do not hold up under close scrutiny. Furthermore, accountants, as professionals, are responsible to society, and society would be best served by greater access to information about services and prices.

RECOMMENDATIONS

The interests of both society and the accounting profession would be best served by permitting advertising by CPAs. I therefore recommend that the accounting profession move to eliminate essentially all restrictions against advertising except those whoch protect against abuse. That is, restrictions should be kept that guard against false, misleading, or deceptive advertising. Furthermore, the new rule of conduct on advertising and solicitation proposed by the AICPA is a good model of such a rule.

SUMMARY

Court decisions and regulatory actions are pressuring changes to allow accountants to advertise, a move that is counter to the accepted professional ethics rules of conduct of the AICPA. Based on current consumer trends for a free flow of information, the AICPA task force on advertising has proposed a new professional ethics rule on advertising which reduces restrictions on advertising. Four interpretations accompany the new rule: (1) advertising should be tasteful, informative and objective; (2) advertising should not be false or misleading; (3) indirect advertising, such as speeches and seminars that enhance professional stature are permitted; (4) any claims that a CPA might make to be an expert are now allowed. Opponents of advertising state that advertising impairs independence, misleads the public, reduces the profession's credibility and dignity, lowers the quality of services rendered, and increases the cost of service fees. Advertising may, however, have positive effects: lower rates because of increased competition among CPA firms, increased demand for CPA services, greater exposure for smaller accounting firms to allow them to compete with larger firms. Whatever decision is ultimately made should be made to insure the best interests of the public and to maintain the honesty and integrity of the profession.

C P A   P R O F E S S I O N A L   E T H I C S :
T H E   A D V E R T I S I N G   D I L E M M A

THE ADVERTISING CONTROVERSY AND ITS CAUSES

Accountants have long prohibited advertising as a form of nonpro-fessional conduct.[2] Under the professional ethics rules of conduct of the American Institute of Certified Public Accountants (AICPA) and most state professional societies, advertising and solicitation by members are pro-hibited. In recent years, however, increasing importance has been placed on the consumer's right of access to information, and this has important implications for restraints against advertising. Judicial decisions based on the concepts of freedom of speech and restraint of trade and actions by regulatory bodies have put pressure on accountants and other professions to lift their advertising restrictions (Sprague, p. 27). The failure to do so could result in governmental intervention. However, whatever happens, any changes in advertising could have a significant impact on competition prices and on other factors affecting accountants (Bravenec, p. 10).

Pressures for Change from the Courts

In the past few years, a number of legal actions have been brought against restrictions on advertising by professional groups, especially law and medicine. These actions and the resulting decisions were based upon the concepts of freedom of speech under the First Amendment and restraints of trade and price fixing under the antitrust laws.[3] The two cases with especially important implications for accountants are the United States Supreme Court decisions for <u>Bates v. State Bar of Arizona</u> and <u>Goldfarb v. Virginia State Bar</u>.

<u>Bates v. State Bar of Arizona</u>. Bravenec (p. 1) states that the Bates decision held that the prohibition by the State Bar of Arizona against newspaper advertising of fees for routine legal services was an unconsti-tutional violation of the First Amendment right of free speech. Because of the similarities between the legal and accounting professions, this decision will undoubtedly be applied to accountants as well. Bravenec (p. 1) suggests that the decision may be much more far-reaching than just permitting newspaper advertising of fees for routine services. The decision may result in a series of changes in the accounting profession similar to those caused by the adoption of the federal income tax or the federal securities acts.

The original charges in the Bates case were that the ban on adver-tising violated the Sherman Act because it tended to limit competition and that it limited the right of free speech under the First Amendment (Bravenec, p. 3). The Supreme Court rules that because the State Bar of Arizona was considered an agent of the state, the ban on advertising did not violate the Sherman Act. However, the Supreme Court ruled that the ban on advertising did violate the free speech issue (Bravenec, p. 4). While the First Amendment had originally been interpreted to apply to matters affecting the public interest (such as political speech), this opinion applied that interpretation to include commercial speech as well. Thus, the interest in freedom of speech was interpreted to be a public interest in the need to be informed rather than a private interest in expression.[4]

While holding that attorneys' advertising should not be subject to "blanket supression," Justice Blackmun (writing the majority opinion for the Supreme Court) stated that certain areas could be regulated. First, "false, deceptive, or misleading" advertising may be regulated, and there would be little leeway for untruthful or misleading expression. Also, advertising claims about the quality of services may be restrained since such claims are not measurable and verifiable and therefore may be misleading. Similar objections may justify restrictions on in-person solicitation ("Supreme COurt Holds," p. 1096). Other possible areas for restriction are those concerning the time, place, and manner of advertising (Bravenec, p. 8).

The Bates decision was based in part on the landmark Virginia Pharmacy v. Virginia Citizens Consumer Council. Hinchey (p. 947) states that this decision held that a state may not completely suppress the publication of price information about legitimate professional services without a compelling reason. For the first time, the First Amendment was held to protect pure commercial speech (Hinchey, p. 947) because of the consumer's need for truthful, accurate, and informative advertising. A key passage of the Supreme Court decision asserts:

> Advertising, however tasteless and excessive it sometimes may seem, is nonetheless dissemination of information as to who is producing and selling what product, for what reason, and at what price. So long as we preserve a predominantly free enterprise economy, the allocation of our resources in large measure will be made through numerous private economic decisions. It is a matter of public interest that those decisions, in the aggregate, be intelligent and well-informed. To this end the free flow of commercial information is indispensable.[5]

Goldfarb v. Virginia State Bar. Another decision with important implications for accountants is Goldfarb v. Virginia State Bar. The Supreme Court ruled that a private voluntary bar association's advertising rule had price-fixing implications and was therefore illegal under the antitrust laws.[6] Since this case involved a private organization and not an agent of the state, the fee schedules of the bar association were not exempt as "state activity." Furthermore, the practice of law was held to be commerce and therefore was not exempt from the antitrust laws as a "learned profession."[7]

2

Pressures from Other Sources

In addition to the legal action discussed above, there have been other pressures for change. Ostlund reports that state attorneys general were advising regulatory boards of the professions to either repeal or not enforce prohibitions against advertising.[8] To illustrate, Sprague (p. 30) reports that Deputy Assistant Attorney General Joe Simms warned the Arizona State Bar:

> When a self-regulated profession publicly and visibly shows basic disregard for consumers and competitive interest, it seems entirely possible that the public may decide that a new system of regulation is necessary.

The Justive Department and The Federal Trade Commission (FTC) were also instituting investigations and legal efforts to force the professions to modify or repeal their advertising rules. In 1975, the FTC announced its intention to examine private and public restraints on free market competition. Special emphasis was given to advertising prohibitions which prevent consumers from making the well-informed choices which foster price competition.[9] The FTC has therefore moved against the American Dental Association charging its ban of advertising of prices for services has prevented competition (Ostlund, p. 60-61). The FTC also moved against the American Medical Association claiming that its ethical band on advertising illegally restrained competition (Ostlund, p. 61).

The FTC has announced a broad-scale investigation of the accounting profession, which is to include an examination of advertising rules of the professional societies and of the state boards of accountancy. The Justice Department is also considering whether the AICPA prohibitions of advertising rule violates the federal antitrust laws. Ostlund reports that as far as he knows, all professional associations that were challenged based on their advertising rules lost their cases in trial courts. While a number of cases are still under appeal, the ultimate outcome is not known (Ostlund, p. 61).

Implications for Accountants

For the accounting profession, danger of legal action exists under both the free speech and anticompetitive issues. In the case of Bates v. State Bar of Arizona, the authority of the state bar association is similar to that of a state board of accountancy. Since such state boards of accountancy would be agents of the state, they could not be attacked for antitrust violations. Therefore, any legal action would probably be under the constitutional issue of free speech. On the other hand, the AICPA and state societies are private voluntary organizations, not state agencies. Therefore, any legal action against the AICPA or a state society would be brought under the antitrust laws (Ostlund, p. 61).

If the accounting profession maintains its current prohibitions and does not reduce them, different groups interested in the consumer's right to know would be critical of such a failure. A government agency, such as the Justice Department, might seek an injunction to prohibit

3

accountants from enforcing or even having those restrictions. If such an agency were successful, all prohibitions against advertising and solicitation might be eliminated, and unrestricted advertising could result, with all its dangers of abuse. The only restrictions remaining would be federal or state laws, and the opportunity for accountants to adopt a reasonable restriction in the public interest would be lost (Ostlund, p. 63).

CURRENT STATUS OF ADVERTISING BY CPAs

As stated earlier, accountants have had prohibitions against advertising for a number of years. Until 1922, the organized accounting profession had no restrictions on advertising.[10] At that time, the American Institute of (Certified Public) Accountants adopted a rule against advertising (Ostlund, p. 49). However, the new rule was not acceptable to some practitioners, and one prominent firm withdrew its membership for 13 years (Sprague, p. 27). Although the rule has been modified and refined over the years, the rule during the past decade has prohibited all paid advertising (Ostlund, p. 59). The current viewpoint of the AICPA toward advertising and solicitation is found in Rule 502 of the Rules of Conduct of the Code of Professional Ethics.

Code of Professional Ethics, Rule 502

Rule 502 of the Code of Professional Ethics reads simply:

Rule 502 - <u>Solicitation and advertising.</u> A member shall not to obtain clients by solicitation. Advertising is a form of solicitation and is prohibited.[11]

This rule is interpreted to prohibit such activities as: (1) advertisements in newspapers or any other medium, (2) holding oneself out in any medium as a specialist, (3) a listing in office buildings directories in a manner not in good taste and not modest in size, and (4) a telephone listing in box or display form or in more than one place in a classified directory (<u>Restatement</u>, pp. 37-39). Thus, the restrictions on advertising, of which the above interpretations are a representative sample, are quite strict as to what is excluded under the current ethics rule. (The complete listing of interpretations is included in Appendix C.)

As justification for the restrictions on advertising, specified in Rule 502, the AICPA in its "Concepts of Professional Ethics" says that advertising and solicitation could encourage representations which might mislead the public and thereby reduce or destroy the profession's usefulness to society." The "Concepts" also prohibit advertising as a form of solicitation, which "tends to lessen the professional independence toward clients which is essential to the best interests of the public" and which "may also induce an unhealthy rivalry within the profession . . ." (<u>Restatement</u>, p. 14). Finally, both advertising and solicitation are condemned as indicating a dominant interest in profits as opposed to a desire for excellence in performance (<u>Restatement</u>, p. 15).

4

Current Extent of Advertising by Accountants

Sprague reports that one of the problems in dealing with professional advertising is to define it. He asks whether advertising must be paid for or whether it must refer specifically to services available for a fee. Many activities of CPAs may bring them to the attention of the public, even when there are no direct attempts to advertise. In fact, most of the large CPA firms have public relations programs and may circumvent the technical prohibitions against advertising under the reported purpose of performing a service for their communities (Sprague, p. 27).

Different forms of activities which could possibly be construed as advertising include the public exposure from speech making, writing books and articles, and preparing informational booklets, papers, or technical guides and then making them available "on request." Furthermore, articles in newspapers and journals may be based on interviews with partners of accounting firms. Sprague reports that it is not difficult to have the press initiate and carry out such interviews and still insure that the desired publicity is obtained (Sprague, p. 27).

Thus, a certain amount of indirect advertising through different forms of publicity is currently done even though the means used are not within the current definition of advertising. Also, the larger and more prominent CPA firms appear in a better position to benefit from this indirect advertising.

STRATEGIES FOR DEALING WITH THE ADVERTISING DILEMMA

In view of the current pressures for a free flow of information on consumers about prices and services, three alternative courses of action exist: (1) make no changes to the current advertising; (2) eliminate all advertising restrictions; and (3) selectively reduce the restrictions. Utilizing the third alternative, the AICPA ethics division has developed a proposed new professional ethics rule on advertising which essentially eliminates the prohibitions against advertising except those deemed to be in the best interest of society and the profession.

Maintain Current Restruction

The first alternative is to maintain the current advertising restrictions with little or no change. This alternative could be termed the traditional approach and may be preferred by most CPAs. McKee reports that a survey revealed that most CPAs, especially the older and more experienced ones, strongly oppose CPAs formally advertising their services.[12] However, as stated earlier, this alternative leaves open the dangers of government intervention. According to Ostlund (p. 63), elimination of all prohibitions against advertising and solicitation could result if no changes are made.

5

Eliminate All Restrictions

The second alternative is to eliminate all restrictions against advertising. Since most CPAs strongly disagree with advertising by CPAs (McKee, p. 70), this alternative would probably be least acceptable to CPAs. However, as stated above, this alternative could be imposed by governmental intervention, if not by selection by the accounting profession. Ostlund (p. 63) reports that if all restrictions against advertising and solicitation were removed, accountants would be able to use any subjective and self-laudatory descriptions they wished. Furthermore, Ostlund (p. 63) believes that the elimination of all restrictions would result in misleading comparative advertising and testimonials and in unrestricted solicitation of other CPAs' clients would result.

Zuckert, however, asserts that because of the many regulatory agencies and other groups already in existence, there is little chance for unscrupulous advertising to run long enough to "impact the public."[13] In fact, California has adopted this approach by repealing all restrictions against advertising (Sprague, p. 30).

Selectively Reduce the Restrictions

The third alternative is to eliminate part of the restriction while keeping or adding those deemed necessary to best serve the interests of society and the accounting profession. This approach is a compromise between the other alternatives and is already being considered by several professional groups. For instance, this approach was used by the AICPA task force on advertising in developing the proposed new Rule 502 discussed below. Also, the New Hampshire Board of Accountancy recently announced that it would no longer enforce the current prohibitions on advertising. At the same time, the Board proposed a new rule which would control advertising to the extent that it contains false and misleading statements (Zuckert, p. 13). In addition, the New York State Board of Regents recently voted to allow advertising of price information by accountants and other professionals. However, advertising that is "sensational or flamboyant," uses testimonials, guarantees results, or claims superiority over other professionals would still be prohibited.[14]

Proposed AICPA Revision of Rule 502

In 1976, in response to the pressures for more information for consumers, the AICPA ethics division appointed a task force on advertising to determine if the interests of the public and the accounting profession would be better served by modifications to the current prohibitions against advertising (Ostlund, p. 59). Ostlund (p. 60) reports that the conclusion of the task force was "that the public had a right and a need for a free flow of information concerning the availability of accounting services, with the flow of information being curtailed only if there were counterbalancing public interests involved."

Accordingly, the task force developed a proposed new Rule 502, which reads:

6

Rule 502 - <u>Advertising or Other Forms of Solicitation</u>. A member shall not seek to obtain clients by advertising or other forms of solicitation in a manner that is false, misleading or deceptive. The direct uninvited solicitation of a specific potential client is prohibited.[15]

The four interpretations that accompanied the proposed new rule are summarized below. First, advertising that is informative and objective is permitted as long as it is in good taste and professionally dignified. Furthermore, no restrictions are made as to media, type of advertising, or frequency of advertising (Exposure draft, p. 1). Second, false, misleading, or deceptive advertising is prohibited since it is not in the public interest (Exposure draft, p. 2). Third, indirect forms of solicitation that enhance professional stature and reputations of CPAs, such as giving speeches and conducting seminars, are in the public interest and are permitted. Finally, a CPA may not claim to be an expert or specialist. While he or his firm may indicate the services offered, he may not state that the practice is limited to certain types of service (Exposure draft, p. 3). (A copy of the proposed new rule and interpretations are included in Appendix D.)

This rule has been submitted to the AICPA membership for a mail ballot. If two-thirds of those voting favor the proposed rule, it will become the new professional ethics rule of conduct concerning advertising and solicitation. If not, Ostlund reports that he is uncertain what will happen. However, he thinks that consumer groups, the media, and possibly legislators would be critical, and the opportunity for the accounting profession to develop and adopt their own reasonable restriction in the public interest could be lost (Ostlund, p. 63).

ADVISABILITY OF CHANGE OF ADVERTISING PROHIBITIONS

There are several factors which must be considered in deciding how accountants should react to the current pressures for change of advertising prohibitions. First, there are several arguments which support prohibitions of advertising as being in the best interests of the profession and the public. At the same time, however, counterarguments show that these assumptions may be either groundless or false. Second, the ultimate effect of a change on accountants themselves should be taken into account. Finally, the responsibility of the accounting profession to society must be considered since a decision on advertising would have a significant impact on the public, as well as, on members of the profession.

Arguments For and Against Advertising by CPAs

There are several traditional arguments to be made against permitting paid advertising by CPAs. Generally, these arguments have a goal of protecting and preserving the professional image and assuring client confidence. Ostlund (p. 60) reports that most of these arguments were considered and then rejected by the AICPA task force on advertising since they felt the arguments did not stand up under close scrutiny in the

7

in the current environment. These traditional arguments against advertising and the consideration of their merit are discussed below.

Advertising impairs independence. Sprague (p. 28) states that the
origin of the prohibition against advertising is sometimes ascribed to a
need to protect and support the CPA's independence in dealing with
clients. Sprague thinks this argument is questionable since prohibitions
against advertising probably predate the rules on independence. Furthermore, Ostlund (p. 60) states:

> No one has yet stated how obtaining a client by advertising
> impairs a CPA's independence, since truthful advertising
> is just a means of informing potential clients that services
> are available. The client must still seek out and select the
> CPA.

Advertising misleads the public. Some accountants argue that the
services offered in this profession, such as auditing and tax, are
highly technical and therefore are only slightly understood by the
public. Advertising of such services could thus mislead the public,
since they would be unable to adequately evaluate the competence in
these fields. If only the less competent CPAs advertise, this argument
could have some merit. However, to answer the question of misleading
advertising, Sprague says that the public will increase in sophisitcation
and will eventually recognize inferior work. Also, statutory and professional regulations against advertising are now enforced more
effectively than they were when the prohibitions against advertising were
first instituted (Sprague, p. 28).

Advertising reduces the profession's credibility and dignity. The
theory for this argument is that the public's confidence in the accounting
profession is best preserved by strict, self-imposed controls over advertising.[16] Ostlund states this argument would be more valid for the past
than for the present because of the current demand by consumers for a
free flow of information. Furthermore, management consulting firms and
insurance companies currently advertise without being considered un-
dignified (Ostlund, p. 60).

Advertising lowers the quality of services rendered. This argument
is based on the concern that if CPAs solicit clients through advertising,
especially on a price basis, the quality of professional work may suffer.
However, Ostlund (p. 60) says "The true professional will render the
services necessary in the circumstances no matter how he obtains the
client." Ostlund (p. 60) fu-ther reports that there are always some who
will lessen the quality of service to obtain an engagement, but this will
occur whether advertising is prohibited or not.

Advertising costs cause increased fees for service. The idea for
this argument is that advertising costs will be merely passed on to
clients in the form of higher fees for services. However, this argument
could be used against advertising by any business. Also, consumerists
claim that advertising may ultimately cause lower fees because the resulting competition would encourage firms to become more efficient in
their operations (Ostlund, p. 60).

8

Possible Effects of Change on Accountants

If advertising by CPAs is permitted under a revised ethics rule, a number of possible effects could result. Concerning the effects on fees for services, the probable results are not easily determined since there could be a tradeoff between higher and lower rates. As stated earlier, lower rates could occur because of the more efficient operations encouraged by competition, and higher rates could occur as advertising costs are passed to the clients.

The small practitioner is currently at a disadvantage in competing with large firms because of their extensive public relations programs. Thus, if advertising is permitted, the small practitioner might be better able to compete by emphasizing personal service, continuity, availability, and less risk of breach of confidentiality, as well as lower overhead and billing rates (Sprague, p. 29). Also, the ability to advertise may help the new CPA in starting his practice, since he could attract clients through advertising (Ostlund, pp. 62-63). About the possible types of advertising used, large firms may use an institutional type of advertising in the national media. However, the smaller firms and local practitioners would probably advertise in the local media (Ostlund, p. 62).

Another possibility is that advertising will increase the demand for the services of CPAs. Sprague (p. 28) reports that studies show that 80% of the American people do not use the services of lawyers because they do not know which ones are best able to help them. This could also be true for accountants. In addition, income tax preparers, such as H&R Block, advertise extensively. Presumably, many of their customers are not being served by CPAs and thus represent an untapped market (Sprague, p. 28).

I conclude from the above that advertising would not result in great harm to the accounting profession as a whole. However, changes within the profession would undoubtedly occur, and the accounting profession would go through an adjustment period. In addition, advertising could actually result in an increased business because of the greater awareness of the public of the services provided by accountants.

Social Responsibility of Accountants

Generally, members of a profession share certain attributes which relate to their responsibility to the public:

Each renders essential services to society.
Each is governed by ethical principles which emphasize the virtues of self-subordination, honesty, probity, devotion to the welfare of those served.[17]

Apparently, the welfare of the public should play an important role in determining the rules of conduct for CPAs. This is emphasized by Kapnick when he says:

9

If accountants are to regain their righ-ful place in our
free enterprise society, we must recognize that we are
accountable not to management, not to government regulators,
not to the profession, but that we are accountable to the
public at large.[18]

Since advertising does inform the public of services deemed essential
to its welfare, the appropriate action should be that which would allow
one the greatest opportunity to make a well-informed choice. As an indication of the importance of advertising as an information source, Crain
reports, "advertising is a major communications artery for the flow of
ideas and information in a free society."[19]

At the same time, however, accountants should attempt to protect the
public against abuses of advertising. The most practical method to
accomplish this would be to restrict advertising practices which are
false, deceptive, or misleading.

CONCLUSIONS

The accounting profession is under significant dnager of legal action
for its advertising prohibitions. If the profession does not act to
reduce its restrictions on advertising, the government will probably
intervene to force that action. Therefore, accountants could lose the
opportunity to regulate themselves in this area.

The current prohibitions against advertising by CPAs are quite strict
and allow little or no opportunity for informing the public about services
and prices. However, accountants already engage in indirect publicity
through such methods as giving speeches and public relations programs.

Accountants can react to the pressures for change in three ways:
(1) by maintaining the current restrictions against advertising, (2) by
eliminating all restrictions, and (3) by restricting only those advertising activities which are counter to the best interests of the public
and the profession. Of these alternatives, the third is most reasonable
since it would allow consumers greater access to information about
services and prices but would still protect against such abuses as
false, deceptive, or misleading advertising.

While there are a number of arguments against advertising by CPAs,
these arguments generally do not hold up under close scrutiny. Furthermore, accountants, as professionals, are responsible to society, and
soecity would be best served by greater access to information about
services and prices.

RECOMMENDATIONS

The interests of both society and the accounting profession would be
best served by permitting advertising by CPAs. I therefore recommend that

10

the accounting profession move to eliminate essentially al restrictions against advertising except those which protect against abuse. That is, restrictions should be kept that guard against false, misleading, or deceptive advertising. Furthermore, the new rule of conduct on advertising and solicitation proposed by the AICPA is a good model of such a rule.

REFERENCES

[1] W. Douglas Sprague, "The Advertising Dilemma," The CPA Journal 47 (January 1977), p. 27.

[2] Lorence Bravenec and Philip Ljungdahl, "Advertising by Accountants: The Upcoming Upheaval." Paper presented at the Southwest Triple A, Dallas, Texas, March 1978, p. 1.

[3] "Supreme Court Holds Lawyers May Advertise," American Bar Association Journal, 63 (August 1977), pp. 1093-1094.

[4] John W. Hinchey, "The First Amendment and the Delivery of Legal Services," American Bar Association Journal, 63 (July 1977), p. 946.

[5] Virginia State Board of Pharmacy et al., Appellants, v. Virginia Citizens Consumer Council, Inc., et al., Supreme Court of the United States, No. 74-895, Slip Opinion (May 24, 1976), pp. 16-17.

[6] Goldfarb et ux. v. Virginia State Bar et al., Supreme Court of the United States, No. 74-70, Slip Opinion (June 16, 1976), p. I.

[7] Lorence Bravenac, Student handout on antitrust law (Spring 1978), p. 1.

[8] Clayton A. Ostlund, "A Discussion of the Proposed Ethics Rule on Advertising by CPA Practitioners," The Journal of Accountancy, 145 (January 1978), p. 59.

[9] Federal Trade Commission, Annual Report of the Federal Trade Commission: 1975 (Washington, D. C.: U. S. Govt. Printing Office, 1975), p. 21.

[10] Federal Trade Commission, "Commission Challenges AMA's Ethical Ban on Advertising," FTC News Summary, 52 (December 26, 1975).

[11] Restatement of the Code of Professional Ethics (New York: American Institute of Certified Public Accountants, 1972), pp. 24-25.

11

[12]Thomas E. McKee, "CPAs' Attitudes Toward Professional Advertising," _The Ohio CPA_, 36 (Summer 1977), p. 72.

[13]Donald M. Zuckert, "Think About Your Advertising Program," _The CPA Journal_, 47 (October 1977), p. 11-12.

[14]American Institute of Certified Public Accountants, _The CPA Letter_, 57 (September 5, 1977), p. 2.

[15]Exposure draft of the proposed new Rule 502, (New York: American Institute of Certified Public Accountants, September 28, 1977), p. 1.

[16]"Should CPAs Advertise?" _The Journal of Accountancy_, 141 (April 1976), p. 64.

[17]Robert H. Roy and James H. MacNeill, _Horizons for a Profession_ (New York: American Institute of Certified Public Accountants, 1976), p. 31.

[18]Harvey Kapnick, _Accounting and Financial Reporting: In the Public Interest_, 1 (Chicago: Arthur Anderson and Co., 1974), p. 49.

[19]"Comments from Advertising," _American Bar Association Journal_, 63 (August 1977), p. 1098.

APPENDIX A

Proposal

13

2007 Langford
College Station, Texas 77840
February 23, 19__

Dr. Elizabeth Tebeaux
Department of English
Texas A&M University
College Station, Texas 77843

Dear Dr. Tebeaux:

In partial fulfillment of the requirements of your technical writing course, English 301, I intend to investigate the upcoming, probable revision of the Professional ethics restriction of advertising by Certified Public Accountants (CPA's).

Purpose

I will examine the current controversy of advertising by professionals, especially as it pertains to the accounting profession. I will look at recent court decisions and other pressures for change which brought about the present situation and will then look at the probable impact on accountants. I will explain the status of American Institute of Certified Public Accountants (AICPA) professional ethics rulings on advertising and analyze the advisibility of change. After exploring alternative ways of reacting to the pressures for change, I will make a recommendation for the best course of action to be taken.

Background

In recent years, increasing importance has been placed on the consumer's right of access to information. Based on the concepts of freedom of speech and restraint of trade, a series of Supreme Court decisions have ruled against restrictions on advertising by professional groups. In addition, investigations by regulatory bodies have been made and litigation filed against professional groups for restricting advertising of services and prices. These actions have great potential implications for the accounting profession. Furthermore, the Federal Trade Commission (FTC) is now investigating the accounting profession's advertising policies. If the accounting profession does not revise its rules in light of the pressures for change, the government will probably either attempt to regulate the profession in this aspect or completely do away with advertising restrictions. The AICPA has developed a revised advertising rule, but substantial resistance by accountants may prevent the change from being enacted. Whatever happens, any changes in advertising policy could have a significant impact on competition, prices, and other factors affecting accountants.

14

Probable Procedure

The procedure I will follow in covering this topic is outlined below.
While I plan to use the format described, this outline is tentative
and may be changed for the final report.

I. Nature and Causes of the Advertising Controversy

    A. Pressures for change
       1. Supreme Court
       2. Federal Trade Commission and other regulatory groups
       3. Consumer groups

    B. Implications for accountants
       1. Possible government regulation
       2. Possible striking down of restrictions

II. Current Status

    A. Professional ethics rule on advertising
       1. Rule 502 and its interpretations
       2. Purposes of the rule

    B. Extent of advertising currentlydone and means used

    C. Needs of the public

    D. Social responsibility of accountants

III. Possible Solutions

    A. Alternative treatments of the advertising problem
       1. No change
       2. Proposed AICPA revision of Rule 502
       3. Other possible rules
       4. Elimination of all rules

    B. Views of accountants

    C. Possible effects on accountants from changes in advertising
       policy

IV. Evaluation and Conclusion

    A. Ways to best serve interests of groups involved
       1. Public
       2. Accountants

    B. Recommended course of action

15

Facilities Available and Not Available

The controversy of advertising by CPA's is very current. Much of the information on this topic has been published in the last nine months and thus is only available in journals, magazines, and newspapers. Therefore, I will probably use mainly journals for the more current portions of the report. I will use a few government publications, especially for citing Supreme Court decisions. I will rely on AICPA publications for current professional ethics rules and interpretations. Background material will come from books and other sources.

Because of the current nature of my topic, relative little published information is available for certain areas of the report. In addition, sources are often hard to find because most indexes and abstracts are not very current. Also, the library's collection of newsletters from the Federal Trade Commission (FTC) was discontinued in 1975. Without this information, I may have to rely on secondary sources for FTC announcements.

Preliminary Problems

As mentioned above, my topic is quite current, and the number of sources is limited in certain areas. While I have found a number of very good articles, I have not been able to find as many as I would like. There-fore, the depth of sources in these areas may not be as great as I would like. A potential problem is that the final report could be too long. If this is the case, I will either eliminate nonessential items or treat them in summary fashion.

Faults of the Topic

I can see no major weaknesses of this topic. However, some published material is judgmental rather than objective. This could indicate emotional bias in some cases.

Merits of the Topic

This topic is of current interest and has important implications for accountants. Research in this area will increase my knowledge of pro-fessional ethics. I will also learn about the attitudes of accountants and the environment surrounding the profession.

Conclusion

In deciding what they should do, accountants are faced with three basic alternatives: (1) do nothing, (2) eliminate all restrictions against advertising, and (3) permit advertising, subject to specified restrictions.

16

Dr. Elizabeth Tebeaux
February 23, 19__
Page 4

The third alternative seems to be the most logical choice of the three.
However, I must reach some conclusion about what level of restriction
would be best.

Sincerely,

Janet M. Barnes

17

APPENDIX B

Progress Report

2007 Langford
College Station, Texas
77840
April 6, 19__

Dr. Elizabeth Tebeaux
Department of English
Texas A&M University
College Station, Texas   77843

Dear Dr. Tebeaux:

In compliance with the requirements of your technical writing course, English 301, I submit this progress report to inform you of the progress I have made in research of my topic, "CPA Professional Ethics: The Advertising Dilemma."

<u>Purpose</u>

As my research progresses, I will continue my examination of the current controversy of advertising by accountants. Therefore, my plans are to look at recent court decisions and other pressures for change which brought about the present situation and then look at the probable impact on accountants. I will explain the status of American Institute of Certified Public Accountants (AICPA) professional ethics rulings on advertising and will then explore strategies for dealing with the pressures for change. After analyzing the need and advisability of change, I will make a recommendation for the best course of action to be taken.

<u>Procedure</u>

The procedure I plan to follow is outlined below.

    I. The Advertising Controversy and its Causes

        A. Pressures for change

            1. Implications of judicial decisions

            2. Pressures from other sources
                a. Regulatory agencies
                b. Consumer groups

        B. Implications for Accountants

            1. Possible striking down of restrictions

            2. Possible government regulation

19

II. Current Status of Advertising by CPAs

    A. Professional ethics rule on advertising

        1. Rule 502 and its interpretations

        2. Justifications and purposes of the rule

    B. Current extent of advertising by accountnats

III. Strategies for Dealing with the Advertising Dilemma

    A. Alternative ways of reacting to the advertising problem

        1. Retention of current advertising restrictions

        2. Reduction of restrictions

        3. Elimination of all advertising restrictions

    B. Proposed AICPA revision of Rule 502

    C. Possible effects on accountants from change

IV. Advisability of Change of Advertising Restrictions

    A. Arguments for change

    B. Arguments against change

    C. Social responsibility of accountants

    D. Needs of the public

  V. Conclusions

 VI. Recommendations

Work Completed

In researching my topic, I have found a number of sources especially helpful. These sources and a brief explanation of how they are useful are listed below.

    "Supreme Court Holds Lawyers May Advertise," American Bar Association Journal, 63 (August 1977), 1092-1098.

        This article explains the impact of recent court decisions upon the legal profession. A recent Supreme Court decision has held that prohibitions against advertising by lawyers violates the First Amendment. This and other decisions and their implications generally apply to accountants because of similarities between the two professions.

Donald M. Zuckert, "Think About Your Advertising Program," The CPA Journal, 47 No. 10 (October 1977), 11-13.

This article presents arguments in favor of advertising by accountants and tells how the profession can ultimately benefit. In addition, the author advises accountants to start thinking about ways to put advertising to use for their firms.

A. Clayton Ostlund, "A Discussion of the Proposed Ethics Rule on Advertising by CPA Practioners," The Journal of Accountancy, 145, No. 1 (January 1978), 59-63.

This article presents information on and an analysis of the proposed AICPA ethics rule on advertising. In addition, the author defines the background for the current advertising rule and presents arguments in favor of reduced restrictions.

W. Douglas Sprague, "The Advertising Dilemma," The CPA Journal, 47, No. 1 (January 1977), 27-30.

This article discusses a number of aspects of the advertising problem: the ambiguities associated with what is (or is not) advertising; arguments for and against advertising; how different segments of the accounting profession would be affected by the proposed ethics change; and the problem of the relationship between solicitation and advertising.

Exposure draft for the proposed new Rule 502, American Institute of Certified Public Accountants, New York, September 28, 1977.

This exposure draft presents the new professional ethics rule on advertising proposed by the AICPA. In addition, it also includes interpretations of what the rule and its provisions should allow or prohibit.

Restatement of the Code of Professional Ethics, (New York: American Institute of Certified Public Accountants, 1972), pp. 14-15, 24-25, 37-43.

This publication contains the code of professional ethics rules and interpretations which were effective March 1,

21

1973, and which are still in effect. The restrictions against advertising, which are currently being challenged, are included in this publication.

Thomas E. McKee, "CPAs' Attitudes Toward Professional Advertising," The Ohio CPA, 36, No. 3 (Summer 1977), 69-72.

This article contains the results of a survey of accountants to determine their attitudes, beliefs, and intentions about advertising by CPAs.

<u>Work Remaining</u>

Before my research on advertising by accountants is complete, I need to determine if certain newspapers, such as the Wall Street Journal, have any recent articles or news items which pertain to my topic.

Sincerely,

Janet M. Barnes

22

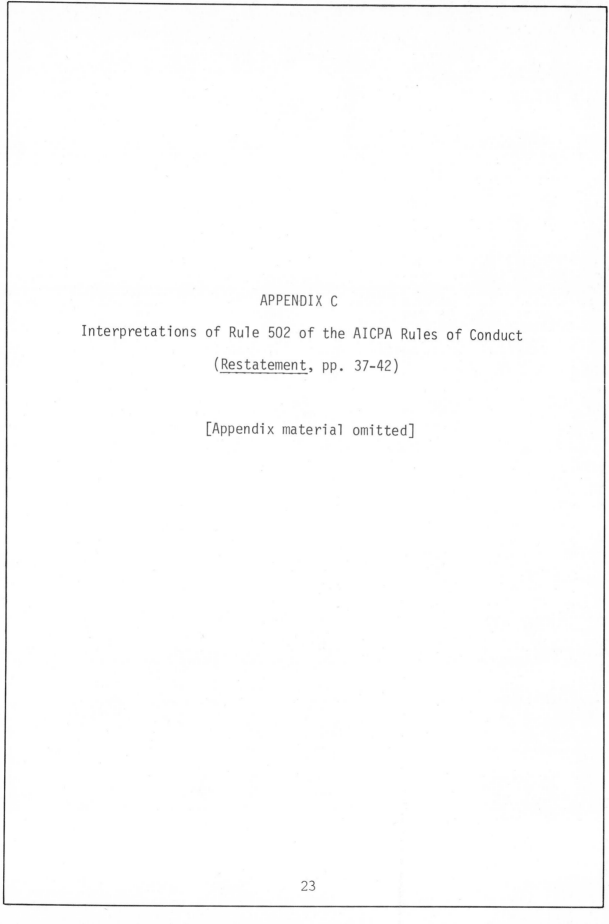

APPENDIX C

Interpretations of Rule 502 of the AICPA Rules of Conduct

(Restatement, pp. 37-42)

[Appendix material omitted]

23

APPENDIX D

New Professional Ethics Rule 502 and Interpretations

Proposed by the AICPA Task Force on Advertising

(Exposure draft, pp. 1-3)

[Appendix material omitted]

APPENDIX E

LIST OF WORKS CONSULTED

Bates et al., v. State Bar of Arizona, Supreme Court of the United States, No. 76-316, Slip Opinion (June 27, 1977).

Darwin J. Casler, The Evolution of CPA Ethics: A Profile of Professionalization, Occasional Papger No. 12 (East Lansing: Michigan State University, 1964).

"Closing in on the Professions," Business Week, 2404 (October 27, 1975), 106-108.

"CPAs Suggest the Watchdogs They Want," Business Week, 2484 (May 23, 1977), 94, 96.

Ralph W. Estes, Accounting and Society. (Los Angeles: Melville Publishing Co., 1973).

Roger Hermanson, Stephen Lock, John Saada, and Robert Strawer, Auditing Theory and Practice. (Homewood, Illinois: RIchard D. Irwin, Inc., 1976).

Leroy Jeffers, "The Lawyer Advertising Case - Victory and Defeat," Texas Bar Journal, 40 (September 1977), 747-748.

"Kentucky Attorney General Supports Bidding Bar," Journal of Accountancy, 139 (January 1975), 20-21.

Stanley D. Robinson, "Recent Antitrust Developments: 1975," Columbia Law Review, 76 (March 1976), 191-235.

"Shall We Advertise," American Bar Association Journal, 61 (December 1975), 1525-26.

"The American Medical Association, et al.," Federal Trade Commission Decisions, 89 (Washington, D. C.: U. S. Government Printing Office, 1977), pp. 296-297.

One of the most useful and prevalent documents in the modern business world is the solicited or unsolicited proposal. You will often respond to a company's request for a proposal (commonly abbreviated RFP) as a prime opportunity to solve their described problems or needs by your firm's specific goods and services. At the operational or supervisory levels of your career, you may contribute to this document by preparing written specifications of the special materials you work with or design. You may be further involved in the research, installation, servicing, promotion, or negotiations that come before and after the actual proposal and are described within it.

A proposal has been called "a hybrid document: part engineering report, part sales brochure, part legal bid." It would be difficult to overemphasize the importance of clear, complete details in describing and explaining what you propose to do for the reader. The magnitude of the project determines the amount of detail to be given, of course. An effective proposal might be broadly described as a well organized, readable document that presents in detail the most believable answer to the problem.

Whether short or long, a proposal is organized so as to present the offered solution in a clear, convincing document that establishes trust between possible buyer and would-be seller and completely covers the customer's need. Technical style of expression is used, with few, if any, first- or second-person pronouns in a formal presentation; however, many good proposal writers recommend a more person-to-person tone, especially in explaining how the proposing company has analyzed the reader's needs. In any case, the tone of the message is pleasant, factual, and nonemotional. The whole document is an actual sales message without the "hard-sell" tactics that characterize many sales letters.

You may find a letter format the most suitable for a short proposal because, although all parts of the genuine proposal go into the message, you can tell all your information in only a page or two. The following one-page proposal for the construction of a Boy Scout building gives enough facts by which the committee could decide to award the contract to this company.

Many proposals use a formal manuscript format such as is common for other business reports, giving an appearance of added importance and carefulness that reflects well upon the proposing company. Though it may not be appropriate to make a big production of a minor and more casual proposal, the amount of money involved is not the deciding factor in choosing a format. A well prepared document, properly subheaded and double-spaced for easy reading, makes a positive impression on the receiver. To present your proposal in this form, you will want to introduce it by a transmittal letter with a person-to-person tone; the letter is part of the frontmatter bound with the main document. Other physical parts you may find useful are listed further on in this text, and any or all of these may be appropriate. Some firms specify the format to be followed in the proposals they request, and the responding company is careful not to violate these stated preferences in preparing the number of required copies. Whether double- or single-spacing is preferred, subheadings and careful paragraphing are essential to a clear, readable proposal. A summary is usually required as a separate part to be placed before the body of a larger formal report.

Here is a comprehensive outline for a proposal; it may be adapted to projects of nearly any nature and size. The main sections represent the customary parts found in any proposal and are usually in the order given. The subsections vary with the specific instance and are included or not, according to the need for details about the subject named. Coverage of any one topic shown in the outline may range from a sentence or two to a bound volume.

Figure 5-24. Proposal in Letter Form

 FOREST W. McNEIR & SON *Contractors*

April 28, 1971

6501 BROMPTON ROAD
HOUSTON 5, TEXAS
MADISON 3-8946

WE PROPOSE TO CONSTRUCT A SCOUT BUILDING FOR SOUTH MAIN BAPTIST CHURCH, HOUSTON, TEXAS, IN ACCORDANCE WITH PLANS AND SPECIFICATIONS PREPARED BY SMART & WHITEHEAD, AIA ARCHITECTS, IN STAGES, WITH THE COST BREAKDOWN FOR EACH STAGE AS SHOWN BELOW.

STAGE #1: To perform all work in accordance with plans and specifications to complete the following items; all exterior masonry walls and all interior load—bearing walls necessary to complete structural portion of building, and including closets #1 and #2 and the janitor's closet, all concrete foundation and floor slab work, all structural steel work, roof decking, all roofing and exterior sheet metal work including gutters and downspouts, all windows and glazing, all exterior doors and frames, all exterior stucco, all exterior painting, and all other work necessary to make the building weatherproof, including exterior hardware. Also, all interior door frames set in load—bearing masonry walls (no interior doors), all underground plumbing work, with water and gas lines run into building (no fixtures) and including underground drain lines from downspouts, electrical service, all electrical outlets shown in load—bearing walls, all ceiling outlets with temporary porcelain receptacles (no permanent fixtures except exterior lighting).

$ 37,465.00

STAGE #2: To pay for the services of architects & engineers.

$ 2,000.00

STAGE #3: To perform all work in accordance with plans and specifications to complete the following additional items: All remaining interior masonry and wood stud walls, with all electrical wall outlets and all door frames (no doors or electrical fixtures).

$ 2,065.00

STAGE #4: To perform all work necessary to complete the following items, in accordance with plans and specifications: Sheetrock ceilings above corridor for return air system, A.C. duct system, with registers, for air conditioning in all rooms except Offices #1 and #2, Kitchen and Board of Review room, install ceiling beams and trim in assembly room, all painting for walls and woodwork except in Offices #1 and #2, Kitchen and Board of Review room, all ceilings, electrical fixtures, resilient floor and base, except in Offices #1 and #2, Kitchen and Board of Review room, and install raised brick platform in Assembly Room.

$ 8,220.00

STAGE #5: To perform all work necessary, in accordance with plans and specifications, to complete the building, including wall panelling and fabric in the Board of Review room, kitchen cabinets, all plumbing and electrical fixtures, all air conditioning equipment, with system complete, all doors, hardware, painting, ceilings, resilient floors and base, carpeting, exterior walks, finish grading and grass planting.

$ 11,250.00

TOTAL COST OF BUILDING $ 61,000.00
                                        FOREST W. MCNEIR & SON, CONTRACTORS

I. Introduction
   A. Identifying statement giving name of proposer and customer, source and date of authority, nature of subject involved
   B. General statement of problem and how proposal will offer to solve it
   C. General qualifications of proposer to succeed in this task, (experience, facilities, and personnel background)

II. Technical Proposal
   A. Analysis of problem into causes, needs, and alternate answers (show of understanding of customer's situation)
   B. Specifications of what proposer offers to do and why
      1. Goods and material to be furnished (described and justified)
      2. Services to be furnished (described and justified)
      3. Guarantees and legal commitments
      4. Work to be done at every stage of project (classifications and number of persons)
      5. Schedule of proposed dates for work phases (test for each stage)
      6. Delivery schedule (means of transportation, site of discharge, target dates)

III. Management-Personnel Proposal
   A. Organizational level at which planning and management would be handled
   B. Qualifications of all persons directly related to project (manager, team members, professional specialists)
   C. Union and other working contracts involved

IV. Commercial Proposal
   A. Statement of explanation regarding proposer's effort to consider budgetary factors
   B. Details of costs of every category

V. Conclusion
   A. Statement of how long proposal will be open
   B. Techniques for communicating about proposal
   C. Statement showing desire to benefit customer in every way

In introducing the message, you identify it as a proposal and tell the date and kind of request that prompted it (telephone conversation, perhaps). You then establish the reader's confidence in your company by assuring the person the situation has been thoroughly studied and that the specific items proposed in this paper comprise the exact solution for these problems and needs. By restating the circumstances in your own terms and telling how your firm has already prepared to handle this case, you show that the customer has put the request into the best possible hands. Long-time experience and wide coverage have a persuasive effect as the reader begins to get a sharp concept of your company's capability; but when you tell how you have directed your capability to this particular set of desires, the customer sees that you are sharing the problem and offering the answer to it.

Having established the facts of your capability and stated the general intention to make your products, personnel, and services fit the customer's needs, you give all the technical details. As you point out the various factors that comprise the whole problem, you propose a solution in specific terms; itemize what things you propose to do; tell why these are best; explain where and how you will do these things; verify the schedule you intend to follow; certify the persons who will be involved in creating, performing, and managing the project; and state the price of these goods and services, separately and totally.

In the concluding portion, assure the reader that your company can and wants to do what you have proposed, and indicate a readiness to discuss or clarify any points.

The following example of a short formal proposal is presented with its letter of transmittal. You will observe that the letter is in conversational tone and gives the most significant facts from the proposal. The short proposal (only six double-spaced pages) adequately covers all parts of the outline, giving specific details for solving each area of the customer's problem. The tone is believable and the style is impersonal and concise. The reader is impressed by the obvious fitness of the proposing company to understand and solve the problem.

Figure 5-25. Letter of Transmittal with Proposal

☆ **BLUE STAR PATROL SERVICE** ☆

324 W. Gramercy
Houston, TX 77002

July 3, 19__

The Fabrico Manufacturing Corporation
1722 Anderson Street
Houston, TX 77037

Attention: Mr. William R. Linke

Gentlemen:

This proposal is in answer to your request for proposal 483, dated June 29, 19__, regarding the installation of an alarm system and patrol service by August 12, 19__.

At a first-year cost of $8,150, Blue Star Patrol Service proposes to install a complete alarm system tailored especially to the needs of the Fabrico Manufacturing Corporation and planned to provide maximum protection against burglaries.

We have considered all aspects of protection for the Fabrico Manufacturing Corporation and can guarantee satisfaction in our systems and patrol service. In order that we may properly install the equipment, the work must begin by August 5, 19__.

We sincerely hope that our proposed equipment, work schedule, guarantees, and services will be accepted by the Fabrico Manufacturing Corporation and look forward to working with you in achieving the best protection possible to prevent burglaries at your plant.

Sincerely yours,

David Jones
General Manager

DJ:hg

Proposal 439 for the Installation of
A Burglar Alarm System and
Patrol Service, RFP 483

Introduction

The Blue Star Patrol Service is pleased to respond to RFP 483, dated June 29, 19_____ from the Fabrico Manufacturing Corporation requesting installation of a burglar alarm system and armed patrol service.

The importance of plant protection from burglaries is of great concern to Blue Star Patrol Service. The reliability and quality of an alarm system and patrol service used by a company are extremely important in protection against burglaries.

It is proposed that the Blue Star Patrol Service install a burglar alarm system and initiate an armed patrol service for the Fabrico Manufacturing Corporation. The installation of the alarm system would be supervised by Mr. Herb Kelpen, who was in the Robbery Division of the Houston Police Department for ten years before joining Blue Star Patrol Service. Under his direction, a team of experienced and reliable technicians would install the system for the utmost protection against burglaries. These same technicians would be available 24 hours a day for immediate service to equipment, should an unforeseen problem arise. Mr. Kelpen would also instruct Fabrico's armed patrolmen in the patrol procedure that would be unique to the Fabrico Manufacturing Corporation's plant in Houston, Texas.

Blue Star Patrol Service has a record of reliability, quality workmanship, and service that would provide full security for the plant. All installation of equipment and services are guaranteed to be of the highest quality. Installation of the alarm system and initiation of the patrol service would begin immediately upon signing of a contractual agreement, and would be operational by August 12, 19 _____, as requested.

Technical Proposal

The following technical proposal takes into account the expressed need that Fabrico has for plant protection against burglaries:

It is proposed that the Blue Star Patrol Service install the Matthews model 434 alarm system in the Fabrico Manufacturing Corporation's Houston Plant. The 434 uses sensitized tape on all windows and doors to detect vibration and breaking. Even the slight vibration produced by a glass-cutter is enough to activate the alarm. Breaking of doors and windows breaks the alarm circuit and immediately activates the alarm.

These alarm systems would be connected to a central console near the front exit of Building A. The console would provide immediate control of the alarm systems throughout the plant, enabling the operator to activate the alarms from a central location. This console provides a 30-second delay for the operator to leave the plant after activation of the alarm systems. It also provides a button that tests the systems and shows a green light if the systems are functioning properly. The console would be connected to Blue Star Patrol Service's central office, and, in case of attempted entry to the plant, would alert the operator there. The operator would alert the patrolmen by radio, and call the police. In case of conventional power failure, batteries would supply the power needed to run the alarm systems. Should a burglary be attemped at this time, the patrolmen would be notified by a radio signal from the console.

The patrol service would consist of two armed men patrolling the plant in an automobile every 45 minutes. These patrolmen would conduct a thorough check of all entrances and buildings and surrounding grounds at the plant, testing locks, lighting, outside material, and parked vehicles. They would respond immediately to any call from our central office. The patrol service would also meet a designated plant officer in the mornings, to open the plant and deactivate the alarm systems.

The installation and reliability of the equipment are guaranteed against defects for five years. The maintenance and testing of the systems are free for one year, and a maintenance contract is offered after that period.

Blue Star Patrol Service would train the Fabrico Manufacturing Corporation key personnel to operate the alarm systems. The training takes only one hour for each person because the activation and circuit test of the alarms is very simple. A copy of the alarm systems' instruction booklet and wiring diagrams would be issued to a designated plant officer after the installation had been performed.

Installation of the alarm system takes one work week, and the patrol service would begin at the time the alarm system was activated. The alarm systems and patrol service would assure the Fabrico Manufacturing Corporation of the most effective protection available against burglaries.

Commercial Proposal

All provisions for the best possible protection at the most economical price have been taken into account in this commercial proposal. The following is a list of itemized costs for the alarm systems and patrol service:

Items	Cost
3,000 feet of sensitized tape	$1,500.00
Matthews model 434 alarm system	2,000.00
Matthews model 240 sound system	1,750.00
Central console	800.00
Installation team wages	800.00
Hookup to central office	100.00
Maintenance and testing	No cost for first year
per year (optional)	500.00
Patrol Service for one year	2,000.00
TOTAL	$9,450.00

The cost of transportation of the equipment and training of key personnel would be absorbed by Blue Star Patrol Service.

Conclusion

Blue Star Patrol Service considers the alarm equipment and patrol service proposed for the Fabrico Manufacturing Corporation to offer the best protection available against burglaries. This protection is proposed at a cost of $8,950 for the first year. Costs for maintenance and patrol service are negotiable after the first year.

To allow for proper installation of the alarm systems by August 12, 1976, the Blue Star Patrol Service cannot commit itself to begin installation after August 5, 1976.

It is hoped that the Fabrico Manufacturing Corporation will realize that all aspects for providing the best protection available have been considered very carefully by the Blue Star Patrol Service in this proposal.

Mr. David Jones, general manager, will handle all negotiations for the Blue Star Patrol Service and will be available for conference in person or by telephone at 783-3618, Ext. 269.

WORK PROJECT 10

Examine each of the following report introductions to see whether they can be improved. Does each contain the necessary element for an introduction? In the space provided, list the elements that are present and those that are missing.

Introduction #1

This manual will discuss the different types of home greenhouses available and the problems that might be encountered in building and operating them. The purpose of this manual is to keep the average person from making the many possible mistakes that can occur in constructing and operating a greenhouse. This report will be broad enough to help an individual decide on the proper size or type of greenhouse and if the greenhouse should be purchased or built. Information is also provided to give the individual some idea of the amount of time needed to properly operate a small greenhouse. Besides the many different types to choose from, other factors need to be considered. After the greenhouse is constructed, continuing maintenance is needed to prevent the continuous problems of insects, plant diseases, extreme heat and cold, and humidity control. All of these problems vary with the type of plants to be grown.

1. Subject of the report

2. Background

3. Major points

4. Purpose of the report

This report will discuss several of the different types of computer graphics and some of their outstanding applications. Computer graphics is playing an important role in education, research, and the entertainment industry. I have included in this report a brief explanation of some basic mechanics involved in computer graphics. In this paper, Computer Graphics has been used as a collective term including computer films, computer-aided animation, electronic scene generation, and computer simulation. The meaning of the different terms will become apparent from their applications, which will be described.

1. Subject of the report

2. Background

3. Major points

4. Purpose of the report

Introduction #3

The subject of this report is the consumer education program for grades four, five, and six. The purpose of this program is to design a curriculum to help students in these three grades make competent decisions in an increasingly complex marketplace and to consider the effects of those decisions on personal finances, the public economy, the community, and the environment.

On March 15, 1962, President John F. Kennedy gave a presidential message in which he stated the four basic consumer rights: the rights to safety, the right to be informed, the right to choose, and the right to be heard. This was the first time that the concept of consumer rights had been clearly recognized by a president. Kennedy's declaration of these consumer rights, along with new consumer laws, both on the national and local level, aided the rise of the consumer movement in America in the 1960s.

Along with the rise of the consumer movement, which had practically deteriorated since World War II, came the renewal of interest in consumer education. Although consumer education became prominent in the public curriculum in the 1930s, it had lost much of its incentive after World War II. However, as the economic situation grew worse, Americans demanded that some type of educational program be implemented.

Today most educators and parents fully realize that children need to be taught how to consume wisely, mainly because children are inundated with advertising from television. They are encouraged to buy, but without proper education they cannot make prudent purchasing decisions. They must learn what to buy, how much to buy, what purpose the product really serves, and how durable the product is. The only way for them to learn how to become good consumers is through careful instruction; elementary schools can design efficient programs which will educate young children to become good consumers.

In this report, I discuss the criteria for developing a proper program for fourth, fifth, and sixth graders. I also compose a group of six classroom sessions to assist the teacher in preparing activities that will attract the students' interest and encourage them to think wisely when purchasing items. This suggested curriculum also shows how to organize a three-year program to develop skills, attitudes, and understandings that contribute to consumer competence and social responsibility. Consumer education cannot be effectively taught in only one year, but working with children during their fourth, fifth, and sixth years in school will help the school to achieve the goals of consumer education.

1. Subject of the report

2. Background

3. Major points

4. Purpose of the report

The subject of this report is redlining and the degree to which it causes urban decay. The purpose of this report is to draw a conclusion about the effects of past discrimination and weigh the potential effectiveness of current regulations aimed at improving the situation. The report examines first the redlining problem and urban renewal. Second, the report analyzes the savings and loan industry and its stand on the issue. By disclosing the results of interviews with savings and loan mortgage officers, the report summarizes research on the fundamentals of mortgage lending to determine if redlining is nothing more than using good business practices. Finally, the report will then describe some available programs designed to save the urban community.

1. Subject of the report

2. Background

3. Major points

4. Purpose of the report

Introduction #5

    This report will study typesetting as an industry in Houston, Texas. This type of study is designed to examine the competitors' marketing practices and policies. Management of printing companies needs this information to do an effective job of plotting marketing strategy and counterstrategy. The purpose of this paper is to analyze the competitive situation among typesetters in Houston.

    1.   Subject of the report

    2.   Background

    3.   Major points

    4.   Purpose of the report

The continued increase in health care costs requires hospitals to operate at an unprecedented level of efficiency if they are to maintain quality care at a reasonable cost to the patient. *Time* magazine reports, "An HEW study found that Americans spent less than three percent of the gross national product on health care at the turn of the century, now spend nine percent, and at the current rate of increase will be doling out twelve percent, or $1 trillion, annually by the end of the century." The purchasing department is vital to the operation of any hospital because it is charged with obtaining the necessary equipment and supplies required for hospital operations and to purchase these at the best cost. The various operating departments of the hospital submit their requests for items to the purchasing department. Purchasing, in turn, contacts suppliers, buys the items, and then disperses the goods to the user departments. Implementation of a computerized purchasing system would be instrumental in streamlining hospital operations and realizing savings in overall costs. In fact, the use of an effective EDP system would reduce the dependence upon people to keep the procurement cycle going. Efficient procurement is the major factor in the effort to hold down the soaring costs of modern health care. The major areas for computerized purchasing are as follows:

1. Inventory control

2. Product referencing

3. Vendor history and performance

The purpose of this report is to show how and why computerized purchasing can make each of these three areas more cost efficient.

1. Subject of the report

2. Background

3. Major points

4. Purpose of the report

244

Introduction #7

The rush to digital technology has been spurred by its technical and economic advantages. Digital logic simplifies cost-effective multiplexing, or packing multiple data channels within one facility. The accuracy of a digital system combined with this cost-effectiveness, makes an almost irresistible combination. The different worlds of analog and digital electronics must frequently be interfaced. Essentially two types of circuits can be used to interface analog and digital circuits. One is for converting analog signals into digital signals and is known as an analog-to-digital (A/D) converter. The other converts digital signals into analog signals and is called a digital-to-analog (D/A) converter. The problem is that A/D and D/A converters have become the bottleneck in applying digital control and computation circuits to analog control systems. Therefore, the purpose of this report is as follows: (1) discuss two types of circuits used to interface analog and digital circuits; (2) discuss the methods for making analog-to-digital/digital-to-analog conversions; (3) describe the basic logic elements used in the implementation of the digital control for digital-to-analog/analog-to-digital conversion systems; (4) describe the various conversion systems; and (5) tell why digital technology is growing.

1. Subject of the report

2. Background

3. Major points

4. Purpose of the report

WORK PROJECT 11

Reports: Informal and Formal

For each of the following assignments, begin by completing the Document Analysis Worksheet. See Chapter 1.

1. Write an informal report describing or analyzing a process in your field. If possible, describe or analyze a process or procedure that relates to some area of your work experience.

   If you choose to describe a job-related process that you think could be improved or changed, develop your report into a recommendation report. Or, develop your analysis as a feasibility study.

2. Write an informal report that incorporates either a detailed or a general description of a mechanism.

3. Write an informal instructions report.

4. Write an informal report that gives instructions for performing a process related to your field of study or for a job-related situation.

5. After examining the plan for a set of directions (Chapter 5), revise a poor set of directions. Write an informal information report to your instructor explaining why the particular set of instructions you have chosen is inadequate. Attach the set of instructions to your report when you submit it to your instructor. Then revise the set of instructions to produce a good, clear set.

   Poor sets of directions are abundant—check those that are included with appliances, car parts, toys, home remodeling items, recreation equipment that must be assembled, and so on.

6. Write a formal set of instructions to perform a process or to operate a mechanism.

7. Write a formal report on one of the following topics:
   • a research report assessing the current status of a major issue or topic in your field.
   • a feasibility study to determine the best or most current approach to a problem in your field.
   • a procedures report for standardizing a process used in a laboratory course in your major or in some area of your job.

8. First write an informal proposal for your formal research report project. Include the following headings: Subject, Purpose, Background, Tentative Outline, Procedure, Facilities Available, Preliminary Problems, Merits of the Proposal, Faults of the Proposal, Conclusion. (See example, Chapter 5.)

9. After your proposal has been accepted and approximately two weeks before your formal report is due, prepare a progress report describing your progress on your formal report. Follow one of the progress report formats listed on page 000.

10. From your research for your formal research report, select a short article. from a journal in your field. Make a photocopy of the article. Then write a descriptive and an informative abstract of the article.

Based on the principles of good style and organization in professional writing, write an informal report analyzing style and organization of the article. Explain, using specific sentences, why the style is good or bad. If the organization could be improved, explain how.

Index